George Washington

George Washington

THE MAKING OF
AN AMERICAN SYMBOL

Barry Schwartz

THE FREE PRESS
A Division of Macmillan, Inc.
NEW YORK

Collier Macmillan Publishers
LONDON

The Free Press
A Division of Macmillan, Inc.
866 Third Avenue, New York, N.Y. 10022

Collier Macmillan Canada, Inc.

Printed in the United States of America

printing number
1   2   3   4   5   6   7   8   9   10

Library of Congress Cataloging-in-Publication Data

Schwartz, Barry
  George Washington: the making of an American symbol.

  Bibliography: p.
  Includes index.
    1. Washington, George, 1732–1799. 2. Presidents—
United States—Biography. 3. Washington, George,
1732–1799—Influence. I. Title.
E312.S39   1987   973.4'1'0924   87-7587
ISBN 0-02-928141-5

For Hal and Sarah

Contents

List of Illustrations

Acknowledgments

As I STUDIED the new republic's extraordinary veneration of George Washington, the example of Emile Durkheim's masterpiece, *The Elementary Forms of the Religious Life,* stood before me, and I worked from beginning to end under its influence. Other scholars who figured prominently in my thinking about heroes and hero worship include sociologists Stefan Czarnowski, William Lloyd Warner, Charles Horton Cooley, and Orrin Klapp, anthropologists A. R. Radcliffe-Brown and Victor Turner, political scientists Charles Merriam and Garry Wills, and historians Merrill Peterson, John Ward, and Thomas Connelly.

To generous colleagues I am equally indebted. Marcus Cunliffe's comments on an early manuscript shaped my subsequent writing in a decisive way. Eviatar Zerubavel's sociological advice helped to make this writing more coherent than it would have been otherwise. Barry Glassner and Peter Hoffer read different parts of the manuscript and their criticisms are reflected in the whole. The final revisions were prepared with considerable assistance from Joyce Seltzer, my editor at The Free Press. I found her standards to be high; her helpfulness, unrepayable.

I could not have begun this work without Bernice Barnett, who spent many long hours gathering archival materials. Ms. Barnett and I were both partially supported by the University of Georgia's Institute for Behavioral Research. Fees for photographs and reproduction of documents were paid by the University of Georgia's Department of Sociology. In addition, many hours of the Department's time were used up by Lori Stapleton, who expertly typed and retyped many pages over many months. She always did the job right the first time; I did not.

To two people I reserve special acknowledgment, for they have been traveling companions and helpers from the start. Eugene Miller, my political science colleague, generously shared with me his great knowledge of America's founding period, and introduced me to sources and materials I would have never found on my own. Janet Schwartz, my wife, is owed the biggest debt of all. Every page of this book has been touched by her refining comment.

T HE GENIUS OF AMERICA, with modest pride, may come forward and say, "The countries of the old world have gloried in their heroes and learned men: I may hope to profit by their example: Greece had a Solon, a Cimon and Epaminondas, and Aristides, and her Demosthenes: Rome in her ancient glory had her Caesars, a Vespasion, a Cato, and Cincinnatus—a Titus and a Cicero: And in modern days her Innocents, her Gregorys, and her Clements—Persia, her Cyrus, Darius, and Artaxerxes: Arabia, her Mahomet: Macedon, her Philip and Alexander: France, her Charlemaign, her Othos, her Henry 4th and Louis 14th: Spain, her Charles 5th and her Gasca: Germany, her Joseph the 2nd: Prussia, her Frederick: Sweden, her Charles the 12th: And England, her Edwards and Henrys—her Newton, her Marlboro, her Chatham and her Wolfe:—Illustrious Names!—the envy and the emulation of the ambitious, or the wise; the boast of their countries; and in them be ye happy, if you can say of them as I can of mine—The deeds of his public and private life withstand the strictest scrutiny of the most jealous eye; and his integrity, like a mountain, repulses and overthrows suspicion: Uniformly just and proper—virtuously great and unexceptionally good: A General, sublimely victorious, descending from the plenitude of human authority, to a private station,—and from a private station, unanimously elected the Sovereign of an enlightened, a free, and a jealous people, without opposition, without distrust, and without envy,—Such is my son: the true model for emulation, and a just example of future heroes."

Pennsylvania Gazette
March, 1791

George Washington

Introduction

On February 7, 1832, the United States Senate and the House of Representatives established a joint committee to arrange celebrations for the one-hundredth anniversary of George Washington's birth. Most committee members were pleased with their assignment, but there were exceptions. Senator Littleton Tazewell of Virginia, upon learning of his appointment to the committee, promptly resigned. "Man worship, how great soever the man," he explained, "[I] will ever oppose." Citing Tazewell's reasons as their own, four of the other twenty-nine members of the committee withdrew. The dissidents knew their colleagues well; "man worship" was precisely what the centennial committee had in mind. On February 13, it proposed that Congress literally canonize Washington by removing his body from Mount Vernon and placing it in a tomb already prepared below the center of the United States Capitol Rotunda; the man and the nation would, thus, become one. In this transfiguration, the committee resolution went on to say, both houses of Congress, and through them the nation as a whole, would "attend and assist."[1]

Most Northerners supported the committee's proposal. Edward Everett of Massachusetts spoke for them as he contemplated Washington's body being lifted reverently from its tomb and escorted to the Capitol by a massive procession of his countrymen. The spectacle would be awesome and "will constitute a transaction unexampled in the history of the world," he remarked. To participate in this event, he added, was a privilege due every American:

> The sacred remains are ... a treasure beyond all price, but it is a treasure of which every part of this blood-cemented Union has a right to claim its share.[2]

Everett's argument made sense to most Northern representatives because they had already claimed Washington as a national possession. Most of the Southerners, however, were unwilling to forget Washington's native Virginia roots, and to them Augustin Smith Clayton's counterargument was more compelling. The task before Congress, declared the eminent Georgia jurist, was to devise a shrine suitable for the perpetuation of Washington's memory. Yet, what could be more suitable than the hero's present resting place, Mount Vernon—the refuge for which he yearned during long years of public service, and on which he lavished every attention when he returned to private life? Mount Vernon had for these reasons already become "the shrine of the patriot's pilgrimage"; what site on earth would be better suited for a permanent memorial? Since Washington had died as well as lived at this place, Clayton saw fit to conclude with a biblical analogy:

> Yes, Mr. Speaker, and with the greatest possible reverence I speak it. Mount Vernon and Mount Calvary will descend to posterity with coextensive remembrance.[3]

No one was surprised by Mr. Clayton's hyperbole, or Mr. Everett's. Most of the Congressmen spoke that way about Washington themselves,[4] and their words were for the most part sincere. These men, after all, grew up at a time when Washington was the singular ornament of the American past. They had come to see him, as had most other Americans, through the eyes of the only popular biographer of their time, the Reverend Mason Locke Weems. They knew what Weems would have said during the debate. Indeed, if someone had taken the Congressmen's laudatory remarks on Washington and interspersed them throughout Weems's life of Washington,[5] no one would have known the difference.

Parson Weems, inventor of the cherry tree story and rector of the nonexistent Mount Vernon Parish, succeeded in transforming the details of Washington's life into a national myth. By mid–nineteenth century, however, a series of more factual, although equally reverent, biographies had been written—by Washington Irving, Jared Sparks, James Paulding, and Joel Headley. Thereafter, post–Civil War biographers, working under the new, Realist influence, criticized the marble-like image rendered in these romantic pre-

War accounts, but the product of their own efforts was not much different. Henry Cabot Lodge, Woodrow Wilson, Paul Leicester Ford, and others tried "to make Washington human," but they could not find much in the way of human failings to attribute to him. It remained for Rupert Hughes and William Woodward, in the 1920s, to portray Washington as a man rather than a monument; yet, many people believed they had pushed their portrayals too far, finding in him more faults than he actually possessed. For a more balanced assessment, more facts were needed, and John Fitzpatrick provided them. His (1931–44) compilation of the Washington papers placed on a more objective foundation his own and subsequent biographies by Douglas Freeman (1948–57), Marcus Cunliffe (1959), and James Flexner (1965–72). More recently, new editions of Washington's papers, and new biographies, have enlarged and deepened our knowledge of his life.[6]

Although Washington's life is now documented in excruciating detail, and treated more dispassionately than ever, we know little about why that life was the object of such intense veneration. Such are the limits of biography. Biographical statements are designed to show what Washington did and why he did it; they are not meant to illuminate in any systematic or detailed way how Washington's achievements and motivations were perceived by his contemporaries, or how these perceptions were shaped by the cultural and social circumstances in which he and his admirers lived. Thus, in 1969 Robert Hay concluded that "a full treatment of the many nuances of the popular view of Washington remains one of the significant unwritten stories in the intellectual history of the United States."[7]

Beginning in the mid-1970s, "the popular view of Washington" became a topic of productive scholarly concern. Michael Kammen's treatment of Washington's place in America's evolving conception of its revolution and George Forgie's analysis of Washington as an object of nostalgia during America's "post-heroic age" are useful models for the study of nineteenth- and twentieth-century perceptions. Recent literature also explores the perceptions of Washington's own contemporaries. Lawrence Friedman, for example, believes that Washington's image reconciled his countryman's strivings for both stability and progress. Jay Fliegelman, following a different track, regards Washington as an emblem of the then-emerging antipatriarchal family. Catherine Albanese and James Smylie consider Washington an exemplification of the new republic's civil religion; most recently, Garry Wills views him as an Enlightenment Cincinnatus.[8]

These works tell much about the different facets of the Washington image as it was perceived by contemporaries and succeeding generations. They do not account, however, for the full power of that image. They do not explain why Washington was adored so intensely by some and so reservedly by others. They say little about his detractors, and when they do discuss them they fail to distinguish between criticisms of Washington motivated by immediate partisan interests and criticism that reflected the ultimate political values of American culture. The connection of these values and this culture to Washington remains to be articulated. A hunger for symbols of reconciliation and legitimacy, a new conception of paternity, an evolving civil religion, a disdain for political strongmen—these elements all figured in the public framing of Washington's image, but they do not capture its full register of nuances and textures. How Washington became a symbol in the first place, and why he remained one despite a succession of serious military failures, are equally important questions which present writings tend to ignore.

It is the range and significance of Washington's shortcomings that make it difficult to understand his veneration on the basis of personal qualities alone. By any standard, Washington was an intelligent and accomplished man, but he was neither brilliant nor self-confident, and his experience (which did not include leadership of large armies) was not precisely suited to the needs of his time. Upon his appointment as commander of the Continental Army, Washington seemed like David facing Goliath, but he had none of David's cockiness. He was "no harum starum ranting swearing fellow,"[9] as one of the delegates to the Second Continental Congress put it. Washington did not promise victory. He did not seek to embolden his followers by rattling his saber or by otherwise affirming the strength of his leadership. "Lest some unlucky event should happen," he warned," I beg it may be remembered, by every gentleman in this room, that I, this day, declare with the utmost sincerity, I do not think myself equal to the command I am honored with."[10] Washington's expression of modesty was not just meant for public consumption. To Patrick Henry, he privately expressed the fear that his appointment would "date my fall, and the ruin of my reputation."[11]

Washington's diffidence proved not to be unfounded. In January 1778, two and a half years after his appointment, Benjamin Rush, a prominent Philadelphia physician and patriot, declared: "The northern army has shown us what Americans are capable of doing with a GENERAL at their head." (The reference is to Gates's victory at Saratoga.) "A Gates, a Lee, or a Conway," Rush continued, "would in a few weeks render [the entire army] an irresistible body of men."[12] More sensitive to the different situations in which Gates, the field general, and Washington, the commander of field generals, labored, Washington's admirers were more appreciative of his achievements; but even they had no illusions as to the quality of his military mind. In hindsight, Washington's own eulogists, like John Daniel of Virginia, admitted that his armies suffered "a succession of disasters and retreats," partly through his own mistakes, and that "it may not be said of him as of Marlborough, that he never formed the plan of a campaign that he did not execute; never besieged a city that he did not take; never fought a battle that he did not gain."[13]

Washington's native capacities could not, as with some of his "self-made" contemporaries, overcome his limited military and political experience. "His mind was great and powerful," said Thomas Jefferson, but that mind, he added, was not "of the very first order.... It was slow in operation, being little aided by invention or imagination but sure in conclusion."[14] Other assessments of Washington's intellect were even less generous. "The great Character," John Adams roared, "was a character of Convention," created by all those who "expressly agreed to blow the trumpet of panegyric in concert.... That Washington was not a scholar is certain. That he was too illiterate, unlearned, unread for his station and reputation is equally past dispute."[15] Benjamin Rush outdid Adams's bitter assessment by telling of a friend who once noticed that Washington, after making a purchase, was unable to count his change.[16] In these two accounts (the first an exaggeration; the second, a lie), we find a caricature of Washington's abilities; yet, the partial truth of these distortions cannot be lightly dismissed. Washington was indeed less educated and less experienced in national matters than many of his contemporaries. In peace as well as in war, therefore, he depended heavily on his advisors. During his first term as President, he confessed to James

5

Madison that "he had from the beginning found himself deficient in many of the essential qualifications" for office.[17] Washington was aware of his shortcomings of intellect as well as experience, making reference on more than one occasion to his "inferior endowments from nature."

Not even personal magnetism, often an important basis of public veneration, could be claimed by Washington. As a writer, he was fluent but lacked elegance, and as a speaker, he expressed himself in a heavy, clumsy manner. In addition, he was not magnanimous toward shortcomings in others. His was a heart, in Jefferson's words, "not warm in its affections."[18] As a general, for instance, Washington believed in discipline and used the whip, gallows, and firing squad to enforce it. "His deeds of severity," pleaded John Mason in his New York funeral oration, "were his sad tribute to justice."[19] To his social equals as well as his wayward soldiers Washington was "the archetypal stranger":[20] stern, distant, and glacial. "Today I dined with the President," wrote his political ally, Theodore Sedgwick, "and as usual the company was as grave as at a funeral."[21] There is also the old story of Gouverneur Morris, another political ally who, on a bet, patted Washington on the shoulder to prove his close friendship with him, only to be devastated by the President's icy stare. Much doubt exists about the veracity of this familiar anecdote, but its content betrays something of the way Washington struck many contemporaries.

Washington possessed many appealing traits; but, his less attractive sides reveal that he was a man not unlike other men, and that other leaders of the Revolution were at least as well endowed with talent and charm as he. But to say this is only to affirm what the worship of Washington entailed: not the recognition of a greatness inherent in the man but the transformation, by society, of ordinary talents and unremarkable characteristics into an image of heroic proportions.

George Washington has been described as a "living 'tribal' totem."[22] Given his undistinguished personal qualities, the analogy seems very appropriate. Totems are objects, usually animals or plants, that permeate the religious life of certain preliterate peoples. These objects are deemed superior in dignity and power—that is to say, "sacred"—not because of their inherent qualities, which are uniformly common and unimpressive, but because they symbolize something greater than themselves: the moral authority of society. In Emile Durkheim's words, "the god of the clan can ... be nothing else than the clan itself, personified and represented to the imagination under the visible form of the animal or vegetable which serves as totem."[23]

Shifting from the primitive world to the modern world, however, we see that symbolic animals and plants are replaced by symbolic leaders. In the process, the line dividing religion and politics becomes blurred. Kings, presidents, and generals, many of whom would not otherwise distinguish themselves by virtue of their talents or achievements, are treated in ways that do not much differ from how their admirers treat God. The similarity between these two kinds of veneration, Durkheim tells us, implies a common source:

> In the present day just as much as in the past, we see society constantly creating sacred things out of ordinary ones. . . . The simple deference inspired by men invested with high social functions is not different in nature from religious respect. . . . In order to explain the consideration accorded to princes, nobles and political chiefs, a sacred character has been attributed to them. . . . However, it is evident that [their] situation is due solely to the importance attributed to [them] by public opinion. Thus the moral power conferred by opinion and that with which sacred beings are invested are at bottom of a single origin and made up of the same elements.[24]

To characterize George Washington as a "living 'tribal' totem," then, is to realize that he was venerated not primarily because he undertook successful military and political enterprises but because in doing so he symbolized the bond between his society's political and religious sentiments.

In ancient times, when political and religious sentiments were indistinguishable, ordinary mortals like pharoahs and emperors were deified by their subjects. In more recent times, especially in countries where the political realm has been institutionally segregated from the religious, national leaders are no longer perceived as gods. Their followers, however, still make use of religious forms to set these men apart—a practice that sometimes engenders controversy. Throughout George Washington's career, many well-meaning Americans voiced alarm about the intensity of his "cult of adoration." To their Protestant minds, the things said and done in Washington's honor seemed "Romish," bordering on "dulia," the homage due angels and saints. (*"Sancte Washington, ora pro nobis"* [Saint Washington, pray for us], John Adams recited in parody of the Roman Catholic supplication.[25]) In truth, Americans thought and felt about God quite differently from the way they thought and felt about Washington. The complaints, however, were not totally unfounded, for common to the veneration of God and the veneration of Washington were conspicuous structural similarities.

The cultivation of beliefs and the observance of rites entered directly into the adoration of Washington, and they were also part of his society's religious heritage. In Washington's society (as in our own), the inculcation of beliefs and ritual attitudes was realized through a twofold spiritual program. "Revelation," the process of coming to know God, was accomplished primarily by the propagation of God's Word. Originally revealed to the prophets, then reiterated and interpreted by the Church's ministers, the Word brought man to a correct belief in the divine character and will. "Adoration," on the other hand, falls more within the sphere of sentiment and action than of belief. By perceptible observances and other external manifestations, including pictures, place names, shrines, and relics, the people of Washington's time acknowledged God's absolute holiness and glory (*Gloria Dei externa formalis*).[26]

Since the veneration of George Washington incorporated both beliefs about his character and conduct, on the one hand, and ritual forms, on the other, he can be seen as the object of a kind of secular religion. One can analyze this religion, of course, but not precisely. To discover how Washington's contemporaries regarded him, we must depend on impressionistic data: private correspondence, newspaper articles and commentaries, poems, orations, eulogies. These documents can show what many literate Americans believed and felt about Washington, and they can also describe the beliefs and feelings of the public at large. In addition, the purchase and display of Washington's portraits, the naming of countries and towns in his honor, the public gatherings that marked his presence, the activities that commemorated his birth and death—all provide evidence of the venerational practices that the new republic adopted toward him. Such data cannot substitute for a methodical sampling of opinion or ritual behavior, but they do furnish, in their totality, a record whose variety and richness make up for its lack of strict representativeness.

From this record, the venerational cult that enshrined, and shaped, the people's image of Washington can be reconstructed. Outside of his intimate circle, it was through this cult alone that Washington came to be known. What his countrymen venerated were representations of the man, not the man himself. Through these representations the meaning of Washington to his country-men can be discovered; by gauging their incidence, and the range of their expression, the extent of his veneration can be grasped.

To understand the content and implications of the veneration of George Washington, it is first necessary to explore, in the con-text of late-eighteenth-century American society, the ceremonial observances through which the people expressed their worship of him, the attitudes which sustained that veneration, and the social functions such veneration fulfilled. Only then can we turn to the moral character that was attributed to Washington, and to the ine-luctable bond between this attribution and the values of his so-ciety. Thus conceived, George Washington appears as both an ob-ject of emotional attachment and an exemplification of moral values. Each understanding overlaps and complements the other. To describe only what Americans believed Washington stood for does not explain why he was set apart and elevated above many other men whose character and conduct closely resembled his; nor does it account for the methods and the functions of that eleva-tion. To describe only the latter, on the other hand, is to ignore what he meant to his countrymen. The two parts of this book ar-ticulate these two aspects of Washington's social role. Each part sweeps through Washington's career, combing out and piling up pertinent fragments and pointing up their distinctive contribu-tions to his image. From this material emerges a fuller understand-ing of how Americans transformed George Washington into a liv-ing monument.

Part One

The
Adoration
of
Washington

1

An Idol for
the Revolution

DOUGLAS FREEMAN CONCEDES in the introduction to one of his seven volumes on the life of Washington, that "the transformation of the quiet Virginia planter into the revered continental commander is beyond documentary explanation."[1] In truth, no combination of written documents and artifacts can in itself account for Washington's rise to fame. Yet, from materials on Washington's life and times, his elevation to national honor can at least be reconstituted, and then perhaps better understood.

Washington was not a charismatic leader in Max Weber's sense: His talents were not exceptional; he had no desire to bring about a radical change in his society; he did not distinguish himself by seizing and exercising power.[2] Nothing about him reminds us of a great conqueror or shaper of history. But if Washington was not a charismatic leader, he was still the object of the most intense display of hero worship this nation has ever seen. To make sense of this veneration, nothing less is required than a revised conception of heroic leadership itself.

"If [society] happens to fall in love with a man and if it thinks it has found in him the principal aspirations that move it, as well as the means of satisfying them," Emile Durkheim observes, "this man will be raised above the others and, as it were, deified.... And the fact that it is society alone which is the author of these varieties of apotheosis, is evident since it frequently chances to consecrate men thus who have no right to it from their own merit."[3] Society transforms ordinary men into great men under

13

very definite conditions. Great men, like other sacred symbols, are created in times of crisis and collective enthusiasm, times when people enter into intense and effervescent relationships with one another. In such times, ideals take on an irresistible momentum, and those who come under their influence "are made to establish the kingdom (or republic) of heaven on earth." Inspired to action, the people yearn for a leader to carry out their plans and thwart the designs of their enemies.[4]

Such was the mood in 1774, when Great Britain closed the port of Boston and imposed other harsh measures on Massachusetts for its violation of the Tea Act. Many Americans were inflamed in sympathy for their sister colony. Everywhere, they were caught up in an outpouring of "hysterical and emotional ideas ... inflammatory phrases ... fear and frenzy, exaggeration and enthusiasm,"[5] all related to a strong belief in the existence of a conspiracy to enslave the colonies[6] and a conviction that British forces were bent on a campaign of plunder and rape.[7] The uproar, however, resulted not in the emergence of a leader but in the establishment of a body, the Continental Congress, which would *appoint* that essential leader. The appointment itself was by no means spontaneous, or even immediate.

In the fall of 1774, Washington served as a Virginia delegate to the First Continental Congress. His role was not a very important one, and he had little to say during the deliberations. But with the prospect of war in the air, the delegates could not help talking about Washington. Most of the delegates to the Congress were Freemasons like Washington, and they had come to know him through the vast network of lodges that had sprung up throughout the colonies.[8] In these lodges many had met the young colonel during his travels, or had heard about his career in the Virginia militia. The delegates knew that Washington's military ventures against French forces in the West were not brilliant ones; nevertheless, he had served honorably, and his military experience, in addition to his membership in the state legislature—not to mention his modest personal demeanor—impressed many of his senior colleagues. It was not until the following year, however, that Washington was to be vested by these colleagues with a national identity.

Not until the spring of 1775, when Americans took up arms at Lexington and Concord, did the nation require such a step. This first military conflict with the British led Americans into a *rage militaire*, which took possession of the Northern and Middle colonies by early summer—precisely the time of Washington's appointment. One Tory observer reported that "the people of Connecticut are raving in the cause of liberty.... The Jerseys are not a whit behind Connecticut. The Philadelphians exceed them both."[9]

News of the fighting set Philadelphia on fire "like a lightning stroke." Residents who earlier sympathized with England renounced their sentiments and took up arms with the militia. "Even our women and children now talk of nothing but of the glory of fighting, suffering, and dying for our country."[10] By the middle of 1775, Philadelphia boasted a militia of over two thousand men. "So sudden a formation of an army," John Adams observed, "never took place anywhere."[11] Later reports from Philadelphia indicated that "the city has turned out 4,000 men, 300 of whom are Quakers. Every county in our province is awakened and several thousand Riflemen on our frontiers are in readiness to march down to our assistance...."[12] The agitation mounted, inciting people to exaggerated claims and unusual modes of conduct. Scholarly John Adams, for example, estimated that Philadelphia turned out "two thousand [soldiers] every day" and, after indicating that he himself was reading military books, announced: "Everyone must, and will, and shall be a soldier."[13] Adams was not psychologically possessed; he had been moved by that superior moral force which floods society during revolutionary periods with "a grandiloquence that would be ridiculous under ordinary circumstances."[14] Abigail Adams was caught up in the same torrent. Concurring with her husband, she described the sound of cannon as "one of the grandest in nature, and ... of the true species of the sublime."[15] Another observer reported: "By accounts from all parts of the country, we find, that they are everywhere learning the use of arms, and seem determined on Liberty or Death.... It is impossible to describe the military ardor which now prevails."[16]

Given the assumed divine sponsorship of the resistance, America's newfound military fervor was amplified by pronouncements from the pulpit. As one minister warned, "When God, in his providence, calls to take the sword, if any refuse to obey, Heaven's dread artillery is levelled against him.... Cursed be he that keepeth back his sword from blood."[17] Other clergymen appeared before their congregations in full military uniform to sign recruits, before taking the field themselves. British reports of loyalist ministers being hung and burned by the rebels were not accurate, but they were symptomatic of the Americans' determination to see God as their ally. Indeed, some ministers who refused to display appropriate zeal for God's crusade were promptly removed by their congregations. As one of the Congressional delegates put it, "It is impossible to conceive of a greater unanimity in the Colonies than that which at present subsists."[18]

A Man for the Times

At this point George Washington might not have been ready for America, but America was ready for him. In May 1775, the Second Continental Congress assembled, anxious and determined to mobilize the colonies for the confrontation with England. That same road on which Washington and the Virginia delegation had passed unnoticed to the First Congress six months earlier was now thick with onlookers. Washington was by now one of the leading members of the Virginia delegation, having been elected to it by only one less vote from the state convention than Peyton Randolph. As commander of the extralegal Fairfax militia in Virginia, he traveled in military uniform and so distinguished himself visibly from his colleagues. Upon arrival in Philadelphia, Washington learned that he had been appointed military advisor for the defense of New York against possible British attack. Several weeks later, word leaked out that he was under consideration for the general command. If that office were to fall to him, however, it would be through "no desire or insinuation," as he put it, of his own. He even induced his friend and fellow delegate, Edmund Pendleton, to argue publicly against him.

In its *Declaration of the Causes of Taking Up Arms*, Congress emphasized: "We mean not to dissolve the union which has so long and so happily subsisted between us." Combining a plea for reconciliation with a threat of armed resistance, this document embodied, if it did not precisely state, the ambivalence felt by many in Congress toward America's relationship with Great Britain. And the choice of Washington as military commander perfectly suited this ambivalence. Proponents of reconciliation could support Washington because they knew his political position on this issue was compatible with (if not as optimistic as) their own. Proponents of separation could also support him, for although still loyal to the King, Washington favored armed resistance to the policies of

16

his ministers. Above all, he was a Virginian, and his appointment would encourage the Southern states to support and participate in the expected hostilities.

On June 16, 1775, the Continental Congress appointed George Washington Commander in Chief of military operations. The quality of the command given to him was strongly conditioned by the uncertainty within Congress. No decision had been made by Congress that directly brought the thirteen colonies into the war being fought in New England. No Continental Army had been raised; there was not yet a nation to fight for. (The Declaration of Independence came a year later.) There was only a commanding general, unanimously supported as a representative of the Congress's will, and it was to this commander, personally, that Congress pledged itself: "[T]his Congress doth now declare that they will maintain and assist him and adhere to him, the said George Washington, Esq., with their lives and fortunes. . . . " And so from the moment he took command, "Washington was more than a military leader: he was the eagle, the standard, the flag, the living symbol of the cause."[19]

As the colonists struggled against Great Britain, they urged each other to renounce their private interests and to concentrate all their energies on the collective military goal. Washington became the focal point of this effort. In exalting Washington, however, the people exalted the policy designed by their representatives. It was not the quality of Washington's persona or performance that accounted for his immense popularity immediately after his appointment, but rather the quality of the duties he was charged to carry out. These duties gave tangible form to the turning point that had already occurred in America's controversy with Britain.

Washington's abrupt ascension to national honor corresponded to a sudden change in the direction of the colonies' political struggle, a strategic change involving the substitution of force for persuasion. His appointment was in effect a decision for war, and the people who agreed with that decision expressed their support in the best way they knew how: by praising its executor. Once the new and fateful course of resistance had been laid out, the conditons were present for the emergence of a hero. Symbolizing the grave decision taken, and the determination to carry it out, Washington became the best-known and most admired man in the colonies. In Philadephia, "thousands" gathered to see him off to the battlefront. In New York, he was escorted by "nine companies of foot [soldiers] in their uniforms, and a greater number of the principal inhabitants of that city than ever appeared on any occasion before."[20] On his way to Boston, where the Massachusetts militia had already begun to hem in the British occupying force, he was repeatedly delayed by enthusiastic crowds. The man was adored before he took actual command of the army.

Sustaining and mobilizing further support for the war, Washington is a clear example of Durkheim's pivotal insight about the social functions of a collective symbol:

> [We] are unable to consider an abstract entity. For we can represent only laboriously and confusedly the source of the strong sentiments which we feel. We cannot explain them to ourselves except by connecting them to some concrete object of whose reality we are vividly aware.[21]

In essence, this is what John Adams meant when, of the situation in 1775, he said: "[Washington's] appointment will have a great effect in cementing and securing the union of these colonies.... Treat the General with all that confidence and affection, that politeness and respect, which is due one of the most important characters in the world."[22] By investing their strong sentiments in Washington, that "concrete object" of which everyone was vividly aware, the people made him into a sacred being. The transformation was sudden and dramatic, because the sentiments activating it were urgent and strong. These sentiments were also immune to certain hard facets of reality.

Thus, Washington's newly acquired heroic stature was evident in the way society not only ascribed to him all manner of perfections but glossed over or ignored his shortcomings. Although a physically imposing man, Washington was not unusually attractive. His face was pockmarked from a youthful bout with smallpox, and his teeth were conspicuously marred by decay. His hips and hands were disproportionately large. Yet, as one of his comtemporaries recalled:

> While a boy at school, I saw him for the first time; it was when he was passing through New England, to take command in chief of the American armies at Cambridge. Never shall I forget the impression his imposing presence then made upon my young imagination, so superior did he seem to me to all that I had seen or imagined of the human form.[23]

After Washington reached Cambridge to assume command of the army, a chaplain wrote in his journal:

> The expression "born to command" is peculiarly applicable to him. Day before yesterday, when under the great elm in Cambridge he drew his sword and formally took command of the army of seventeen thousand men, his look and bearing impressed everyone, and I could not but feel that he was reserved for some great destiny.[24]

Benjamin Rush, who later became a leading critic and disparager of Washington, got caught up in the excitement. "If you do not know General Washington's person," Rush explained to a friend, "perhaps you will be pleased to hear, that he has so much martial dignity in his deportment, that you would distinguish him to be a General and a Soldier, from among ten thousand people: there is not a king in Europe but would look like a valet de chambre by his side."[25] Likewise, whereas few women were attracted to Washington during his youth, in 1776 a prominent lady confessed in her diary to "a womanly admiration of a noble exterior."[26]

The appreciation of Washington's countenance and physique was the result rather than the cause of a renown that had yet to justify itself in any other way. The means of expression of this renown, moreover, were not limited to aesthetic judgments. While Washington was still encamped in Boston, and before even a shot was fired on his command, books were dedicated to him, children were named after him, and ships were named after both him and his wife.[27]

To sustain his reputation, of course, Washington would have to act in his capacity as military commander, but during the first, heady year of the war, he did not have to do very much. Indeed, the first public actions to bring him acclaim were not the fighting of battles but the drafting of letters. When Washington issued a public warning to General Gage about the mistreatment of American prisoners, and when, in an equally well publicized letter, he refused to accept a communication from General Howe, whose term of address—"George Washington, Esquire"—denied the legitimacy of his military rank and mission, the public was positively delighted. The first letter, said Benjamin Rush, "captivated the hearts of the public and his friends." The second letter Rush described as a "masterpiece," which "raised his character higher than ever in the opinion of Congress and his friends." Congress passed a resolution of its own congratulating the General for standing up to the British the way he did.[28]

In March 1776, the British (outgunned but not defeated) withdrew their troops from Boston, precluding significant combat with the Americans. Before seeing a demonstration of Washington's military prowess in pitched battle, Congress voted him a gold medal, and he was applauded throughout the land. The local homage was especially keen. The Massachusetts Assembly praised his achievements in a formal address. Harvard, in turn, voted him the honorary degree of Doctor of Laws.[29] It was clear that his military skills were secondary to his symbolic role as defender of the nation's rights.

In the first year of the war, then, there was more shouting than fighting. Washington traveled to Massachusetts to assume command of the army. He wrote a letter protesting the treatment of prisoners. He waited out the British at Boston. Each action was important and, from the American standpoint, meritorious, but somehow the approbation they evoked was disproportionate to the magnitude of their achievement. Applause for Washington seemed to be determined more by sentiments associated with events than by the military significance of the events themselves. Collective enthusiasm for his mission and his role, resisting sober deliberation, kept Washington aloft.

Indeed, Washington filled critical social needs as the colonies took their first steps toward nationhood. By identifying with him, Americans could articulate their own stake in the war and justify their personal sacrifice. At the same time, Washington's greatness embodied a faithful representation of something that was impersonal and objective. It gave voice to each individual's feeling that outside of him there existed something greater than him. By choosing Washington as a symbol of this transcendent entity, Americans communicated their ideals to one another. Through him, they expressed their sense of moral harmony, their common attachment to a new political unity. George Washington—or, more precisely, the idea of George Washington—was essential to America's militant arousal and to her incipient national consciousness.

By summer 1776, the military fervor had been dissipated by the realities of a year of war. Still, the initial craze was repeatedly invoked as a moral standard, creating the image of a golden era when martial enthusiasm was everywhere joined to a zealous commitment to self-sacrifice.[30] The need to preserve this intangible sense of collective effervescence was met by connecting it to things concrete and visible. A few months after Washington received his commission, there appeared the immensely popular "New Song," whose very first stanza made use of the new military commander as an emblem for the colonies' martial sentiments: "Since WE your brave sons, insens'd, our swords have goaded on, / Huzza, huzza, huzza, huzza for WAR and WASHINGTON."[31] Other poetic outbursts added clarity to what Washington stood for: "In spite of Gage's flaming sword, / Or Carlton's Canadian troop, / Brave Washington shall give the word, / And we'll make them howl and whoop."[32]

The people's enthusiasm was sustained by their commander's bloodless victory at Boston. And although Washington was soundly defeated in his first (and poorly managed) pitched battle at Long Island, the loss was rarely attributed to him. Newspaper accounts stressed the enemy's numerical superiority and indicated that a retreat was the only alternative to surrender or suicidal counterattack. Washington's own role in this withdrawal was thought to be heroic. From one eyewitness the nation learned that he "flew like a guardian angel to protect and bring off his brave troops. . . . The retreat was conducted with the greatest secrecy. . . . There never was a man that behaved better upon the occasion than General Washington; he was on horseback the whole night, and never left the ferry stairs till he had seen the whole of the troops embarked."[33] After more than two months of further withdrawal, Washington suddenly took his army into New Jersey and dealt the enemy sharp and effective blows. By January 1777, most Americans were convinced that their Washington was a great warrior whose prowess had on three different occasions (at Boston, Trenton, and Princeton) humiliated the numerically superior British veterans. Praise for Washington was boundless. William Hooper, a delegate to Congress from North Carolina, declared him to be "the Greatest Man on Earth."[34] "Had he lived in the days of idolatry," announced a writer in the *Pennsylvania Journal*, "he had been worshipped as a god."[35]

A Graven Image?

On February 19, 1777, several weeks after the Battle of Princeton, John Adams rose to address Congress. The debate was routine enough: whether a number of candidates for major general should be approved by Congress, as was customary, or passed down for Washington's approval instead. First, Adams registered opposition to the proposal allowing Washington to choose his own general staff; but he then made a startling statement about Washington himself—something rarely said before by any important political leader, and rarely heard before in any important political body:

> I have been distressed to see some of our members disposed to idolize an image which their own hands have molten. I speak here of the superstitious veneration which is paid to General Washington. Although I honor him for his good qualities, yet in this house I feel myself his superior.[36]

In the early weeks of 1777, the American people and Congress had been carried along by a renewal of the same revolutionary enthusiasm that had triggered the rebellion's onset a year and a half earlier. Adams himself had been moved by those first emotional currents; but now, as he affirmed the dignity of the new government ("this house," as he called it), he pleaded for a restoration of calm deliberation and reason. The delegates who had heard Adams's statement knew it was not motivated by personal enmity, for Adams was the very man who in June 1775 had fought for Washington's appointment and guided it through committee. Adams was the man who, despite the pain of seeing another "wear the laurels which I have sown," had spoken warmly of Washington in private correspondence and discussion, and even suggested the striking of a gold medal for him after the Boston campaign.[37]

Adams's rebuff, rather, was directed not against Washington but against his own colleagues. That the masses were enthralled by the new hero was to be expected. What bothered Adams was that his fellow delegates to Congress, all men who should know better, felt the same way. Adams made clear what he was worried about. At stake in excessive veneration of Washington was not the General's reputation, but the principle of civilian control of the military. The very sentiments aroused by successful resistance to tyranny, Adams implied, might create a new tyrant, a tyrant made all the more formidable by the acclaim of the people themselves.

Adams's speech was significant as the first public expression since the war's onset of America's ambivalence toward "great men." It also indicated the extent to which the veneration of Washington had grown.

Two months after he made his address to Congress, Adams wrote to General Nathaniel Greene a letter containing an oblique criticism of Washington's lack of military aggressiveness—but he never mailed it. "Not sent, being too impolite," Adams wrote on the margin.[38] This little incident revealed what Washington had become—a person so venerated as to be immune to criticism. Benjamin Rush, too, wrote letters critical of Washington, but unlike Adams he did mail them. Rush never lived it down.[39] He became the bearer of the worst stigma any public figure of his time could possess: that of being unfriendly to Washington.

By any objective account, the twelve months that followed the date of Adams's speech were not good ones. In late 1777, the victories at Trenton and Princeton were negated by devastating losses. Washington had failed to stop the British offensive at Brandywine. His attack on the enemy force at Germantown was repulsed. Philadelphia fell and the government fled to York, in the Pennsylvania hinterland. On Christmas eve the American army was not on the offensive, as it had been a year before, but was recuperating at Valley Forge. Within a single year, Washington's military fortunes had dropped from their highest to their lowest point—at which time John Adams, then thought by some to be in sympathy with the cabal seeking to replace Washington, summarized the public mood (and protected his own reputation) by declaring the General the "Center of our Union."[40] Despite subsequent ups and downs on the battlefield, almost four years would pass before a decisive change in the military situation took place. During this stalemate, a French correspondent took the measure of Washington's reputation:

> Through all the land he appears like a benevolent god; old men, women, children they all flock eagerly to catch a glimpse of him when he travels and congratulate themselves because they have seen him. People carrying torches follow him through the cities; his arrival is marked by public illuminations; the Americans, though a cold people who even in the midst of troubles have always sought the dictates of methodical reasoning, have waxed enthusiastic about him and their first songs inspired by spontaneous sentiments have been consecrated to the glorification of Washington.[41]

Two months later, American and French forces achieved a decisive victory at Yorktown. American newspapers gave full accounts of the public reaction to this victory. As Washington worked his way back north, he found himself an object of ceremony in every village and town. Civic celebrations, including poetry, oratory, illuminations, and newspaper hosannas, gave proof that he had become the savior of his country. Seen in the context of his entire public career, however, the victory at Yorktown was less a cause of Washington's brilliant reputation than an occasion for the public to affirm and express a reverence that had already been long established.

A Different Kind of Hero

How could a man so modest in accomplishments be admired so much?

Where strength is virtue and weakness vice, mediocrity generally brings contempt. But this was not so in the case of Washington. He became a great general without the stunning victories that are traditionally associated with martial genius. Washington's military reputation was based on attributes of another kind.

From the very beginning, Americans needed a figure to symbolize their revolt; that need, however, explained neither the choice of Washington nor the legitimacy of that choice. Washington was, in fact, chosen and legitimated by Congress. Along with all general officers selected by Congress, he acquired instant legitimacy because his appointment came out of an honored process of reconciling regional interests and opinions. While today we might not see this as a very good way to choose a commanding general, much less a hero, Americans of the revolutionary period saw things differently.

Two principles dominated the political culture in which Washington's activities were judged. The first was the Anglo-American heritage of civil control of the military. Scarcely present anywhere else in the eighteenth-century Western world, this heritage induced Americans to evaluate Washington's conduct in light of civilian concerns as well as military efficiency. His mandate to form and discipline an army was a mandate to create a force that would not only win battles but also subject itself to the public will. The second principle embedded in America's political culture was decentralized power. It vested in the states a legitimacy which transcended that of the central government, rendering the latter dependent on the former for resources needed to carry out "continental" (i.e. national) enterprises. This arrangement placed a premium on the military commander's ability to prosecute the war with limited supplies, to coordinate his military activities with troops under state control, and to accept and work with the resulting inefficiency.

Civil supremacy and state autonomy—these were essential, non-negotiable supports in the architecture of the new republic, and their erosion would have been considered more devastating than a return to British rule. Given the weightiness of these concerns, it is understandable why John Hancock, a man with no war experience, seriously considered himself a candidate for the command given Washington. And if Hancock's conception of that command was naive as to its military aspects, few were inclined to exaggerate those. Washington was certainly preferred over Hancock because he had once been an active soldier; however, the men who chose Washington were as much impressed by his experience in the Virginia legislature as by his experience in the Virginia militia. Their reasoning was prophetic. From the very beginning of his appointment, Washington found himself in the role of not only a war leader but also a diplomat negotiating civil-military and state-national boundaries. His duties, in this regard, were pressing. Through eight years of war, Washington's correspondence with state governors and legislators was almost as voluminous as his correspondence with members of the Continental Congress, even though it was to Congress alone that he was formally obligated.

In the strictly military realm, too, Washington's duties were far more expansive than those now commonly assigned to commanding officers. Recruitment, acquisition of supplies and weapons, and other routine functions now carried out by staff were then the commanding general's responsibility. No one who has even skimmed through Washington's twenty-five volumes of wartime correspondence (more than any other American officer has produced) can doubt that he took that responsibility seriously. Washington was, by far, more of an administrator than a fighter. He was the army's ambassador to civil authority, its chief administrator, and its top strategist and warrior—in descending order of importance. At least, that is how the most influential men of his time regarded him. The perception of the masses could not have been much different. During the tedious war years, Washington's regard for civil authority and his concern for the maintenance and well-being of the army were repeatedly mentioned in the public media, and were as much a part of his public identity as were his activities on the battlefield.[42]

The Americans' restrained conception of their commander's fighting role reflected their ambivalence toward military leadership in general. To be sure, they wanted a soldier to help express their defiance of "the Ministry" and to defend their land, but they wanted no part of a professional soldier committed solely to the craft of war. Thus, a few weeks after his appointment, Washington was personally addressed by the New York Congress: "[We] have the fullest assurances that whenever this important contest shall be decided ... you will cheerfully resign the important deposit committed into your hands, and re-assume the character of our worthy citizen."[43] Lacking tested institutional constraints on the ambitions of strong leaders, and with the ever-present examples of Caesar and Cromwell to justify anxieties about the imposition of dictatorship, Americans at war looked not to their best military man for direction but to the military man in whom they had the most trust. One commentator thus justified his preference for a native-born commander over the superbly trained and experienced Charles Lee, declaring that "the colonies are not so wrapped up in General Lee's military accomplishments as to give him preference.... "[44] As to Washington's own training and accomplishments, "[t]he General very well knows," said Henry Laurens (future president of Congress), that "we are, and will continue to make suitable allowances for all defects seeming or real.... "[45]

By "suitable allowances," Mr. Laurens did not mean unconditional tolerance of failure. But the margin of tolerance that was allowed for by Laurens and his congressional colleagues helped to protect Washington from the one serious challenge to his command. When Philadelphia fell to the British, General Horatio Gates, fresh from victory at Saratoga, contemplated a project, along with General Thomas Conway, Thomas Mifflin, and others, to disparage Washington in the eyes of Congress and force his retirement. These men felt they had good reason to seek Washington's dismissal. They believed the Commander in Chief had made strategic and tactical errors which contributed to the fall of New York and Philadelphia. Yet, the plan never got far beyond the circle of its own designers. Elbridge Gerry, for example, was unable "to make any Discoveries that can justify Suspicion of a Plan's being formed to injure the Reputation of [Washington] or remove [him] from office." Likewise, Eliphalet Dyer assured his correspondent "that there is not the most distant thought of removing General Washington, nor ever an expression in Congress looking that way." And while Henry Laurens was aware of certain disagreements between Washington and the Congress, he assured Lafayette that "it would be very easy to convince [Washington] there has not anything been designedly done or omitted to affront him."[46] The name subsequently given to the anti-Washington operation, the "Conway Cabal," explains why so many delegates to Congress were for so long unaware of it. The conspirators kept their views secret because they felt they were in a minority. They were right. "Washington or no army!" was the cry of the vast majority of officers who learned about the conspiracy.[47]

The defeats that led to the loss of Philadelphia convinced few in the military, or elsewhere, that Washington should be replaced. Competence entered into part, but not all, of this general assessment. From Brandywine, where Washington's defense line was outflanked, reports attributed defeat to a "misfortune" bearing no relation to "the propriety of his whole conduct in opposing the enemy's march to Philadelphia." Likewise, if Washington failed to take Germantown, where another enemy force was deployed against the capital city, he did give the British what they themselves called their worst "drubbing since Bunker's Hill." But even if there were some doubt regarding his military talents, it mattered little. In the long run, it was character and motivation that Americans prized above all else. "[Concerning] the affairs of Long Island and Fort Washington," explained one commentator, "I intend no reflection on the judgment of the general officers whose opinions may have been the foundation of those disasters, for their opinions certainly proceeded from a spirit of enterprise and true intrepidity, a spirit which, I trust, will never be severely condemned by us, however it may fail of success."[48]

Acutely suspicious of the aspirations of men in power, few Americans were willing to base their judgment of any officer solely on his military skill. This attitude applied with special force to the Commander in Chief. Washington was indispensable to the cause not because of his narrow technical aptitudes but because he had become, through the good will occasioned by his mediation of national, local, and military interests, a focal point of America's political consensus. He had become almost everyone's "representative man." Benjamin Rush, though critical of Washington's military performance, confessed that he "is idolized by the people of America and is tho't to be absolutely necessary for us to ... carry out the war."[49] Not the man's prowess in battle but the man himself is what united and animated the nation.

Ways of Imagining Greatness

Strong religious convictions reinforced the people's allegiance to Washington. Battles might be lost, but in the ultimate success of the war most Americans felt confident. Past experience had already shown the great logistical problems experienced by European armies fighting on American soil, and the colonists felt that they could well exploit this disadvantage.[50] But the belief in ultimate victory shared by most Americans was motivated more by religious sentiments than by technical considerations. Before Washington's appointment there had already been several skirmishes with the British, and in most of these (at Great Bridge, Nantucket, Hog Island, Gloucester, Ticonderoga, Lexington, and Boston), the American militias had given a good account of themselves. These small victories inspired confidence, largely because the press and pulpit ascribed a religious significance to them. "One source of the revolutionaries' confidence lay in their obedience to God. A religious vocabulary voiced many of the calls to serve in the Continental Army and to promote its cause. . . . God intended His punishment of war-makers only for Britons, and He entrusted its execution to Americans. . . . This explanation obviously allowed only one outcome—American victory."[51] The prevailing belief in providential intervention put God on America's side, and rendered every occurrence on the battlefield a manifestation of the Divine Plan.[52]

Washington's role in this "legend of providential intervention"[53] was understood in terms of an important aspect of the prevailing covenant theology. Specifically, the story of the Israelites' exodus from the land of Egypt provided Americans with a model of their own experience with England,[54] enabling them to transform a complicated geopolitical struggle into familiar religious terms. This paradigm, depicting America as a land promised and granted by God, had been deeply rooted in the collective consciousness from the very beginning of settlement. When the Massachusetts colony, in the mid–seventeenth century, undertook to codify its law, it looked back instinctively to the Exodus and adopted the

Mosaic code as its own. So when the late eighteenth century Americans searched for precedents to aid them in understanding the meaning of their war with Britain, they turned again to the Exodus. Americans believed—indeed in most cases, took for granted—that their contest with Britain was a matter of history repeating itself, a recapitulation of an ancient struggle for liberty. For this reason, the initial design for the Seal of the United States, devised in 1776 by Thomas Jefferson, Benjamin Franklin, and John Adams,[55] depicted on one of its sides Egypt's Pharoah in an open chariot passing through the Red Sea in pursuit of the Israelites. On the opposing shore stood Moses, illuminated by rays from a Pillar of Fire, extending his arm toward the sea and causing it to overwhelm Pharoah and his hosts. The motto: "Rebellion to Tyrants is Obedience to God." (See Fig. 1.)

It seemed foreordained, at least in hindsight, that someone would play the leading role in the American Exodus drama. When Washington emerged, he was the most plausible Moses. A few days after the British army evacuated Boston in March 1776, the Reverend Leonard, in a service attended by Washington, preached a sermon "well adapted to the interesting [important] event of the day," from Exodus xiv:25: "And He locked their chariot wheels, and caused them to drive heavily; and the Egyptians said, 'Let us flee from the face of Israel, for the Lord fighteth for them against the Egyptians.'"[56] This parallel was important for Washington, because it embodied the criterion for his success as military commander. Based on a recognition of Great Britain's power, this standard did not require decisive military victory. Citizens of the "New Israel" knew that Moses, the leader of their spiritual predecessors, prevailed not by annihilating his enemies but by preserving his followers from annihilation. Not by his own powers did he do so, but by force of the Covenant. Correspondingly, the military retreats of the "American Moses" were often defined not as defeats but as acts of deliverance, and they were followed by prayers of gratitude.[57] Thus the successful retreat from Long Island was made possible by the Lord of Hosts, who intervened "by sending a thick fog about two o'clock in the morning which hung over Long Island while on New York side it was clear." Similarly, when the British General Howe hesitated before taking Philadelphia, it was said that "he stopped short on the borders of the river, as if afraid that the waters of the Delaware, like another Red Sea, would overwhelm the pursuers of the injured Americans, who had in many instances as manifestly experienced the protecting hand of Providence, as the favored Israelites."[58]

But if his religious countrymen could find even in Washington's failures the delivering hand of God, that discovery did not detract from the praise accorded him on the occasions of real victory. Convinced that God's favor depended on each man's effort within his own calling, the Protestant people of America had no trouble reconciling their applause for personal success with their belief in divine intervention. Disastrous or repeated failures would probably have shattered this rationalization, but Washington's failures, according to newspaper accounts, seemed neither serious nor frequent, and victory came often enough to convince pious America that its commander was a man who had earned the right to remain the agent of Providence.

In short, the earliest manifestation of the worship of "godlike Washington," as Americans came to call him, did not depend—could not have depended—on technical genius, nor even on persistence and fortitude (which became apparent only with the passage of time). Washington's deification answered instead to the new nation's need to articulate and concretize the fervent beliefs and emotions of its citizens and the intangible virtues of their cause.

Biblical precedent for George Washington's military role was discovered in the heat of the first several months of war. That was no coincidence. Times of excitement and danger, of "collective effervescence," are times when men enter into relations with the realm of the sacred. The nature of that realm, however, must be properly understood. Sacred things differ from profane things not as good differs from evil but rather as the extraordinary differs from the mundane. Thus, great men of evil may be godlike—morally inferior, it is true, but nonetheless endowed with extraordinary powers, and treated accordingly.[59] The extraordinary powers in whose presence Americans found themselves in the tumult of 1775–76 were sacred powers of two kinds: the benevolent, godlike power symbolized by George Washington and the malevolent, Satanic power represented by George III. Positive rites of praise performed in reference to Washington were accompanied by negative rites of condemnation directed against the King.

Thomas Paine's *Common Sense* set the stage for the ritual degradation of the King by its systematic revelation of his "true" character: Paine transformed the former "Father of his People" into the "Royal Calumniator," the "cruelest sovereign tyrant of the age." The newspaper media, too, disparaged the people's protector. George III became "George the fool," George the "monster in human form," whose "name darkens the moral sky and stinks in the nostrils of the world." Another commentator expressed a similar sentiment in verse: "One prayer is left, which dreads no proud reply, / That He who made you breathe, would bid you die." Along with the symbolic assaults—the removal by angry crowds of the King's coat of arms from courthouses, churches, taverns, and shops; the destruction of royal portraits and statues—came the ultimate malediction: "God bless Great Washington; God damn the King."[60]

However, to conceive George Washington as a god and George III as a devil is to miss both the ambivalence of the attitudes held in regard to them and the irony in the symbols through which these attitudes were expressed. Specifically, Americans paid homage to Washington through venerational forms once reserved for the King.

The Americans' continued use of monarchical forms extended far into the past. People in crisis fortify themselves by embracing their culture's most meaningful experiences. Incorporating traditional patterns of belief, feeling, and conduct, these experiences become "root paradigms,"[61] stable points of reference for interpretation of the current situation. During their war for independence, Americans came under the influence of two such paradigms: the first, the Exodus, attached them to their religious roots; the second, monarchy, made firm the grip of their political roots. The two models were not equivalent in salience and influence. As a remote event which no American knew firsthand, the Exodus provided dramatic metaphors for political experience. As an immediate power to which most Americans had recently been subject, monarchy was the stuff of political experience itself. Out of this experience were carried vital modes of thinking, feeling, and acting which Americans transferred to their new leader. Linked to the institution of kingship, Washington's stature could develop around symbols of authority already established in the American mind.

If the Revolutionary War effectively overthrew and disposed of the substance of monarchy, the cult of the monarch could persist in a new republic. Thus Americans remained in the grip of monarchical tradition long after they had established their new government. Having venerated a king until 1775, they had learned to attach themselves to the state through regard for a single individual.[62] Perhaps because they did so with little conscious reflection, Benjamin Franklin believed in "a natural inclination to Kingly Government."[63] Although others did not attribute this inclination to nature, they were acutely aware of its power and endurance. In a remark addressed to the young generation of Americans born and reared under a republican regime, Rufus King, a representative of the older generation (and an official in Washington's presidential administration), wrote:

> You young men who have been born since the Revolution, look with horror upon the name of a King, and upon all propositions for a strong government. It was not so with us. We were born the subjects of a King, and were accustomed to subscribe ourselves "the Majesty's most faithful subjects"; and we began the quarrel which ended in the Revolution, not against the King, but against his parliament.[64]

Rufus King's memory was accurate. Just a few months after the official Declaration of Independence, "A Farmer" delivered his opinion on the political inclination of the Americans. It is a "monarchical spirit," which "is natural from the government they have ever lived under." This tradition, he added, is reinforced by the existing social structure, with its "great distinction of persons and difference in their estates or property." Several years later Jefferson would concede: "We were educated in royalism; no wonder if some of us retain that idolatry still."[65]

The number of people Jefferson referred to cannot be determined; it was almost certainly a minority. Yet, old forms get filled with new content. Long after monarchy was repudiated as an institution, it continued to furnish the cognitive schema for linking America's masses to a republican state. George Washington became George III's symbolic successor. "The Father of His People" was replaced by "The Father of His Country." The common name, George, lent irony to a transition that became apparent soon after the start of war. Thus the last stanza of the previously mentioned "New Song" concludes: "And George, his minions trembling round, dismounted from his throne / Pay homage to America and glorious WASHINGTON." Another conception of Washington as the new embodiment of America appeared shortly after the Battle of Trenton: "God save the King, the British heroes cry'd / And God for Washington! Columbia's sons reply'd."[66] The tune of the traditional anthem "God Save the King" remained the same; however, its lyrics were changed to "God Save Great Washington." On newly minted coins Washington's face appeared and the King's disappeared; but the style was often the same, as in the Georgius Triumpho coin (Fig. 2), patterned directly after the coin that bore the image of George III.

Naming patterns, too, showed that Washington had replaced the monarch as America's source of political identification. From the very beginning of New World settlement, English colonists named their most important places after royal governors and kings. With the onset of war appeared a new name on the land. Fort Washington and Washington Heights appeared on Manhattan Island in 1776. Shortly afterward, counties in North Carolina, Maryland, and Virginia and towns in North Carolina and New Hampshire were named after the American commander. In 1781, Washington County was formed in Pennsylvania. In 1782, the college in Chestertown, Maryland, was renamed Washington College.[67]

Traditionally, royal dignity was honored not only by naming practice but also by observance of the king's birthday. Here, too, George Washington replaced George III. In 1781, about ten months before the siege of Yorktown, General Washington's birthday was celebrated at a special dinner attended by American and French officers. A year later, after the Yorktown victory, the public celebrations began. In Richmond, Virginia, Washington's birthday was observed with "utmost demonstrations of joy." Several months before the official termination of the war there were dinners and toasts in Cambridge, Massachusetts; New York City; and Talbot Court House, Maryland. Plans were laid to make the celebrations permanent.[68]

Into this incipient cult of veneration flowed the outpourings of poets. Production began early. Upon Washington's assumption of command in 1775, Phillis Wheatley, the nation's first black poet, sent Washington a note explaining that his appointment "excite[s] sensations not easy to suppress." To the note she attached a poem of praise. The poem concludes with a wish that, for many, must have seemed a little more than metaphorical: "A crown, a mansion, and a throne that shine / With gold unfading, Washington! be thine." Every subsequent military event evoked a barrage of venerational odes. Prominently displayed in newspapers through-out the colonies, the best of these verses helped banish from the public mind all thought of the once glorious king, and attributed his former qualities—his "great soul," "godlike virtues," and "in-born greatness"—to the new hero. Americans had lost a monarch but gained something better: a demigod, whose merit "Fame's thousand tongues confess."[69]

To the monarchical symbolism of the Washington cult no me-dium contributed more than iconography. The importance to the people of icons as political symbols was apparent from the very beginning of the rebellion. Thus, in New York's Bowling Green Square on July 9, 1776, a British observer recalled how

> an elegant equesterian statue of our most gracious sovereign was openly profaned by the sacreligious hands of traitors, set on by public orders of seditious leaders, who called themselves gentlemen; who had often in the most solemn manner appealed to heaven as a witness of their immaculate loyalty to that amiable prince, whom now they insult in pamphlets and printed speeches, with the title of "Royal Brute"; ... after shamefully mutilating the highest ornament of New York, they carried it about in scandalous procession treating a noble image of the sacred Majesty of Britain with indignity most atrocious, most im-pious, and diabolical.[70]

Against a background of mock funerals for the King, the passage of laws denying him public praise, and a torrent of verbal abuse carried by the press, the iconoclasm at Bowling Green was a nat-ural accompaniment to the public announcement of indepen-dence made earlier in the day. The full significance of the destruc-tion of the King's statue at Bowling Green (if not of the equestrian features of the statue itself) was recognized by European engrav-ers as well as by American artists, who would later use that event as a background emblem in their paintings of Washington. A rev-olutionary turning point in American history was symbolized by an unoccupied royal pedestal (Fig. 3–4).

After independence was declared, American artists launched a campaign to create for the nation a new, republican effigy. Among the conventions exploited for this purpose was the riding horse—a symbol of *royal* power that went back to antiquity. In one variant of this convention, the leader stands beside a horse tended by an aide or servant, as in both the portrait of Charles I and the 1780 engraving of Washington. In a second variant, Washington is scarcely distinguishable from Napoleon as he sits astride his steed, with fierce martial expression, ready to meet the enemies of the state. Another symbol of military power exploited by the republican artist was the armor of the ancient warrior—whereby the fully clad father of the newly established republic takes on an appearance similar to George III himself (Figs. 5–8).

In none of these engravings is it insinuated that Washington might be welcome in the actual role of monarch. On the contrary, the titles affixed to some of his pictures, like "George Washington, Esquire" and "Farmer Washington" underscore his membership in a nonhereditary landed gentry. Not as a reincarnation of aristocratic authority but as a rebel against that authority (disdaining even its most conciliatory gestures) is how Washington was regarded. Yet, these republican motifs were expressed by use of the same artistic devices employed previously to acclaim kings.

Monarchical elements insinuated themselves into the meaning and use as well as the substance of the Washington portraits. Most educated Americans believed that portraits of rulers had an edifying effect upon the people, and their belief was part of a long tradition. As a young man, Julius Caesar is said to have been so moved by a statue of Alexander that he immediately determined to emulate him. Icons of the early church (which derived theoretical justification from imperial Roman statuary) were designed to awaken and direct the people's moral sensibilities and so provide an aid to salvation.[71] After the images of Christ, the Virgin, and the saints were cast out of late-sixteenth-century English churches and replaced by Queen Elizabeth's, it was assumed that the new icons would promote "civile discipline" by stirring in men's minds the virtues of secular piety and reverence.[72]

Similarly, when the Pennsylvania legislature in 1779 commissioned Charles Willson Peale to execute a likeness of Washington for its statehouse, it did so for the expressed purpose of promoting public morals. Contemplation of the General's portrait, its sponsors hoped, "may excite others to tread in the same glorious and disinterested steps which lead to public happiness and private honor."[73] Peale finished his sacred task, the icon was displayed, and the public adored it. All went well—until the painting was irretrievably defaced by vandals. In the reaction to this desecration one is reminded of the way Britons had reacted several years earlier to the desecration of the King's statue. The parallel tells something of what Washington had become to his countrymen:

Last night, a fit time for the sons of Lucifer to perpetuate the deeds of darkness, one or more volunteers in the service of hell, broke into the State House in Philadelphia, and totally defaced the picture of his Excellency George Washington.... Every generous bosom must swell with indignation at such atrocious proceedings. It is a matter of grief and sorrowful reflection that any of the human race can be so abandoned.... A being who carries such malice in his breast must be miserable beyond conception. We need wish him no other punishment than his own feelings. "The motions of his spirit are black as night, and his affections dark as Erebus" [the son of Chaos and Night].[74]

Disseminating the Image

That same attitude which led Americans to regard the Washington portrait as a sacred object—something to be protected and cherished—goes a long way to helping us understand its widespread distribution. Precedents for such dissemination are numerous. Primitive people placed images of their sacred totem on everything that belonged to them: helmets, shields, weapons, utensils, tools, walls, doors, canoes, funeral piles—even their own flesh. The ancient Greeks felt forlorn and abandoned when enlightened legislators removed images of their gods from public display; they were restored because the people needed a tangible representation of their gods to contemplate and adore. The movement to introduce icons into the early Christian church was instigated for the same reason. Legitimation of political authority, like that of spiritual authority, was harnessed to the custom of making images of the gods. Dispersion of the ruler's portrait, however unlifelike, satisfied his subjects' desire for a tangible representation of him, and so made him ubiquitous, like the gods.[75]

In eighteenth-century America, the first major efforts to disseminate Washington's image were made by Charles Willson Peale. In 1776 and 1777, Peale had completed a number of portraits (all commissioned by private subscribers), of which one—a 1776 painting ordered by John Hancock—was immediately mass-produced (Fig. 9). Copies of Peale's portrait gave to a people scattered from Massachusetts to Georgia (just as copies of the King's image gave to a people scattered across the globe) a common icon. At the sound of the great man's name, the same picture flashed into everyone's mind. Reproduced in books, magazines, children's primers, broadsides, sheet music, and bank notes, the Peale portrait brought Washington to the immediate presence of those who would never otherwise have been able to see him.

Many of these representations were too crude to resemble any human being, let alone Washington; but if the people were concerned only to have authentic likenesses of Washington, then the more accurate engravings would have quickly driven out of the market the inferior versions. In fact, the crude engravings continued to be used to the very end of the century and beyond, despite the availability of better copies. The tolerance accorded the portraits' technical failings reveals something of their social function. Americans wanted a representation of Washington not only to satisfy their curiosity as to what he looked like but also because they felt a need to represent the intangible things Washington stood for by means of a material sign, no matter how technically inaccurate that sign might be (Figs. 10–11).

Peale was to create for the republic many representations of Washington. His last wartime project, commissioned in 1783 by the trustees of Princeton College to replace "the picture of the late King [George II] of Great Britain, which was torn away" (by a cannon ball, during the battle of Princeton),[76] underscored the symbolic function that all his portraits fulfilled.

The royal countenance was displaced by many other efforts. Congress had voted in 1783 for the erection of its own equestrian statue of Washington. Although that project was never funded,[77] many painters, including John Trumbull, William Dunlap, Joseph Wright, and James Peale Polk, supplied their private patrons with life portraits of the great man. Most of these portraits, copied by the original artist, were later engraved, with a view to meeting an insatiable demand from the public at large. A republican version of the monarchical icon was mass-produced:

All over the land, at the close of the war, his beloved image was substituted on banner, seal, parlor wall, journal, and bank note, for royal physiognomies: and Rip Van Winkle was not the only conservative absentee, who increduously rubbed his eyes at the appearance of our republican chief on the tavern sign so long radiant with a kingly visage. In every museum in America, his majestic figure stood prominent among the wax groups on which children gazed with delight, solemn in black velvet, ruffles, and hair-powder; grotesque [illustrations drawn on translucent material and illuminated from behind by fire] on festal nights, Liverpool [kitchen] ware, primitive magazines, the figure-heads of ships, the panels of coaches, and engraved buttons, rude cotton prints, and melancholy samplers, every object in the economy of trade and domestic life, was decorated, more or less truthfully, with that endeared and hallowed countenance. . . . [78]

Such was the significance of the Washington image and the uses to which it was put at the end of the War of Independence. To almost everyone who lived at that time, Washington had become the new symbol of national consciousness. The uproar that took place in every town he passed through, the places named for him, the birthday celebrations held, the poetry written, the images graven in his honor—these are things of which no American could have been unaware. They enabled the new republic to continue to focus its attention "on one person doing interesting actions," rather than dividing its attention among "many, who are all doing uninteresting actions."[79] Thus did a new venerational cult sustain America's tendency to concentrate its political affections. Thus did Washington remain the object of that cult long after the conditons that first gave rise to it had disappeared.

The Americans' intense approbation of George Washington was shaped by both the military situation they faced and the unstable world in which they lived. As new situations arose, the magnitude and quality of that approbation would take a new course, one that would transform an honored military hero into a Founding Father. If Washington became the object of venerational sentiment previously invested in a king, his reputation would also prove indispensable to the building of republican institutions. The transformation, however, was an ambivalent one.

The presence of monarchical elements in America's veneration of Washington reminds us that throughout the eighteenth century, America, though jealous of its liberties, was not egalitarian; it was a society of deference, a society "consisting of an elite and a nonelite, in which the nonelite regard the elite, without too much resentment, as being of a superior status and culture to their own, and consider elite leadership in political matters to be something normal and natural."[80] Indeed, the virtuous members of this elite class, these "strong rods of community," were "looked up to as fathers," for their benign influence was considered the ultimate guarantee of society's well-being. On the continued vereration of such rulers, American political thinkers believed, depended the stability of government itself.[81]

John Adams's statement in Congress on the "superstitious veneration" of Washington, however, reflected the other side of America's political culture. If eighteenth-century Americans admired virtuous leaders, they deplored hero worship ("idolatry," as they were more likely to call it)—they wrote against it in their public and private correspondence; they spoke against it in their conversations and in their speeches and sermons. Believing that all authority, social and political, must be distrusted and constantly scrutinized, most Americans saw in even their most popular leaders the potential for tyranny. They took seriously Samuel Adams's warning: "Let us beware of continental and state great men."[82]

In this attitude toward leaders is to be found a deep paradox. Political fears that in themselves would inhibit hero worship rested on assumptions that actually promoted it. The very importance that Americans attributed to powerful men rendered them objects of both esteem and suspicion. Ambivalence, not intensity, therefore, made American hero worship distinctive. This duality of admiration and fear, this proneness to self-examination, played a key part in the American people's wartime reaction to George Washington. Praise for Washington erupted in the midst of martial enthusiasm, and its evolution seemed to be unaffected by the course of events. The praise itself was bombastic; its volume, massive. But the people who participated in this cult of veneration rarely lost themselves in it. Their attachment to Washington was at once emotional and rational; they contemplated their own venerational passions. And if this capacity for reflexive deliberation, this self-inhibiting and self-correcting inner reflection, was not unique to eighteenth-century Americans, it was carried further and with more urgency by them regarding their attitude toward Washington than by any of their European contemporaries with respect to the leaders they admired. Some Americans did more reflecting than others; some did so more publicly than others; but in the aggregate, and even during the headiest days of the war, they never tired of questioning the sources and consequences of their own approbation.

2

Hero Worship and Nation Building

O Washington! how do I love thy name! How have I often adored and blessed thy God, for creating and forming thee the great ornament of human kind!. . . . Our very enemies stop the madness of their fire in full volley, stop the illiberality of their slander at thy name, as if rebuked from Heaven with a "Touch not mine Anointed, and do my Hero no harm!" Thy fame is of sweeter perfume than Arabian spices in the gardens of Persia. . . . Listening angels shall catch the odor, waft it to heaven, and perfume the universe![1]

That is how Ezra Stiles, president of Yale University, saw George Washington at war's end, in 1783. Few Americans disagreed with Stiles, and the succeeding years of peace did nothing to change their opinion.

The years spent by Washington in private retreat, far from diminishing his reputation, made his reputation all the more secure. To a people that feared ambitious men, the retirement itself was grounds for approbation, proof that Washington pursued neither power nor fortune in return for his military service. And so, whenever he left Mount Vernon, he was greeted by formal ceremonies, salutes, and flattering addresses. To Washington's regret, Mount Vernon itself had become a "must see"—a shrine as much as a stopover—for every prominent traveler in Northern Virginia. Coins bearing Washington's image multiplied and found their way into every pocket in the republic. Like most of the wartime engravings, the coinage proclaimed Washington's symbolic role by associating him with national emblems. On some coins, the laureled chieftain, depicted on the head, is joined, on the reverse side, to the goddess of liberty (who holds Liberty Pole and Liberty Cap), to the goddess of justice (who holds her scales), or to intertwined olive branches representing unity. On another coin Washington's image appears on both sides, as if the great man needed no symbolic context other than himself (Fig. 12).

The portraitists, too, continued their work. Antoine Houdon, Joseph Wright, Robert Pine, and the Peale family all sculpted or painted him from life. So fast and furiously did they follow one another that Washington found himself "altogether at their beck." At first he protested, but having realized what he had become, "Now no dray moves more readily to the thill [wagon] than I to the painter's chair."[2]

The grounds for Washington's continued popularity were revealed in statements offered during the increasingly elaborate celebrations of his birth. An editorial in the *New York Gazette* asked: "After the Almighty Author of our existence and happiness, to whom, as a people, are we under the greatest obligation? I know you will answer 'To Washington.'" In the same issue of the *Gazette,* a poet sung: "Glorious deeds he has done, / By him our cause is won / Long live great Washington!"[3] The apotheosis was complete. Having delivered his country from the yoke of British tyranny, Washington had become the reason for America's present well-being. He would be the reason for America's future well-being, too. Returning to public life as leader of the Federal (Constitutional) Convention in Philadelphia, he was met by the joyous chiming of bells.

Yet, the enthusiastic reaction to Washington's arrival in Philadelphia bothered many citizens. Not the man praised but the praise itself was the basis of their concern. Unchallenged, the panegyric was beginning to border on blasphemy. Many pious Philadelphians who saw the Washington cult rejuvenated at the Federal Convention must have recalled one "Mary Meanwell's" letter to the *Freeman's Journal,* written five years earlier, after the Yorktown campaign:

> Having read Mr. Bradford's paper of Nov. 21, these words struck me, "WASHINGTON, THE SAVIOUR OF HIS COUNTRY." I trembled and said, "Shall we attribute to the arm of flesh, what the Almighty has done for America? I respect our great general, but let us not make a GOD of

him!" It must give him pain, and cause him to blush, when he finds that "What is due to our Creator is attributed to him."

The first of the ten commands, which forbid idolatry, is now before me. For this reason, Sir, I am not ashamed to date this from the time that my Bible suggested the thought to me, when I recollected what I read in Mr. Bradford's paper and compared it with the Almighty's command.[4]

In deification there are also political dangers. Miss Meanwell recognized this in her follow-up letter, which described the excessive praise of Washington as an offense "to every principled whig."[5] With this assessment many readers must have agreed. If the overwhelming and seemingly unconditional praise of Washington helped to mobilize the aspirations and sentiments of the rebelling colonists, it might also allow Washington to assume power outside the law and to use that power to impose his will upon others, with the help of the army he then commanded. William Tudor had expressed this concern two years before Yorktown. Even though final victory was then far from sight, he warned of its consequences as he spoke of Washington in a public address:

> Bondage is ever to be apprehended at the close of a successful struggle for liberty, when a triumphant army, elated with victories, and headed by a popular general may become more formidable than the tyrant that has been expelled. . . . Witness the aspiring CROMWELL! . . . A free and wise people will never suffer any citizen to become too popular—much less too powerful. A man may be formidable to the constitution even by his virtues.[6]

Tudor's speech articulated an apprehension that had been felt by others. In late 1777, almost a year after he had warned Congress against its "superstitious veneration" of General Washington, John Adams expressed relief that the American victory at Saratoga was not masterminded by him. Adams explained: "If it had been, idolatry and adulation would have been unbounded; so excessive as to endanger our liberties, for what I know. Now, we can allow a certain citizen to be wise, virtuous and good without thinking him a deity or Savior."[7]

In view of these anxieties, what Washington did not do during the final phase of his military career was more important than his positive accomplishments. As John W. Daniel later put it, "he left mankind bewildered with the splendid problem of whether to admire him most for what he was or what he would not be."[8] Indeed, what Washington was, in the popular view, was shaped to a great extent by what he chose not to be. The facts of the matter were many and well known. The main point was recognized by the Marquis de Chastellux during his 1781 travels: "This is the seventh year that [Washington] has commanded the army, and that he has obeyed the Congress; more need not be said, especially in America, where they know how to appreciate all the merit contained in this simple fact."[9] The observation was a sound one. Despite many wartime disagreements with Congress, Washington faithfully deferred to its policies and so affirmed the then cherished but not yet established principle of civilian control of the military. When given emergency dictatorial powers by Congress, he never abused them. Despite his great popularity, which could have been used as a cushion against military setbacks and a weapon against Congress, Washington made it known to Congress that he was ready to resign his command at any time. Even more, he showed himself to be a great ally when Congress was itself in need. During the Newburgh crisis, when Washington could have taken over the government by military coup, he dissuaded his unpaid officers and men from taking action against the vulnerable and financially bankrupt Congress. And not only did Washington sternly rebuke those who wished to restore the monarchy around him; he hastened to surrender his military power at war's end and returned to private life. Washington's wartime conduct stilled the fears of those who saw in his prestige the seeds of tyranny. That Washington had placed himself above suspicion, and that his reputation largely hinged on this achievement, is the key to understanding his postwar role in national affairs.

A New Political Order

After the trials of war, America confronted the task of nation building. It was in the context of this task that the veneration of Washington assumed a new and critical significance.

The primary role of charismatic leaders, according to Max Weber, is the creation of new institutions; yet, in Weber's formulation, the radicalism of these leaders, their alienation from the stable structures of society, prevents them from taking part in the consolidation of such historic changes as they bring about. For this task, disciples of an administrative bent of mind are needed, men who can incorporate new ideas and new ways of doing things into the normal functioning of society. It is all a matter of an effective division of labor: Old orders can be brought down and new ones conceived by charismatic leaders, but it takes noncharismatic types to bring heaven to earth, to translate innovative ideas into stable institutional structures.[10]

But this was not the case in America's transition from war to nation building. The activities that culminated in the Federal Constitution involved more than mundane organizational work; they were infused by, and contributed to, the same kind of social climate as that which prevailed during the war. The years of war and nation building were "hot years" of collective enthusiasm and effort. In both periods, Americans experienced a special closeness to one another. They were all caught up in *la vie sérieuse*—engaged by transcendent issues, animated by ideals, and vividly aware of the relationship of these to the great man in their midst.

The man himself helped to translate his followers' enthusiasm and ideals into a new order. Having presided over the dismantlement of the old order, Washington was, in this respect, his own successor, but he played the successor role in a unique way. Americans knew that history was filled with examples of authoritarian leaders who exploited their personal popularity to legitimate policies and actions that brought the government under their personal control. In contrast, Washington used his popularity to legitimate the policies and actions of others. Many took part in the formation of the government; Washington's role was to stake his reputation on the outcome. He sanctified the new system not by controlling it but by simply identifying himself with it. Correspondingly, loyalty to Washington the individual held the government together until the people could learn to be loyal to the government itself.[11]

Whether Washington's presence was essential to the creation of that government is difficult to say. Had he died earlier, the names of other notable Americans might have been invoked successfully to mobilize support for the new federal system. But Washington did not die, and many Americans believed that the national authority could not have been established without him. During the American nation-building period, therefore, Washington's reputation was more than a collective representation of national values; it was a positive force in its own right. The prestige conferred upon Washington during the War of Independence was an inter-est-gathering deposit, later drawn upon to promote and ratify the Constitution.

In the absence of legal precedent, the Federal Convention re-quired the prestige and authority of Washington's presence.[12] However, most observers felt that Washington's participation was essential to the success as well as the legitimacy of the convention. Prior to the meeting, James Monroe, in a letter to Jefferson, sug-gested that "the presence of General Washington will have great weight in the body itself, so as to overawe and keep under the demon of party [sectional interests], and that the signature of his name to whatever act shall be the result of their deliberations will secure its passage thro' the union."[13] "Because a FRANKLIN and a WASHINGTON are among the number of those who gave ap-probation to it," Alexander Hamilton also expressed confidence that the new Constitution would be ratified.[14] Monroe and Ham-ilton were both right. Everyone knew that Washington presided over the creation of the Constitution and was the first to sign it. Praise of Washington filled newspapers sympathetic with the Con-stitution in an effort to exploit his identification with it. His pres-tige was invoked at every state convention, and opponents of the Constitution were obliged to rationalize their disagreement with him. A letter to Jefferson concerning Virginia's ratification bears a conclusion that must have been applicable to many other states: "Be assured," wrote James Monroe, "that General Washington's influence carried this government."[15]

Washington's influence was instrumental not only to the accep-tance of the Constitution but also to its very conception of the government's executive branch. From the extreme Whig delegates of some of the Northern states, there was strong opposition to proposals for executive power. This power, the critics believed, would in effect, if not by design, give the President the rights of a king. Sensitive as all delegates were to the prospect of executive abuse, the convention nevertheless provided for a strong presi-dency. These powers were not unlimited, but the assumption that Washington would be their first custodian seemed to diminish the need for checks that had been imposed elsewhere. Governments established by state constitutions limited the tenure of important positions for the expressed purpose of inhibiting their power. For this same reason, much criticism and debate ensued when the six-year Senate term was proposed to the Federal Convention.

Yet, no limits at all were placed on the President's term, and there was no serious debate about it. Certain that no other man would be President, it seems as if the delegates did not want to shortchange themselves, or insult Washington, by placing a time limit on his incumbency. As South Carolina's Pierce Butler put it in a letter about the Executive's powers, "Entre nous, I do not believe they would have been so great, had not many of the members cast their eyes toward General Washington as President; and shaped their ideas of the powers to be given a President, by their opinions of his Virtue."[16] To the question whether these powers might be abused by one of Washington's successors, William Lewis of Pennslyvania could find no better reply than "General Washington lives, and as he will be appointed President, jealousy [suspicion] on this head vanishes."[17] Evidently, the public's image of Washington had blended so deeply into its image of the presidency as to make the two virtually inseparable. The presidency was Washington; Washington, the presidency. In subsequent years, incumbents might benefit from the dignity of this high office; in 1789, the office benefited from the dignity of its incumbent. Washington's reputation legitimated the presidency.

However, at a time when political suspicions ran so high, few would have had total confidence in any President, not even Washington. And so, after the Constitutional Convention (so named only in hindsight) adjourned, James Monroe praised Washington's willingness to forsake his retirement in favor of the public good, but then added:

> Having however commenced again on the public theatre the course which he takes becomes not only highly interesting [critical] to him but likewise to us: the human character is not perfect; and if he partakes of those qualities which we *have too much reason* to believe are almost inseparable from the frail nature of our being the people of America will be lost. . . . [18]

Whether Washington would become a charismatic dictator, as Monroe feared, remained to be seen. But if no one could be totally certain of Washington, they could be more certain of him than of any other conceivable prospect for the presidency. He was voted into office without a single dissent.

The perception of Washington at the time of his election to the presidency differed in one significant respect from the way he was perceived during the early part of his career. The instant veneration that he enjoyed upon his military appointment was generated in a context of great emotional fervor. The excited expressions of praise for the man preceded any concrete achievements on his part, and it is fair to assume that most men filling the role of Commander in Chief would have been as much esteemed as he was. In this sense, the initial phase of Washington's career as a national symbol was largely determined by society's need to personify its revolutionary consciousness.

In contrast, the postwar praise of Washington invariably made reference to what he did and did not do as commanding general, and singled out those aspects of his performance that did most to alleviate America's traditional fear of political power. Although the popular antipathy to strong leaders did not prevent Washington's abrupt deification in 1775, it did require assumptions about his "disinterested" motives, his respect for the role of citizen-soldier, and the way that morality, rather than genius, contributed to his military greatness. Only at war's end were these assumptions verified by actual performance; and in the context of public preoccupation over the redistribution of institutional power, this verification transformed Washington into an absolutely credible symbol of the nation's political morality. Thus, the second phase of Washington's veneration was largely based on his actual wartime conduct. Given the quality of that conduct, particularly his refusal to exploit public support for personal gain, his reputation in 1789 seemed higher and more secure than ever.

Yet, the presidential duties that Washington was about to assume would complicate his role as a national emblem. Attached for the first time to the power of a nation-state, the Washington cult was celebrated more intensely, and more extravagantly, than ever. This very development, the spurring on of a hero cult that already verged on idolatry, intensified prevailing conflicts of interest and provoked hostilities that would bring Washington's reputation to a point lower than anyone would have dreamed when he took office.

President—or "Perpetual Dictator"?

For the crowds that gathered in New York to greet Washington on his inauguration day, nothing could have been more remote than the prospect of his becoming an object of hostility. "I have seen him!" exclaimed a young lady in the crowd, "and though I had been entirely ignorant that he was arrived in the city, I should have known at a glance that it was General Washington: I never saw a human being that looked so great and noble as he does. I could fall down on my knees before him."[19] What a day it was for Washington: the culmination of a voyage that took him through all the major towns between Mount Vernon and the capital. By traveling the countryside, making appearances, attending fetes, receiving honors, and giving addresses, Washington reenacted the "royal progress" by which ancient kings took symbolic possession of their realm.

Yet, as the fifty-seven-year-old President-elect set out on his "progress," he was disturbed "by feelings not unlike those of a culprit who is going to the place of his execution." When the end comes, he hoped, it would be inconspicuous. "[N]o reception," he wrote to Governor Clinton, "can be so congenial to my feelings as a quiet entry devoid of ceremony."[20] Everywhere, however, the turnout was effusive. Every town Washington passed through was festooned with flags, emblems, and slogans. Mounted escorts were sent out to receive him. At the sound of the clattering entourage, applause; at the sight of the man himself, pandemonium. Then the addresses, the toasts, the fetes. Then the farewell, to the roar of crowds and cannon. As the procession worked its way north, the crowds grew bigger and the ceremonies more elaborate. Twenty thousand people witnessed his passage through Philadelphia. At Trenton—his most memorable stop—Washington was met by a white-robed choir of ladies who serenaded him with a ballad as they strewed blossoms in his path:

> Virgins fair, and Matrons grave,
> Those thy conquering arms did save,
> Build for thee triumphal bowers
> Strew, ye fair, his way with flowers—
> Strew your Hero's way with flowers.[21]

In New York, site of the inauguration, the din was overwhelming. The city had virtually closed down for the occasion, as thousands of citizens, so dense in their assemblage as to make movement difficult, pressed for a sight of their hero. A few people were heard to say that they could die content, having cast their eyes at last on the savior of their country. Others shuddered at the sublimity of the occasion itself, which was "beyond any descriptive powers of the pen to do justice to—How universal—and how laudable the curiosity—How *sincere*—and how *expressive* the sentiments of respect and veneration".[22] The scene was enough to make the most self-assured man apprehensive. In Washington, it produced shivers. He told his diary that the "display of boats . . . the decorations of the ships, the roar of cannon, and the loud acclamations of the people . . . filled my mind with sensations as painful (considering the reverse of this scene, which may be the case after all my labors to do good) as they are pleasing."[23] Prophetic indeed were these sensations. In time, Washington's darkest premonitions would be realized.

Washington's forebodings were based on the possibility of failure. However noble his intentions, he feared that inexperience and inadequate ability would make him a bad President. He did not realize that more than political skill would be necessary to deal with his problems. Washington was promoted to national honor not because of his achievements but because the timing and manner of his military appointment made him a symbol of the people's aspirations. His decline, too, would be brought more by social circumstances than by actual performance. Although Washington's presidential actions were sometimes unpopular, these actions play only a secondary role in explaining the opprobrium concentrated against him. That same idealism and enthusiasm that made Washington a hero would later induce some Americans to see him as a villain, but with this twist: The very reputation that Washington feared losing became the source of all his troubles.

Neither the vision of a beloved leader enticing unsuspecting admirers to monarchy, nor the prospect of Washington being such a man, was new in America. These ideas occupied many minds in wartime, and they were to reappear with greater force, and much greater consequence, in the 1790s. To idolize a servant of government, like a general, was one thing; but when idolatry attached to the very head of government, the least suspicious of men could sense the danger of tyranny. Even an admirer like John Trumbull, who had extolled Washington in his poetry, detected "the odour of incense" at his inaugural celebration and regretted that the country had idolatrously "gone through all the Popish grades of worship. . . . "[24] The very rituals and forms that helped instill in the majority a respect for the new political authority thus invoked in others traditional fears of authority itself. And since affection for Washington remained strong enough to allow his government to pursue whatever policies it pleased, many Americans were concerned to know whether the Constitution's theoretical restraints would really work in practice. Could popular support embolden a President to ignore the law of the land in favor of his own ambition? This question rekindled discussion about whether the public's boundless esteem for Washington might undermine the principles of republican government.

John Adams was probably contemplating a Washington presidency when he surmised in 1787 that if the great man had a child of his own, he or she would be "demanded for marriage by one of the royal families of France or England, perhaps by both." So great an impression would this invitation make on the pride and vanity of Americans, Adams thought, that every precept of republicanism would be sacrificed to its acceptance.[25] Many shared Adams's apprehensions. In 1790, an article appearing in the *New York Journal* complained of the plan to display the President's portrait in New York's City Hall: "The injudicious flattery of the people," warned the writer, "have often intoxicated their rulers and sanctioned their usurpations."[26] Another citizen found the panegyric surrounding Washington redounding to "the shame and disgrace of republican dogmas."[27] Benjamin Rush put the same point in a religious framework. "We have not instituted divine honors to certain virtues in imitation of the inhabitants of Paris," he said (in reference to the new secular religion established in France), "but we ascribe all the attributes of the Deity to the name of General Washington. It is considered by our citizens as the bulwark of our nation. God would cease to be what He is, if He did not visit [punish] us for these things!"[28]

Although some of these remarks were politically motivated, it would be a mistake to dismiss them as such. That Washington's political opponents saw his prestige as his most dangerous attribute is itself evidence of the seriousness with which many Americans saw the matter of hero worship. Nor would it do to ascribe these critical remarks to envy alone. Many of Washington's contemporaries, especially those who were closest to him, did begrudge him his fame; but their apprehensions of its political consequences were articulated at too high a level of principle, and with too much precision and perceptiveness, to be based solely on malice. The broodings of republican iconoclasts were more directly informed by the political realities of the time and by the premises and paradigms of their culture.

Americans in the postwar period cherished liberty, but when they drank toasts to it, they often qualified themselves. "To liberty without licentiousness" was the common offering. Licentiousness meant disorder, and the only remedy for disorder, history had taught, was tyranny. There would be no question of how the tyrant would appear: He would be wearing a crown. For some, however, the equating of kingship with tyranny made no sense. They hoped, in fact, that a new political arrangement, combining monarchical stability with republican liberty, could be devised. Such opinions only intensified apprehensions about the restoration of the crown, an idea that had been in the air since the end of the war.

Postwar political uncertainty, economic disarray, and the renewal of regional antagonisms rendered these apprehensions plausible. John Jay observed that "[i]f faction should long bear down [overwhelm] law and government, tyranny may raise its head, or the more sober part of the people may even think of a king." In New England, where the rebellion had originally started, Crevecoeur noted that many "[a]re so weary of the [Government] ... that they sigh for Monarchy and that a very large number of persons in several counties would like to return to English domination." To a people that had previously defined the importation of a Dutch king as the cornerstone of its Glorious Revolution, the rumored movement to recruit a foreign prince to restore order in America did not seem implausible. Nor was there much dispute when Luther Martin of Maryland claimed that some of his fellow delegates to the Federal Convention privately favored a restoration of monarchy. Prominent British leaders put stock in such claims. In 1790, one of the Canadian governors reported that "a republican government does not seem calculated for the disposition and genius of the people in the states." The newly ratified Constitution, another report concluded, is but "an experiment" paving the way for a more "energetic" government. In addition, some of the more optimistic British officials hoped that Ohio, Kentucky, and Vermont would move toward an arrangement with England (which still controlled land adjacent to these territories) rather than with the United States.[29]

Despite these opinions, most political observers felt that the new nation's commitment to republicanism was strong and the prospect of monarchy remote. The (heavily Anti-Federalist) Republican minority shared the first view, but not the second. Many Republicans believed that conditions were ripe for a plot to impose a new monarchy upon an unwilling people. The only question was whether Washington was the man to bring about the transition to monarchy. On first sight, the prospect of his doing so might have seemed absurd; but then, "[t]yrants seldom rise up in a day and seize the privileges of a people, but artfully endeavor to lull them into security, and represent to their imaginations the blessings of monarchical or aristocratic government."[30] If Washington was not the man to represent the blessings of monarchical government, some of his contemporaries might have asked, then why is his praise so often expressed through the emblems of monarchy? In 1792, for example, William Sullivan's wood statue of Washington (Fig. 13) was presented to the New York public in Bowling Green Square—atop the very pedestal that once supported the image of George III. Hindsight tells us, of course, that it was convention and not ideology that made the employment of royal symbolism inevitable. Yet, conventions are heavy with ideological implications. In Gilbert Stuart's *Lansdowne* painting, which is regarded by some to be the very epitome of republican state portraiture (Fig. 14), Washington wears a sword as he stands by his writing table, but his plain black attire defines the weapon he carries as a symbol of impersonal civil power. Beneath the table is the Constitution; upon it, the *Federalist* and the *Journal of Congress*. The painting tells us that Washington is executing the will of others, not his own.[31] But to regard the *Lansdowne* as a distinctly republican portrait is to assume that every viewer's reaction to it is determined by its substance alone. Eighteenth-century viewers were probably moved more by form than by content, and that form fell squarely within the monarchical tradition of state portraiture:

[I]f the English state-portrait played its part in perpetuating a great and honorable tradition, it also furthered the spread of that tradition to other lands. Undoubtedly the painted images that served as the king's *alter ego* in the assembly chambers of the colonies are responsible for the fact that the basic sixteenth century formulas came to be used for chief executives and other worthies in the United States. In particular the full-length type with one arm or hand resting on a piece of furniture became as common for the American official portrait as it was for the European.[32]

Stuart's Washington bears comparison to David's Napoleon. In both paintings, the head of state stands before the furnishings of office, heavily decorated with national symbols. In the background, massive doors and high ceilings, or heavy drapes and pillars, signify the dignity and power of the state. Both paintings show the head of the state standing before an ornate, thronelike chair. Earlier prototypes of the state portrait, like those of Elizabeth I, Philip II, and Charles IX, make use of these same props to convey to the viewer the awesome powers of his ruler (Figs. 15–18). No wonder that President Washington was addressed by one of his critics as "George I, Perpetual Dictator of the United States."[33]

Tension between monarchical and republican strains in American political culture brought the venerational cult of George Washington to an unprecedented level of scrutiny during the new government's formative years. The growing apprehension was evident in the reflections of John Adams. Although personally resentful of Washington, whose overwhelming fame had undermined his own claim to the attention of posterity, Adams's opinions were representative of those held by many contemporaries, and they were influential as well. They antagonized part of the general public, but they also supplied food for thought to many political and cultural leaders.

In his August 1785 letter to an acquaintance, John Jebb, Adams declared that the most pressing political issue of the day was the people's attitude toward its leaders. For years the colonies had been ruled by men of wealth who renounced their private affairs to assume public positions of power and responsibility, and who returned home, unpaid, when their obligations were fulfilled. But the system was not without its compensations. In return for their services, these men expected, and usually received, not only the people's gratitude and respect but also their acquiescence to the government over which they presided. In place of this system of *noblesse oblige,* Adams favored a strictly bureaucratic government in which the public's obligation to its leaders was acquitted by cash payment.[34] Adams must have been anticipating the establishment of such a government, and Washington's role in it, as he considered the people's attitude toward Washington's wartime services.

Adams made no charges against Washington himself; he issued

no apocalyptic warnings about the tyrant lurking behind the idol. He spoke instead of the subtle dangers inherent in uncritical adulation, and dissected two symbolic gestures that sustained the public's adulation of Washington: his voluntary resignation from the military and his willingness to perform public service without pay.

> It was a general sentiment in America that Washington must retire. Why? What is implied in this necessity? ... Does not this idea of the necessity of his retiring, imply an opinion of danger to the public, from his continuing in public, a jealousy that he might become ambitious? and does it not imply ... a jealousy in the people of one another, a jealousy of one part of the people, that another part had grown too fond of him, and acquired habitually too much confidence in him, and that there would be danger of setting him up for a king? Undoubtedly it does, and undoubtedly there were such suspicions; and grounds for them too.[35]

Beneath the high regard for Washington, Adams detects a widespread sense of uneasiness. Many declared that the public *should* be suspicious of Washington; Adams declared that it already was, and justifiably so.

Next, Adams took up Washington's refusal to accept a salary for his military services—another gesture that endeared him to his countrymen. But Adams was not so naive as to think the public got off scot-free. By refusing compensation, he observed, Washington indebted the citizenry to himself, rather than the other way around. Benefits that cannot be reciprocated in one currency, Adams warned, must be repaid in another. In this instance, submission substitutes for money:

> Now, I ask, what occasioned this dangerous enthusiasm for [Washington]? I answer, that great as his talents and virtues are, they did not altogether contribute so much to it as his serving without pay, which never fails to turn the heads of the multitude.... There should have been no such distinction made between him and the other generals. He should have been paid, as well as they, and the people should have too high a sense of their own dignity ever to suffer any man to serve them for nothing. The higher and more important the office, the more rigorously should they insist upon acknowledging its appointment by them and its dependence upon them.[36]

Adams concluded by reiterating that his qualms had nothing to do with Washington himself. Washington was an honest and virtuous man, he averred, and his acts of benevolence were sincere; but precisely such acts had for centuries induced the people to turn otherwise disinterested patriots into tyrants. Now Adams could put his finger on the nub of the problem. "I think that it has been the people themselves who always created their own despot."[37]

That heroes are not born but made, that they arise from the way people act toward them, that they are manufactured by society itself—these were convictions that would inform another effort to keep the Washington cult within the limits of republican propriety.

Knowing how deeply Adams resented Washington's fame, one might see his cautions about despotism as a symptom of envy rather than a conclusion drawn from a detached study of the facts. Yet, these same suspicions were expressed in 1792 by men whose attitude toward Washington was somewhat friendlier than Adams's. These men were members of Congress, and they were concerned with a problem different from the one Adams raised. They were not bothered at all by Washington's popularity, and they were pleased, not dismayed, by the people's gratitude toward him. Rather, their concern was to ensure that the enormous prestige presently attached to the man be permanently segregated from the office he occupied. Only then could the nation be assured that Washington's prestige would die with him and not be passed on to Presidents of lesser character.

The discussion began when the House of Representatives ordered Alexander Hamilton, then Secretary of the Treasury, to prepare a plan for a national mint. Within the text of Hamilton's report was a brief discussion of the "devices" to be used on coins. These devices, or images, he noted, were "far from being matters of indifference, as they may be made the vehicles of useful impressions."[38] Hamilton was talking about the moral uplift often afforded by the slogan, emblem, or portrait engraved on coins. Accordingly, in January 1792, the Federalist-controlled Senate agreed, in the Mint Act, that upon each denomination of coins there should be impressed the head of the President. The plan was rejected by the House of Representatives, where Republicans had a slight majority. Political interests certainly affected this vote; but, the substance of the House's reasoning should not be confused with its supposed "motives." In an institution like the House, where about half the membership took pride in identifying itself as neither Federalist nor Republican, that reasoning would have to make moral, not political, sense to be persuasive.

John Page, a fellow Virginian who had fought with Washington against the French, the Indians, and the British, spoke on behalf of the majority. Page, a Republican, was even more concerned about monarchical tyranny than was Federalist Adams:

> We have all read, that the Jews paid tribute to the Romans, by means of a coin on which was the head of their Caesar. Now as we have no occasion for this aid to history, nor any pretense to call the money of the United states the money of our Presidents, there can be no sort of necessity for adopting the idea of the Senate.[39]

To those who denied that a mere image on a coin could produce harmful effects on society, the Representative conceded that "as long as the people were sensible of the blessings of liberty, and had their eyes open to watch encroachments, they would not be enslaved." But, he continued, "if they should ever shut them, or become inattentive to their interests and the true principles of a free government, they, like other nations, might lose their liberties." Page's statement, like Adams's, assumed that the public's attitude toward monarchy was not one of disdain but, at best, one of indifference. For this reason, "it is the peculiar duty of the Representative of a free people to put them upon their guard against anything which could possibly endanger their liberties."

Representative Page then gave voice to his fear of political ambition, adding to it a new dimension: the abuse of fame. Whereas honorable men pursued fame as a prize for virtue, ambitious men pursued it as a prize for power. Recognizing in the production of state icons the most tangible proof of fame, Page cautioned his colleagues and constituents "of the danger, not merely of imitating the flattery and almost idolatrous practice of Monarchies with respect to the honor paid to their Kings, by impressing their images and names on their coins, but . . . to add as few incentives as possible to competitors for the President's place." Cabals, corruption, and animosity, Page warned, "might be excited by the intrigues of ambitious men, animated with the hope of handing their names down to the latest ages on the medals of their country."[40]

The majority in the House of Representatives agreed with Page, and eventually Congress decided on a substitute for the proposed Washington head: the emblem of Liberty—a device that was, in Representative Williamson's words, "consistent with Republican principles."[41] Washington himself, strongly opposed to the original Senate plan, applauded the outcome. He probably agreed with his friends in Congress who viewed that plan as a blow rather than a boon to his reputation.

The Mint Act debate nicely captured the conflicting duties that Americans faced: their obligation to render gratitude to Washington for his virtue and service, vis-à-vis their obligation to ensure that the show of gratitude not be too elaborate, and not take inappropriate forms. The dilemma was resolved by a balancing act. Everyone who took an interest in the mint debate knew that more than a score of Washington-head coins were already in existence when this debate began[42] and no one had complained about them. Furthermore, few Americans thought that the ideals of the republic had been undermined when, ten years earlier, a Continental Congress had empowered itself to commission an equestrian statue of Washington. But these acts of veneration were deemed proper because they were undertaken by agencies in which Washington played no part. Thus, monarchical danger inhered not in the use of the Washington image itself but in the promulgation of that image by a government over which Washington himself presided. By refusing to allow this to happen, the Congress created a separation of powers not provided for by the Constitution, a separation of the personal popularity and influence of the President from the prestige and authority of his office. In doing so, Congress and the people could maintain their sincere affection for Washington with increased assurance that similar affection for popular men of the future would not be misused.

This same stricture—the ban on rulers' celebration of their own power—applied to etiquette as well as iconography. Etiquette—which, to the twentieth-century eye, appears to be the most trivial aspect of political conduct—takes us to the source of Washington's eighteenth-century troubles.

The Manners of Office

The new federal government was acutely aware that its decisions would affect the conduct of future governments. Precedent was therefore the guiding concern in the Mint Act debate, but it

proved to be even more important in the matter of state ceremony. Whereas debates over the use of the President's image on
coins were largely confined to Congress, ceremonies of state were
topics of widespread public commentary. The coinage dispute
failed to engage the public at large because it concerned decisions
made about Washington by others; the controversy over executive
ritual was much more extensive and heated because it involved
the decisions and conduct of Washington himself.

In this light, Representative Theodorick Bland could challenge
the very integrity of the government by criticizing the awkward-
ness of its Chief Executive's bows, which were "more distant and
stiff" than those of a king. To this comment Washington made no
direct reply, but in a letter to an acquaintance he expressed regret
that the issue should be raised at all. Levees (formal receptions,
about which more later) and other state ceremonies were not meant
to convey political pretensions; they were merely ways for the
President to make himself accessible to the people without being
overwhelmed by them. As to the comment on his parlor manners,
Washington replied:

> That I have not been able to make bows to the taste of poor Colonel
> Bland (who, by-the-by, I believe never saw one of them), is to be re-
> gretted, especially too, as (upon these occasions), they were indiscrim-
> inately bestowed, and the best I was master of, would it not have been
> better to throw the veil of charity over them, ascribing their stiffness
> to the effect of age, or the unskillfulness of my teacher, than to pride
> and dignity of office, which God knows has no charms for me?[43]

Few would have doubted the sincerity of Washington's reply, but
toward the ritual itself he was expressing an attitude that was alien
to his time. He was in effect dismissing the routine he followed
as an "empty form," a "mere ritual," an artifical performance
bearing no relationship to the real world of power and privilege.
In a society of ascribed role structures and deference, this dis-
claimer carried little conviction. Refined men and women of
Washington's generation took ritual seriously; they saw it as an
expression, and preserver, of orientation and boundary. Since ritual was so earnestly regarded and used as a political form—as a
guide for living in a hierarchical society—Washington could not
escape the political implications of ceremonies in which he had
agreed to participate. The charge that Colonel Bland had lodged
may have been wrong insofar as it applied to Washington's inten-

tions, but that charge bore some political truth, for it was symptomatic of Washington's new relationship to the American people. As first President, he had to act in ways that, in the opinion of many, set him apart from the people.

The administrative and executive duties of the American presidency require most of its incumbent's time; yet, the ceremonial occasions in which he must participate possess a visibility that governance alone cannot possess. These dual sets of functions become problematic when the same person fails to perform both satisfactorily, particularly when the ceremonial functions that person is called upon to perform—functions which invariably involve the granting and receipt of deference—carry implications that are at variance with his executive actions. The English solution to this problem is to assign these two sets of duties to two different sets of people: executive duties to the Prime Minister and Parliament; ceremonial duties to the Crown. A successful revolution against the Crown ruled out this solution in America. During its formative period, the American government therefore placed upon its chief officer, George Washington, the responsiblity not only of executing republican policies but also of assuming the leading role in acting out republican ritual. The situation was aggravated by the fact that there was no established body of republican ritual for the new government to enact. In the late eighteenth century, no precedent for state ceremonies existed outside the monarchical tradition.

Yet, two years earlier, on the eve of the Federal Convention, Washington had dealt successfully with a similar dilemma. He effectively distanced himself from the Society of the Cincinnati, a hereditary veterans association to which many Americans ascribed monarchical designs. Washington was never tainted by his presidency of the society because he publicly called for its reform and promised to renounce his office if his call were not heeded. And when the leadership of the partially reformed society was offered to him a second time, he rejected it. All these things Washington did on the advice of Thomas Jefferson.[44] As President of the United States, however, he found himself under the influence of other advisers, and caught up in new enterprises.

Every new enterprise faces uncertainty and the possibility of failure. When properly performed, rituals reduce these hazards by bringing "more vividly to the mind through symbolic performances certain centrally important processes and norms."[45] When improperly performed, rituals make these processes and norms more obscure. Thus, in Washington's new administration, impoverished observances would sanction democratic, leveling impulses inappropriate to a society that had yet to develop the prerequisite attitudes and institutions. On the other hand, ostentatious observances, all too familiar to a people recently under the sway of monarchy, would fail to acknowledge the new republican institutions.

If ritual and ceremony are forms of communication, Washington's people were not very good communicators. The symbolic structures they created were too formal and elaborate for the preponderant currents of opinion. For any society there is an optimal level of simplicity or extravagance that state observances might take. Few regimes hit the mark exactly; Washington's erred on the side of extravagance.

The direction of that error was no accident. Alexander Hamilton, no less than John Adams, believed that "the public good requires as a primary object the dignity of the office should be supported." Mindful of the negative reactions they might arouse, Hamilton nevertheless recommended that certain ceremonial forms followed by European courts be adopted in carrying out the affairs of the American presidency. Prominent among these forms was the levee, an arrangement for receiving visitors that required the President to appear weekly for half an hour and, as Hamilton put it, "converse cursorily on indifferent subjects with such persons as shall strike his attention and at the end of that half hour disappear."[46] There were also weekly tea parties and official dinners, all formal affairs whose every detail was reported in the Federalist press and read with great interest.

Supporters of Washington's government sought to affirm its authority in other ways. On the matter of presidential title, for example, a Federalist majority in the Senate favored "His Highness the President of the United States of America and Protector of their Liberties." The Federalist press had ideas of its own, including "Your Magistracy" and "Your Supremacy." But if Washington was pleased with the simplicity of the title eventually agreed to, "President of the United States," he did not think it unseemly to furnish his office with a carriage drawn by six cream-colored horses—or, when he felt it necessary to travel horseback, to adorn his white steed with leopard cloth and gold-trimmed saddle. The display of these and other accoutrements of authority, along with the more bombastic annual celebrations of the President's birth, gave to the levees and other courtly affairs a more powerful meaning than they might otherwise have had.

In the new government's ceremonies, many Americans, perhaps the majority, found welcome signs of national dignity—signs that showed America to be a "respectable nation," a place where important visitors could witness the same forms and manners that prevailed in the most stable and powerful states of Europe. The people's pride in their government was reinforced by the ritual forms through which the government expressed pride in itself. However, these forms were not new and indigenous; they were copied directly from the European courts. The Republican critics were very much aware of this imitation and preoccupied themselves in trying to understand the motives behind it. Their analysis aroused fears that Washington, or his counselors, or both, were determined to move along the path of European monarchs.

The storm broke early. On June 15, 1789, only a few months into the first administration, an observer in New York's *Daily Advertiser* complained that "Levees, Drawing Rooms &c. are not such strange, incomprehensible distant things as we have imagined; and I suppose, that in a few years, we shall have all the paraphernalia yet wanting to give the superb finish to the grandeur of our AMERICAN COURT!"[47] As the end of Washington's first term approached, the tempest grew more, not less, intense. In the *National Gazette,* one "Cornelia" made capitalized reference to "THE DRAWING ROOM" before exhorting readers to "fashion men to virtue, but not to the servility and adulation of royalty."[48] From another correspondent—a month later and in the same newspaper:

> It appears from some late publications, that a new order of citizens has been created in the United States, consisting only of the *officers* of the federal government.—The privileges of this order, it is said, consist in sharing, exclusively, in the profits of the 25,000 dollars a year allowed for the President's table, and in the honor of gazing upon him once a week at his levees.—It remains only to give this new order a name, and assign it a proper coat of arms and insignia; I shall therefore propose that it be called *the most noble order of the goose.* . . . [49]

A few days later, another article appeared in the *National Gazette.* Now "A Farmer," in more serious tone, declared that even moderate men have been "awakened into resentment by the monarchical practices of the administration," and expressed the hope that the President "will be no longer misled by evil counselors" and "abolish every custom which can call in question the sincerity of his professions."[50] A month later—in March 1793—the tirade continued. The recitation of odes, the spectacle of citizens assembled "to shuffle to the President's honor," and all the "monarchal farce" of the President's birthday celebration were condemned, along with "the absurdities of levees and every species of royal pomp and parade."[51] In yet another article, one "Mirabeau" entreated the President directly to do away with the ostentation of his office, for "Americans have emancipated themselves from the trammels of monarchical fashion, as well as from the trammels of monarchical government; and they would be inclined to suppose that every attempt to introduce the one, would be but as the harbinger of the other."[52]

Vituperation

John Adams and John Page, members of different political factions, had agreed on two things: that excessive veneration of any one man in a republic was dangerous, and that, should this danger be realized, it would be not only through the machinations of the man himself but also through the uncritical enthusiasm of the people. If Washington were ever succeeded by a tyrant, therefore, the people would have only themselves to blame. Those who criticized the symbols and ceremonies of the presidency entertained a different opinion. They, too, condemned hero worhsip and were vocal in denouncing the public's gullibility; yet, the weight of their criticism fell not on the people, as with Adams's and Page's strictures, but mainly on Washington's administration. Blame for the republic's drift toward tyranny, they seemed to be saying, resided in the pernicious rituals of its government. Washington himself, according to many press reports, took part in these only at the prodding of his advisors—but that made no difference. Through some undefined yet irresistible force, the monarchical forms he had adopted would lead to a monarchical government.

Yet, why were the federal government's rituals regarded in this way? It was true that many of the observances involving the President were borrowed from monarchical tradition, but it was not as if Americans were unfamiliar with them. Washington was neither the first nor the only public magistrate in America to hold high-toned receptions or to be treated with courtly deference. Nor was he the only one to live in a comfortable mansion, don handsome attire, or ride in a fancy coach. In these respects, the colonial governors and, later, the state governors had already set a fine example. Thus it was not the ritual and symbols themselves that made for public controversy.

Since anti-administration sentiment was concentrated among Republicans, one might assume that criticism of Washington's role in presidential ritual was merely a retaliation for his administration's economic policies, which strongly favored commercial interests. However, there is no evidence to suggest that public support for Washington was less intense in the noncommercial, Republican strongholds than in the commercial areas, where Federalism was strong.[53] On the contrary, the accounts of Washington's presidential tours tell of warm and enthusiastic welcomes everywhere. Though support for the new administration was highly correlated with economic interests, support for Washington himself was universal.

The attitudes that Washington and his government adopted toward political opponents might help explain more plausibly their criticism of his political rituals. Washington's adminstration was, of course, faced with opponents from the very beginning. Expressing themselves at first through individual petitions, the various antagonists of Federalist policy eventually formed a network of "Democratic (later called "Republican") societies" under the leadership of Jefferson and Madison. The Federalists looked on these opposition groups in much the same way leaders of other new states regard their rivals. "At best, Republicans often seemed governed by obstinacy, envy, malice or ambition. At worst they were seditious and treasonable."[54] The Republican press, for its part, told of Federalist meetings where "[t]he horrid crime of differing in opinion with [Washington and Adams], and the damnable sin of having a partiality for one foreign nation in preference to another, were most charmingly chaunted forth. . . . "[55] Washington's own public condemnations of the "self-created" societies lent validity to this complaint.

Republicans were also angered by the Federalists' suspicion of the masses. The common man was thought to be a natural constituent of the Republican party, and to Federalists that made its goals suspect. At the edge of democracy, the Federalists believed, hung anarchy. "Let it stand as a principle that government origi-

The Exodus recovered . . . *The Seal of the United States*
(First Design), by Benson J. Lossing, after the verbal
description (From Gaillard Hunt, ed., *The History of
the Seal of the United States,* Washington, D.C.: Department of State, 1909)

A king turned inside out . . . *Georgius Triumpho,* 1783
coin (Illustration from *Guide Book of United States Coins,*
© 1986, Western Publishing Company, Inc. Used by
permission)

LA DESTRUCTION DE LA STATUE ROYALE A NOUVELLE YORCK.

Die Zerstorung der Koniglichen Bild | La Destruction de la Statue royale
3   Saule zu Neu Yorck   AParis chez Basset Rue St Jacques   a Nouvelle Yorck

Declaration of independence . . . *La Destruction de la Statue Royale*, by an unidentified artist (Courtesy of the Library of Congress, Washington, D.C.)

Independence achieved: a vacant pedestal . . . *Washington and the Departure of the British Garrison from New York City* (1790), by John Trumbull (Courtesy of the Art Commission of the City of New York)

5

Horse and servant: republican will . . . *Washington* (1780) by Noël Le Mire (National Portrait Gallery, Smithsonian Institution, Washington, D.C.)

6

Horse and servant: monarchical pride . . . *Le Roi à la Chasse* (Charles I), by Anthony Van Dyck (The Louvre, Paris)

7

Man of the people in princely armor . . . *The True Portraiture of his Excellency* (1783), by John Norman (McAlpin Collection, Print Collection, The New York Public Library, Astor, Lenox and Tilden Foundations)

The true PORTRAITURE of his Excellency
George Washington Esq.
In the Roman Drefs, as Order'd by Congrefs for the Monument to be erected in Philadelphia, to perpetuate to Posterity the Man who commanded the American Force through the late glorious Revolution

8

The armored prince . . . *George the IIId* (1778), by Robert Pollard (Courtesy of the Library of Congress, Washington, D.C.)

GEORGE the IIIᵈ
King of Great Britain, France and Ireland.
Printed for I. Robson Newcastle upon Tyne.

9

The first national icon . . . *George Washington* (1776), by Charles Willson Peale (The Brooklyn Museum, Brooklyn, New York)

His Excellency General
WASHINGTON

A lifelike replacement for the King . . . *His Excellency General Washington*, frontispiece for *A Primer*, 1779, after a 1776 painting by Charles Willson Peale (The Historical Society of Pennsylvania, Philadelphia)

11

FARMER WASHINGTON.

PHILADELPHIA:

Unlifelike, but familiar . . . *Farmer Washington* (1785), by an unidentified artist after a 1776 painting by Charles Willson Peale. The caption, "Farmer Washington," was added in 1799 (Courtesy of the Trustees of the Boston Public Library)

12a

12b

12c

12d

The circulating icon . . . *Washington-head Coins*, post-war period (Illustrations from *Guide Book of United States Coins*, © 1986, Western Publishing Company, Inc. Used by permission)

nates from the people," Jeremy Belknap, a New England clergy-man, wrote to a friend, "but let the people be taught . . . that they are not able to govern themselves."[56] Belknap's principle was shared by almost all Federalist leaders, including Washington. Many of these men came to believe, in fact, that anything supported by the public at large must be contrary to the national interest.

This supercilious attitude could not have produced mutual trust between the people and the administration. However, in a society ruled for more than 150 years by its elite class there was no reason to assume that the people as a whole expected to be regarded as a full partner in government. It was equally unlikely that colonial and state governments were any more hospitable to the claims of hostile factions than was the Washington administration. Although Washington's political opponents were distressed by his intolerance of dissent and by his distrust of what the Federalists called "democratic levelism," Washington's attitudes were not uncommon, and these attitudes alone cannot account for the quality and vicious intensity of the attacks made upon him.

Although candid criticism of Washington began shortly after he became President and continued throughout his first term in office, he was so popular in 1793 that his reelection was welcomed by most Republicans, and even endorsed in the anti-administration press.[57] During his last four years in office, however, Washington's reputation suffered damage. The amount of damage was actually no more than a big dent, but on so smooth and shiny a surface it showed up prominently. "You have no idea how deeply the public confidence is withdrawing itself from the President, and with what avidity strictures on his conduct are received," declared John Beckley. "Gratitude no longer blinds the public mind."[58] Likewise, one "William Tell" observed that the man whom Americans once admired as a God was now falling into contempt.[59] In his private diary, Nathaniel Ames wrote: "Better his hand had been cut off when his glory was at its height, before he blasted all his Laurels."[60] Jasper Dwight was more direct: "That you have lost some of your glorious celebrity is not to be denied," he announced in a public letter to Washington on the occasion of his Farewell Address.[61] "Heavens, what a change!" wrote Charles Adams to his father. "But four years ago and we thought the voice of calumny dared not attack this man."[62]

An unpopular foreign policy precipitated this transformation. The first fruit of that policy, the so-called Neutrality Proclamation (1793), did not bear heavily on the material well-being of any significant sector of the population, but it did offend the political sensibility of many. Not only did American neutrality betray an old friend, France, in favor of an old enemy, England; it also sided with a monarchy at the expense of a republic. The reactions to it were explosive. Something akin to the 1775–76 *rage militaire* took possession of many people. One manifestation of the hysteria, as John Adams revealed, focused directly on the President: "Washington's house was surrounded by an innumerable multitude, from day to day huzzaing, demanding war against England, cursing Washington, and crying success to the French patriots and virtuous Republicans."[63] As crowds raged against Washington, they looked back. "American Whigs of 1776 will not suffer French patriots of 1792 to be vilified with impunity,"[64] cried Freneau.

Two years later, when the Jay Treaty was negotiated, the public outrage was even greater, for this measure ignored economic interests as well as obligations to an old ally. And there was another, sinister implication. When Washington flatly denied the House's request for access to papers connected with the treaty (an act which, in the eyes of many Republicans, weakened the popular branch of government relative to the "aristocratic" Senate), the insinuations accelerated: Washington had asserted "monarchical perogative" and defied the will of the people.

Many found this diagnosis plausible. Washington had already been criticized for both his pro-British attitudes and his appointment of Anglophiles to important executive posts. Even moderate Republicans believed, for example, that Alexander Hamilton was working behind the scenes with other members of his faction to form "an alliance with the crown of Great Britain and finally with the aid of that government to ESTABLISH A MONARCHY IN AMERICA."[65] But now Washington himself came under the gun. Once thought to be under the influence of monarchists, the President was now considered a monarchist himself. On this point, the criticism was most explicit: Washington was condemned not for tyrannical designs in general but for designs that would lead to a particular kind of tyranny. The precision added credibility to the charges. In a society still saturated with monarchical symbolism, and still under the influence of many who would tolerate, even welcome, a new monarchy, the attribution to Washington of a desire to be king was the most plausible form of attack. The attack itself was pressed forcefully.

Republican newspapers made public the charge that Washington had become "the *head* of a British faction."[66] One writer, referring to Washington's defiance of the House, exclaimed: "It matters not to seven eighths of the people whether their petitions have been despised by George Guelph [George III] or George Washington."[67] Another correspondent saw Washington as a "usurper with dark schemes of ambition," a son of "political degeneracy."[68] Old age forced the President off his horse and into a carriage, but critics saw instead another sign of "supercillious distance."[69] Along with his wife, Martha, "our gracious Queen,"[70] Washington showed himself as "the omnipotent director of a seraglio [sultan's palace] instead of the first magistrate of a free people."[71] For another writer, he was "titular St. George"—so designated by those who "worship at the shrine of Mount Vernon."[72] Another writer saw Washington as a Nebuchadnezzar greedily savoring unhallowed praise;[73] another mockingly offered him a crown; a third found in him "all the insolence of an Emperor of Rome."[74] In short,

> We have given him the powers and prerogatives of a King. He holds levees like a King, receives congratulations on his birthday like a King, receives ambassadors like a King, makes treaties like a King, answers petitions like a King, employs his old enemies like a King, shuts himself up like a King, shuts up other people like a King, takes advice of his counsellors or follows his own opinion like a King.[75]

The "discovery" of Washington's "true" motives and aims put his private life and, retroactively, his past in an entirely new light. "Gambling, reveling, horse racing and horse whipping" had been the essentials of his education, his critics declared. In private transactions he was "infamously niggardly," a "most horrid swearer and blasphemer" despite religious pretensions.[76] The unselfish and patriotic Virginia planter had become the un-Christian slaveholder, whose ambition and greed were too vast to be satisfied locally.[77] The unsalaried patriot was now the embezzler of public funds;[78] the conqueror of a British army was now the military incompetent, whose inferior intellect and education were covered over by the achievements of true soldiers. "His modesty is conformable to his abilities ... he never pretended to possess great ones."[79] (The problem was congenital: "Nature had played the miser when she gave you birth."[80]) The new criticism mounted in volume and ingenuity. Thomas Paine's extended character assassination, "Letter to General Washington"[81] (reminiscent of his insults to George III in *Common Sense*) was advertised for sale in Republican newspapers. Notorious forgeries, prepared by the British during the war to discredit the American commander, appeared in the opposition press as newly discovered evidence of Washington's degeneracy. These "private letters"[82] showed that Washington was a traitor from the very beginning. In one commentary on these letters, we learn that

> You, though you assisted us in the war, were never an advocate of our independence, that all you wished was that we should enjoy the immunities of British subjects, that a reconciliation should take place between the mother country and her colonies, and in short, that you labored to prevent our independence.[83]

Washington's actual retirement from office brought him no relief from criticism. On the very day the new President, John Adams, was sworn in, Benjamin Franklin Bache, in the guise of "A Correspondent," explained to his *Aurora* readers the significance of the old President's departure. It was not that a bad man had left office but that, in his leaving, the republic itself was preserved:

> If ever there was a period for rejoicing, this is the moment—every heart in unison with the freedom and happiness of the people, ought to beat high with exultation that the name of WASHINGTON from this day ceases to give a currency to political iniquity, and to legalized corruption.... When a retrospect is taken of the WASHINGTONIAN administration for eight years, it is a subject of the greatest astonishment, that a single individual should have cankered [corrupted] the principles of republicanism in an enlightened people, just emerged from the gulph of despotism, and should have carried his designs against the public liberty so far as to have put in jeopardy its very existence. Such however are the facts, and with these staring us in the face, this day ought to be a JUBILEE in the United States.[84]

No doubt, the political opposition had an interest in discrediting the prop and figurehead of the Federalist establishment. Yet, public disgust occasioned by the cruelty of the Republicans' onslaught moved them further from, not closer to, that goal. So dramatic was this popular backlash that even the most agitated Republican could not have failed to see its effect. Indeed, the attacks on Washington's past and present motives went so far beyond the prevailing norms of decency that level-headed opponents of his policy were certain that the attacks had been deliberately planted by administration officials to generate public support. Withal, the abuse continued. Even brief readings of the *Aurora* and other opposition newspapers give one the impression that many Republicans were running amok. Something more than a contest between contending political parties seemed to be at stake.

The Paranoid Style

How, then, did Washington's reputation lose credibility and appeal? Nothing in the actual conduct of Washington's government gave strong reason to assume that it was unlike existing state governments in its zeal to uphold republican ideals. Republicans thought the Federalist policies wrong—but the motives of those who designed those policies were rarely challenged. Most Republicans regarded most Federalists as patriots devoted to the cause of liberty and to the national interest; how best to achieve these goals was the issue that divided them. But a minority of Republicans felt differently; they saw beneath the administration's actions not an ill-conceived policy but a secret plot to restore aristocratic prerogatives, to convert the republic into a monarchy, and to enslave the people.

The tendency to link otherwise independent events via the assumption of a hostile intrigue is part of a recurrent pattern in American political thought. A series of historical episodes going back to 1798 led Richard Hofstadter to attribute this "paranoid style" to political minorities.[85] Had Hofstadter gone back further, he might have linked these episodes to a tradition that was once part of the mainstream of American thought, a tradition that was eventually enlisted in the service of both antimonarchism and antifederalism.[86]

Visions of plots by men in high circles held a privileged claim on the American imagination. From the very beginning of the eighteenth century, colonists were convinced that the Church of England had a secret design to abolish the smaller Protestant denominations and assimilate their members. This conviction persisted to the 1760s and was a conspicuous part of the context in

which the Stamp Act itself was received. "[T]he stamping and ep-
iscopizing of our colonies," declared Jonathan Mayhew, were "only
different branches of the same plan of power."[87]

Nothing did more to sustain the belief in a British conspiracy
than the reprisals taken against the colonists' defiance of the tea
tax measures in 1774. These reprisals, or "Intolerable Acts," flowed
from plans that were, it was said, "systematically laid"—from designs "settled," "fixed," and "calculated" to subdue the colonies.
The "system of slavery fabricated against America" derived not
from momentary bad judgment or evil, but was rather "the off-
spring of mature deliberation."[88]

As the details of the conspiracy against America became
"known," few fingers were pointed against the Crown. As late as
1774, the King was viewed by most Americans as their protector,
the only barrier between themselves and the scheming ministry.
That this eminently decent man had been duped by his inner circle was a plausible assumption, for "the best and greatest of monarchs," as one representative observer put it, may often be de-
ceived by pernicious schemes. . . ." Under the venerable name of
King George, said another, ambitious ministers "daringly attempt
to shelter their crimes."[89] Eventually, however, Americans came to
believe that George III could not be as innocent as was commonly
supposed. As the crisis came to a head, the axiom "The King can
do no wrong" was condemned in the press. Actions of the King
himself accelerated and emboldened public discussion. His disregard of the Congress's Olive Branch Petition, and his two acri-
monious proclamations against the "traitors" and their rebellion,
helped convince many that he was the guiding force in the plot
to enslave America.[90] No such plot existed, but it was the belief
in its existence that propelled the American colonists into rebellion.[91]

The motives ascribed to external enemies in the mid-1770s derived from a conspiratorial theory of political power that could
be applied to internal enemies in the 1790s. Behind the measures
taken by Britain during the prewar period, Americans saw the
cunning of a corrupt ministry. The ultimate protector of their
rights, the only obstacle to designs against liberty, in their view,
was the King. Behind the policies of the early Federalist period,
many Americans saw plots laid by an aristocratic Senate and evil
administration counselors. The ultimate safeguard of the people's
rights, the only impediment to secret plans against liberty, was be-

lieved to be the President.[92] On the eve of war, Americans came to see the King as an accomplice to the ministerial conspiracy rather than its opponent; by the start of the second Federalist administration, many Americans concluded that Washington was the main figure in the Federalist plot. Stunned by his presumed betrayal, Washington's opponents swore against him the same enmity that an earlier generation of Americans had sworn against the King. No wonder that Jefferson could write at this time that "all the old spirit of '76 is kindling."[93] The point was made by Freneau as well: "The spirit of 1776," he said, "is again aroused."[94]

Freneau was right. To read the anti-Washington tirades is to be reminded of the pamphlets, speeches, and sermons that raged against George III on the eve of the Revolution. The similarity is no accident, for conspicuous in both outpourings was the work of the same type of men. By reiterating their opposition to con-stituted authority in the 1790s, these men not only relived their own lives but also restored for thousands of other lives the spirit of the Revolution. Not every critic, not even a majority of critics, fit this description; but many did, and among these were men so equipped and situated as to make themselves and their fellows heard above the voices of Republican moderates. These men had gained a prominent place in the opposition press, and they used it to publicize their claims against Washington.

Those who knew the authors of these radical commentaries must have recognized merely a new rendition of, for them, an old theme. The leaders of the anti-Washington and Anti-Federalist crusade of the 1790s were men who would be designated by any political es-tablishment as professional radicals, men whose allegiance shifted according to who was in and out of power. Opposition to power, along with a tendency to excess in accusation and rhetoric, was the one constant in their public lives. Before Philip Freneau tongue-lashed President Washington in the *National Gazette,* he had written odes to General Washington and composed satires against his adversary. Before Thomas Greenleaf insulted Washington in the *New York Journal,* he and his father (the latter losing his post as Justice of the Peace as a result) had written inflammatory arti-cles against the British.[95] Before William ("Peter Porcupine") Cob-bett assailed Washington, he faced prosecution in England for po-litical agitation[96]; before James Callender let loose his barrage against Washington, which included an outrageous toast to the President's "speedy death," he had been indicted for sedition in

Scotland for his intemperate political discussion about abuses of government. Indeed, upon arriving as a fugitive in the United States, Callender was immediately identified as a scandalmonger. Under the Adams administration, Callender would be imprisoned for sedition, but his venom was not reserved for the Federalists alone. He would eventually rip into President Jefferson, his old protector and patron, even more viciously than he pilloried President Washington.[97] Before William Duane, an assistant editor for the *Aurora,* raised his voice against Washington, he had been expelled from India by the British for his clamorous antigovernment writings. Duane, too, had first been attracted to, then repelled by, Jefferson, the first Republican President.[98]

Before Benjamin Austin turned on Washington, he had distinguished himself first as a hater of monarchy, then as a demogogic agitator, promoter of riots, and all-around favorite of the mob. (John Quincy Adams remembered his flooding of a town meeting with 700 men "who looked as if they had been collected from all the jails on the continent.") Even by the standards of the 1790s, Austin was an anachronism. "He liked the political vintage of 1775 too well," observed a biographer, "to accept the new wine of federalism."[99] Before Thomas Paine damned Washington he, too, had railed against the British, with exceptional force and consequence. Paine's inconstancy succeeded only in estranging everyone in respectable society, both Federalist and Republican.[100] Other men of similar background and attitude campaigned against the first American establishment. James Cheetham, for example, arrived in the United States just after Washington left office; but he bought a half-share in the last of Greenleaf's newspapers, *Argus,* soon enough to vent his spleen on Washington's successor, John Adams. Only a few years earlier, this member of England's radical Constitutional Society had been arrested and charged with conspiracy to overthrow the British government.[101]

In their stinging attacks against Washington and his establishment, these men touched on key elements in the American political legacy; they embodied the continuity between the anti-British crusade of the 1770s and the Anti-Federalist crusade of the 1790s. Yet, their campaign was not undertaken in a social vacuum. It was the public's readiness to assign malicious intentions to actions that might otherwise be ascribed to bad judgment that made the anti-Washington movement as effective as it was. Against a background of levees and birthday celebrations, of administration attempts to canonize its leader by impressing his image on coins, of national offices filled with men believed to be sympathetic to what Jefferson called "monocratic" (monarchical-aristocratic) rule, and of a popular majority that showed itself gullible to the claims of its government, the radical branch of the opposition defined measures taken by the incumbent Federalists not in light of their apparent merits and weaknesses but as elements of a broader, carefully devised scheme of oppression. However innocent they seemed, every action of the President and his government added to the critics' body of evidence that pointed to conspiracy. Thus, a treaty that betrayed a republican ally, France, and undermined domestic interests through its concessions to Great Britain was not merely ill-advised; it "must impress every upright mind with horror and must carry conviction to the soul of every man, who is not in the plot against his country's liberty and peace."[102]

Divorced from their social context, these charges would seem less than implausible; they would be unintelligible. Restored to that context, they reveal a strong and enduring element in American life, the tendency to attribute disagreeable, although manifestly straightforward, acts (like the 1765 Stamp Tax) to dark, conspiratorial designs. The malicious criticisms leveled against Washington can thus be seen as expressions of that same bent of mind that animated the Revolution itself.

Venerated by All

As a man who cherished reputation above all other earthly things, Washington found the attacks on his character less bearable than any other hardship of public life. Yet, he must have been consoled by the realization that his critics were in a small minority, and that many Americans saw them, as he did, engaged in a conspiracy of their own, a conspiracy to "Frenchify" the nation, sabotage the Constitution, and restore the old confederation. And if, from the very beginning of his presidency, a few condemned Washington for kingly arrogance and ostentation, a far greater number saw in him paternal solicitude and simplicity. When he arrived in Charleston, South Carolina, in the spring of 1791, shortly after the second anniversary of his presidency, a visitor observed that "all look up to him as the saviour of the country, all respect him as the founder of our States and cherish him as a father who would come to see for himself if his children are happy.

He appears among us without any display, with no escort except his virtues, with no retinue except a secretary and the enduring memory of his beautiful and glorious deeds."[103] The critics' inability to understand the sincerity and depth of feeling beneath such tributes to Washington helps to explain why their all-out attack on him was bound to fail.

No objective observer would have misunderstood the people's attitude toward their new President. When Washington left New York in 1790 for a "Northern Tour" through nearby New England, he was met with tumultuous welcomes. A year later, he was received with similar enthusiasm in the distant states of the South. Washington's reception in Charleston, the South's largest city, magnified the adulation he had received in the more than thirty other towns and villages he had visited during his "Southern Tour"—and showed not only how sincere but also how universal his veneration had become. It was a perfect reflection of how American citizens everywhere felt about him.

Thirteen neatly uniformed naval captains rowed Washington into Charleston harbor, where he was quickly surrounded by forty boats and ships, each profusely arrayed with colorful bunting, each alive with banners and streamers, each filled with noisy spectators waving welcome. A barge carrying musicians and singers pulled beside the President, and, reenacting the traditional reception for waterborne English monarchs, serenaded him on his way to shore. (That part of his welcome must have caused the guest to wince. If critics reacted so violently to his courtly, yet subdued, levees, what would they think about this bombastic reception?) As he disembarked, cannons roared and church bells rang. A committee led by the state governor and chief city magistrate greeted him and, after a round of introductions, led him to a massive parade in his honor. Through all this, "an uncommonly large concourse of citizens" (more than a majority of the city's population, according to one correspondent) "reiterated shouts of joy and satisfaction."[104]

After the parade, Washington heard a series of public addresses. The speakers all expressed strong affection for the new government, and even stronger affection for him. To assure Washington that that affection was no less profound in the remote South than it was elsewhere in the nation, the intendant [mayor] and wardens of Charleston revealed "a peculiar satisfaction in declaring their firm persuasion, that they speak the language of their constituents in asserting that no body of men can exceed them in attachment to his public character, or in revering his private virtues. . . ." The city's merchants, in their own address, underscored the point— "that we yield to *none* in sincere respect and attachment to your person. . . ."[105]

As he relaxed alone that night, Washington may have wondered about the contrast between his critics' accusations and the people's feelings. Acting on his initial perception—that the critics' disdain for his "pomp" and "haughtiness" was shared by at least part of the public at large—he had deliberately displayed on this day, as previously, an air of diffidence. When praised as the single cause of America's military and political achievements, for example, he took pains to point out in his reply that the nation's well-being "rests not on the exertions of any individual."[106] But most Charlestonians did not seem to know what he was talking about. As the days passed, it became increasingly certain that they saw him as the sole deliverer and embodiment of their nation.

On the evening of his second day in the city, Washington dined with local, state, and foreign dignitaries. His table was set under an imposing triumphal arch, and as toasts were drunk to his government, cannon volleys were fired off. On the third night, he attended a public ball at the Exchange Building. Within clear sight of that building, in Charleston harbor, a ship, brightly illuminated, displayed the letters VW (for *Vivat Washington*—Long Live Washington) on its largest sail. The entrance to the building itself was decorated by his portrait, along with the inscription *Deliciis Patriae* (Delight of the Nation). Inside, the pillars were entwined with laurel, and throughout the great hall were placed messages in English, Latin, and French: "With grateful praises of the hero's fame/We'll teach our infants' tongues to lisp his name"; *Magnus in bello* (Great in war); *Hominis jura, defendit et curiat* (The law of man defended and preserved); *Diogène aujourd'hui casseroit sa lanterne* (Today Diogenese would throw down his lamp). As Washington greeted each of the two-hundred and fifty ladies in attendance, he noticed other pictures of himself, and other inscriptions, embroidered on their dresses and ribbons.[107]

Washington might have felt like a monarch, but it was through no contrivance of his own. No courtly levee, no stuffy reception arranged by his own staff, ever produced such adulation. It was a spontaneous and sincere excitement. "Bells have been ringing every day since his arrival," a correspondent observed on Washington's fourth day in Charleston. "Our city has been in such a bustle all this week, and every body so much taken up by our beloved President, that little or nothing like business has been done. . . ." As the week drew to a close, the consensus grew. What a delight, exclaimed one of the city notables, "to observe the man whom we most venerate *venerated by all*" (Italics in original.)[108]

Reflecting on all this during his next stop, Savannah, Washington recalled that "the continual hurry into which I was thrown by entertainment—visits—and ceremonies of one kind or another, scarcely allowed me a moment that I could call my own—nor is the case much otherwise here."[109] Nor was the case much otherwise in the other places he visited during his three-month, 1,900-mile tour.[110] These receptions, all as warm as they were hectic— and, most importantly, all devoid of partisan reference—convinced Washington that his appeal transcended politics. It showed "that the President was as popular in the Southern states as he was in Federalist New England."[111] The importance to Washington of this fact cannot be exaggerated. He returned to the capital knowing far more about public opinion and sentiment than did his critics. He knew that his support was strong enough to sustain even controversial policies.

Behind any controversial measure introduced during Washington's second term, some Americans might have been disposed to look for a plot, but only a few Americans were so engaged in that search as to be impervious to Washington's own words and judgments. Thus, after the details of the Jay Treaty became known, and condemned, in almost every part of the Union, Thomas Pickering, then Secretary of War, declared that the tumultuous opposition could be halted only by a proclamation of the President's intention, withal, to accept the treaty. Washington's formal acceptance came in mid-August; several months later, William Plumer of New Hampshire observed that "the incomparable answer of our great Chieftan is very popular with the sovereign people. More than nineteen-twentieths approve it."[112] The degree of support was as high in Philadelphia as in New Hampshire. Once opposed by ninety-five percent of the citizens, Benjamin Rush lamented, the treaty was now "approved of, or peaceably acquiesced in, by the same proportion. . . ." The connection between this sudden change of opinion about the treaty and Washington's approval of it was, in Rush's view, self-evident. The respectable people he knew who strongly opposed the treaty when they first read it, suddenly embraced it when they learned of President Washington's decision.[113] Thomas Jefferson, too, was forced to concession: "Congress has risen: [but] one man outweighs them all in influence over the people, who have supported his judgment against their own and that of their representatives."[114]

Whether or not the people supported Washington despite their own convictions, as Jefferson asserted, cannot be accurately determined. What is certain, however, is that during the first, critical eight years of its existence, the government attained through Washington's popularity a stability it might not otherwise have possessed. And, detractors of Washington paid a high price for their criticism—at least those who held or aspired to public office. Personal attacks on Washington were as counterproductive in the South, where Republicanism was strong, as they were in the Federalist states of the North. While traveling in North Carolina, Robert Goodloe Harper (a South Carolinian) made this point in his letter to Alexander Hamilton.

> The old man never stood higher or firmer than he does through these states. [Absalom] Tatom, one of the North Carolina members, lost his election for speaking dis-respectfully of him. . . . That a man should oppose the [Jay] treaty, [the people] could account for and bear; it was natural, they said, for men to differ in opinion on such subjects; but it was inconceivable to them that any man, without improper motives, a bad heart, or a most perverted judgement, should speak with disrespect of the old man, as they call him, or do any act which implied a want of confidence in his integrity. . . . The Election for Electors in this state is made by the people. While it was understood that General Washington would consent to be reelected, no man however popular, had the least chance of becoming an elector if he was understood to be opposed to the old man. Ever since he has declined, some very popular Candidates, it is thought, will be very much injured in the election, by their known dislike to him.[115]

The attitudes that Mr. Harper described were part of a cult that had fully established itself during Washington's first presidential term. By 1791, two years after he took office, the "monarchical" and "idolatrous" celebration of his birthday had become a national custom. There was hardly a town anywhere too small to have at least one ball or banquet on that day to honor Washington.

In Philadelphia, the capital, as in all large cities, the celebrations were especially elaborate:

> Tuesday the 22d inst. being the anniversary of the birth of the PRES-IDENT OF THE UNITED STATES, when he attained to the 59th year of his age—the same was celebrated here with every demonstration of public joy. The Artillery and Light Infantry Corps of the city were paraded and at 12 o'clock a federal salute was fired. The congratulatory compliments of the members of the Legislature of the Union—the Heads of the Departments of State—foreign Ministers, officers, Civil and Military of the state—the Reverend Clergy—and of Strangers and Citizens of distinction, were presented to the President on this auspicious occasion.[116]

Three years later, the animosities excited by the Jay Treaty induced the Congress to drop the practice of adjourning on the President's Birthday. Nationwide, however, the birthday pageants were more glittering than ever. Not only did supporters remark on the "unusual joy and festivity" of the occasion, but also opponents, like James Madison, acknowledged an "unexampled splendor" in the public demonstrations.[117] These exhibitions differed from those held during Washington's regional tours and other travels, when local citizens turned out to greet and honor him. Washington's Birthday involved multiple celebrations, simultaneously observed by every city and town in the country. It was a national event, equaled only by July Fourth in enthusiasm and resplendence. The birth of the nation and the birth of Washington had become commemorative touchstones for the American people.

The Federalist establishment, it is true, gloried in the Washington's Birthday celebrations, but to regard them as mere political choreography is to miss an essential feature which linked them to other forms of public ritual. By providing the members of society with a periodic occasion to reaffirm their common national sentiments, the observance of Washington's birthday took on the character of a religious rite. "There can be no society," said Durkheim, "which does not feel the need of upholding and reaffirming at regular intervals the collective sentiments and the collective ideas which make its unity and its personality." These occasions "do not differ from religious ceremonies, either in their object, the results which they produce, or the processes employed to attain these results."[118] In both ceremonies, civil and religious, a synchronization of activities produces a synchronization of sentiments. From this unity results a more acute sense of the sacred. (A mocking newspaper reference by a Republican critic to Washington's Birthday as America's "Political Christmas" underscores the point.[119]) Washington's Birthday was indeed a sacred day: a time for communion, a time when the sanctity of the nation, and the strength of the people's attachment to it, could be reaffirmed. The Washington's Birthday observance seemed like a religious communion because on that day "we feel our natures raised by the contemplation, and dignified by an alliance with its object." Observers noticed that the riotousness and drunkenness that marked other public gatherings during the year were on this day totally absent. Like any religious liturgy, the Birthday rites extolled good and condemned evil: They "nourished in our bosoms public spirit, disregard of unmerited opprobrium, contempt of whatever is base, and the admiration of everything which is truly great, noble, and illustrious."[120]

The religious quality of the Birthday celebrations was also evident in the sanctity of its object. Sacred figures perform feats deserving of pious gratitude, and they enjoy immunity from criticism. Likewise, when Washington's Republican opponents disparaged the recognition of his birthday, the faithful could be assured that what they were hearing was more profane than dogs "baying the moon." Citizens everywhere beheld

> with indignation the malicious attempts of a few ungrateful persons, to tarnish the glory of this justly renowned hero and republican, [but] it is highly gratifying to perceive, that the body of the people entertain that undiminished sense of his virtues, which the grateful heart, from a recollection of past services, cannot but acknowledge him to possess.

And so the communion, and the nation, was preserved. "All ranks of citizens vied with each other in mutual congratulations [to] the *Man who unites all hearts.*"[121]

July Fourth oratory carried the same message. On this holiday, no one's name was venerated more often than Washington's, and none were condemned more violently than his detractors'. To oppose Washington, every American was told, was to be an enemy of national unity. Robert Forsyth's 1796 Princeton College speech was representative, and almost all who heard it, or read it in the newspapers, agreed with its conclusion:

> Faction! curst offspring of hell begot on mercenary interest! . . . [T]hou has dared to shew they horrid visage for a moment, crawling from the

infernal pit, and to spit thy venom and sulphur on the untarnished, the immortal glory of Washington! his powerful genius shall crush thy head, and plunge thee down again into the abyss from whence thou hast sprung! O Washington! whose name, on every return of this anniversary, I shall pronounce with enthusiasm along with the sacred name of *country.*[122]

The nation's regard for Washington was attested to in other ways. It was expressed in the increasing number of counties and towns named after him, including the Territory (District) of Columbia, which had earlier been designated the nation's permanent capital. The "Washington Marches" remained a favorite of the public and were played on almost any pretext. Francis Hopkinson's "Toast" (1778) and "Seven Songs" for Washington (1788) also remained popular. Of the production of poems there was no end. Graven images abounded. The Mint Act, which forbade impressions of Washington's image on federal coins, did not stop state and local institutions from producing them or from importing them from Great Britain. With equal zeal, painters continued their work. The subject was reluctant, but the need for his likeness was too strong to be resisted. During his presidency alone Washington sat at least once, and often more than once, for no less than fifteen different artists. "No American, and few world figures before the age of photography—except, possibly, Louis XIV and Napoleon—sat for portraits as often as Washington did."[123] Enriching the nation with up-to-date likenesses of its hero, the artists also enriched themselves. Gilbert Stuart, who sought sittings with Washington to repay his debts, found himself in April 1795 with a backlog of thirty-nine requests for copies of his portraits. These, according to his daughter, he dashed off at the rate of one every two hours.[124] Other artists did not do quite as well, but they made more money with Washington than they would have made without him.

At the end of his second term, then, Washington remained the new nation's hero and emblem. He held a virtual monopoly on the public's affection and overshadowed anyone who stood in his presence. Even his successor to the presidency, John Adams, on his own inauguration day, complained to his wife about the wet eyes cast upon his predecessor, Washington, who sat beside him as he made his public inaugural address. When that speech was done, the multitude ran after Washington, not Adams, and gave thunderous voice to its affection for him.

Hero Worship and the Forging of a Union

How could Washington for so long retain his extraordinary prestige, expecially in the presence of that vocal minority which sought to subvert it? Although his own professions of disinterestedness, along with his impeccable conduct in the presidential office, blunted the attacks of his critics, they do not in themselves account for the intensity of his supporters' adulation, nor do they explain why these supporters constituted an overwhelming majority.

The ideals that Washington stood for were the most important aspect of his cult, and the most appealing of these ideals was national union. The people seemed to realize intuitively that there could be no liberty without union, and when they expressed praise of Washington, the benefits of union were often affirmed in their next breath. "When WASHINGTON lived," one of his mourning countrymen recalled, "we had one common mind—one common head—one common heart—we were united—we were safe."[125] Without Washington, the nation would have had many minds, many heads and hearts, and would have been weak and unsafe. Those who drew this implication at his death in 1800 must have heaved a sigh as they turned to their old (1789) *Display of the United States of America* (Fig. 19), with its thirteen interlocking rings (representing each state and its population) forming a halo around the dominating profile of the first President. The feelings evoked by this icon of the Federalist Era embodied the most important social use of the Washington cult.

In recent years, behavioral and social scientists have studied at length the integrative functions of hero worship. Sigmund Freud believed that the common bond that ties people to their leader also ties them to each other. He clarifies the underlying social dynamic expressed in the veneration of Washington when he describes the way individuals are united through their internalization of a common "ego ideal."[126] Georg Simmel enlarges on this point by explaining that "[t]he subordination of a group under a single person results, above all, in a very decisive unification of the group"; it is "the cause of a commonness which in the absence of it could not be attained and which is not predetermined by any other relation among its members."[127] Freud's and Simmel's insights provide a useful preliminary account of how hero worship brings unity to a diversified society. But before we can fully understand the unifying role of George Washington, it is necessary to further explore the structural problems faced by this nation.

In the last quarter of the eighteenth century, the problem of social order was paramount in the minds of America's leaders. During the Revolution, soldiers brought with them to the battle-front local attachments and prejudices that were often ignored in the presence of a common enemy. When the war was over, however,

> the frenzied spirit of dissention burst forth, and spread among a people ... with rapid and deadly progress. ... [C]onvulsions which shook the first states of our union to the centre—the bands of our union and government dissolving ... were the existing effects of this dissention. ... [128]

The writer was not exaggerating. Samuel Osgood, contemplating the prospects of a national regime replacing the then present confederation, announced: "Time will tell whether our union is natural; or rather whether the Dispositions and Views of the several parts of the Continent are so similar as that they can and will be happy under the same form of Government. There is too much reason to believe they are not."[129] Osgood's pessimism reflected the states' determination to maintain their political autonomy; the sectionalist split between Southern, Middle, and Northern states; and the deep provincialism and religious insularity of the states' several populations. In this context, and in view of practical economic and political needs, social integration was an urgent goal.

The "jealousies of so many independent sovereignties," Isaac Parker, a Massachusetts lawyer, believed, "would be appeased by nothing but the all controlling popularity of Washington."[130] Most Americans would have shared Parker's conviction, and their consensus attained its most dramatic ritual expression in the public ceremonies that commemorated Washington's birth. These observances expressed the nation's conception of the man, but they also expressed the nation's conception of itself. Recall the observance at Philadelphia, particularly its participants: congressmen, federal department heads, state officials, and city representatives. The common participation of national, state, and local representatives affirmed (and was meant to affirm) the integration of national, state, and local authority. To this end the press contributed by printing accounts of various celebrations held throughout the country. The universality and similarity of these celebrations revealed a source of commonality that would have otherwise been less visible.

Perhaps nothing attests so well to the integrative features of the Birthday observances as the toasts offered in Washington's honor. Taken separately, these offerings admit of little significance; considered in the aggregate, however, they convey a coherent statement about the nation's major conflicts and their resolution. They reproduce both the reality and the ideal of federal union. The toasts drunk in Boston's Concert Hall on February 22, 1796, furnish an example:

1. The Day: the Birth-day of virtue, valour and partriotism.
2. The President of the United States: may the gratitude which he has implanted in the hearts of his countrymen, be as lasting and extensive as his virtues.
3. The Vice-President of the United States: may Americans never forget the blessing they owe to his firmness, nor the truth his talents have explored.
4. The Congress of the United States: may the wisdom which preserved our tranquility, continue predominant.
5. The Governor and the Commonwealth of Massachusetts.
6. The Marquis de la Fayette: may the gloom of a despot's prison be soon exchanged for the embraces of his father Washington in the land of freedom.
7. Governor Gilman: may his example be imitated by all the rulers of the free; and the gratitude of his fellow citizens be the reward of his patriotic firmness.
8. The Legislature of Massachusetts: May it prove a bulwark against the assaults of . . . insidious enemies.
9. The people of France: a speedy termination of their toils, glorious as the hopes of their patriots, and splendid as their victories.
10. John Jay: may virtue, independence and patriotism, be eventually successful.
11. The Mechanical Association of Boston: may they ever preserve the spirit of 1787, by which they insured to Massachusetts, and to the United States, the Federal Constitution.
12. The Hon. Mr. Harper: may every legislator, like him, calmly investigate measures, and when convinced of error, have independence to renounce it, and to embrace truth and reason.
13. The town of Boston: may the cradle of American Liberty exist in the Temple of Order, good government, and unadulterated republicanism.

14. The Heroes who fought with and supported our beloved Washington thro' the glorious struggle which established our independence.

15. As this was the first day of the most glorious son of liberty, may this anniversary be the last of contention amongst her sons.[131]

These fifteen toasts, one for each state in the union, reflected particular as well as common attachments. References to Lafayette, then confined in France's "despot prison"; to the present "toils" of the French people; to John Jay, negotiator of the controversial treaty; to the Mechanical Association, whose efforts helped to ratify the Constitution over Anti-Federalist opposition; to Robert Goodloe Harper of South Carolina, a former Republican leader who converted to Federalism—these expressed New England's strong Federalist persuasion and so lent weight to the Republican claim that Washington's Birthday was a factional rather than a national occasion. The remainder of the toasts, however, acknowledged a reality that transcended faction—namely, the three great realms of intersecting authority: national authority, represented by the President, Vice-President, and Congress; state authority, represented by the office and person of the governor as well as by the Massachusetts Legislature; and local authority, represented by the town of Boston. This hierarchical structure was sanctified by the last two toasts—one commemorating the sacrifices made for its establishment, the other recalling the end for which those sacrifices were made: national unity. The tension between local, state, and national integrity was thus expressed and resolved during the celebration of Washington's birth. Thereby Washington became a part—a leading part—of the fabric of union.

No one took this role more seriously than Washington himself. His 1783 Circular Letter, or "Legacy" as he called it, was an explicit attempt to lend his reputation to the support of a strong national government. The ill-conceived ceremonies he followed as President were meant to dramatize the dignity of that government, just as the showing of the presidential flag in the Northern and Southern Tours was meant to add to its visibility. Continued references to "consensus" in his presidential addresses underscored Washington's personal conviction that national unity was at once problematic and vital. Recognizing himself to be the central figure of the new republic, he believed that he could contribute to this unity by publicizing his personal stand against political and regional interests. The belief proved to be sound. However much it angered his political opponents, Washington's publicly stated determination to rise and stay above the nation's "self-created societies" and "factions" helped perpetuate his role as a national symbol and engendered support for the ideal of union. Thus, when Washington visited Boston during his 1789 Northern Tour, he found an imposing arch erected in his honor (Fig. 20). The words inscribed on the face of the arch were familiar ones: "TO THE MAN WHO UNITES ALL HEARTS."

At the same time that most Americans regarded Washington as a symbol of union, however, they regarded him as a symbol of liberty as well. Many Anti-Federalists saw him as a buffer—a protector of popular rights against aristocratic privilege—rather than a unifier. No citizens, however, were more sensitive to Washington's role as an upholder of liberties than the religious minorities. These groups were less anxious to cultivate what they had in common with other Americans than to sustain what kept them apart. Washington recognized this, just as he recognized the tenacity of regional and economic interests, and he took pains to explain precisely what national unity meant to him. He carried to his countrymen a vision of "organic" rather than "mechanical" solidarity, a union based on difference and interdependence rather than uniformity of belief and conduct.[132] Washington's understanding of the kind of integration appropriate to a modern state was not shared by the most powerful Protestant establishments, the New England Congregationalists and Presbytarians; but other religious groups could not have been more pleased. The Baptists, for example, were delighted when the nation's hero urged them to "be persuaded that no one would be more zealous than myself to establish effectual barriers against the horrors of spiritual tyranny, and every species of religious persecution." The Quakers rejoiced to know that the new President considered them "exemplary and useful citizens," despite their refusal to aid him in war. Catholics, who were in many respects the most despised of the religious minorities, saw an end to persecution when the chief magistrate assured them that all citizens "are equally entitled to the protection of civil government. . . . And I presume that your fellow-citizens will not forget the patriotic part which you took in the accomplishment of the revolution, and the establishment of their government." Jews found in Washington's policy an unprecedented expression of friendship from a head of state: "It is now no more that toleration is spoken of, as if it was by the indulgence of one class of people, that another enjoyed the exercise of their inherent natural rights." The Universalists, disdained by the pious for their liberal religious views, were congratulated by Washington for their "political professions and practices," which were "almost universally friendly to the order and happiness of our civil institutions. . . ."[133] Acknowledging in each instance that respect for diversity was a fair price for commitment to the nation and its regime, Washington abolished deep-rooted fears that would have otherwise alienated a large part of the population from the nation-building process. For this large minority, he embodied not the ideal of union, nor even that of liberty, but rather the reconciliation of union and liberty.

If Washington's great prestige helped resolve tensions in one aspect of the social structure, it produced even greater tensions in other respects. Strong and long-standing resentments occasioned by one man's virtual monopoly over the people's regard and affection lay at the core of the problem. One commentator articulated these resentments by asking:

> Can the President doubt that *he alone* is the fountain of the tranquility and happiness of the United States? As well might he doubt, that *his* single *arm* conquered the armies of Great Britain, and established the independence of our common country. Will it be believed that such men as Gates, Green [*sic*], Franklin or Adams had any agency in our emancipation? This would be as absurd as the opinion that the armies of the United States had a share in the glory of the revolution, or that the statesmen in congress had contributed to its success. The tranquility and happiness of the United States grew out of the President as a watermelon grows out of a field in Jersey. . . . Omnipotent in power as well as in fame, he alone holds tranquility and happiness in his right hand and not even "his man Timothy" [Pickering, then Secretary of State] can put in a claim to a share in dispensing our unparalleled prosperity.[134]

This statement appeared in the opposition press, but it must have struck most Americans—even those whose political views were consistent with Washington's—as sound.

Federalist leaders like John Adams and Alexander Hamilton were known to be resentful of Washington's reputation. As products of a culture that regarded fame as the only just reward for public service, these men were dismayed by the fact that one person had been given credit for a great enterprise that required the sacrifice and exertion of an entire society. Even more, this focusing of collective gratitude on the figure of Washington could only undermine others' belief in the reputational benefits of self-sacrifice and public duty. Although every patriot was obliged to renounce personal ambition and was entitled, in theory, to a measure of fame in return, the stark reality was that only one man found himself thus compensated.

Between the moral imperative of justice and the social imperative of unity coiled a tension that could never be resolved, and from this tension arose agonizing contradictions. On the one hand, John Adams could assert despairingly in his letter to Benjamin Rush that "[t]he history of our Revolution will be one continued lie from one end to the other. The essence of the whole will be that Dr. Franklin's electrical rod smote the earth and out sprang General Washington. That Franklin electrified him with his rod—and thence forward these two conducted all the policy, negotiations, legislatures and war."[135] Rush, of course, agreed, and affirmed the necessity of rescuing from oblivion the entire cast of revolutionary heroes and giving *them* "first place in the temple of liberty."[136] On the other hand, Adams knew too well the public benefits that flowed from his and others' obscurity. His ninth discourse on Davila recognized that

> when the emulation of all the citizens looks up to one point, like the rays of a circle from all parts of the circumference, meeting and uniting in the centre, you may hope for uniformity, consistency and subordination: but when they look up to different individuals, or assemblies, or councils, you may expect all the deformities, eccentricities, and confusion, of the Polemick [polemic] system.[137]

Adams's acute observation was as well founded as his resentment. The great leaders of the Revolution—Hamilton, Jefferson, and Adams himself—were not only men of strong ideological convictions; they were also the representatives of regional interests, and their personal relationships were marked by adversity. Had they been elevated to the same level as Washington, they could have been worshipped only as local gods, representing (respectively) the Middle States, the South, and New England. Sectional cleavages, instead of being resisted, would then have achieved symbolic expression and, in that measure, been legitimized. Thus, a "monotheistic" form of hero worship was precisely what was needed in post-Revolutionary America. Only a cult like Washington's, a cult powerful and exclusive enough to deflect local sentiments onto a common object of symbolic orientation, could have contributed to the integration of society. This point was acknowledged along the entire political spectrum. In 1792, for example, even Thomas Jefferson, though opposed to many of Washington's policies, pleaded that he accept another term as President, declaring that "North and South will hang together as long as they have you to hang on."[138]

The cult devoted to the adoration of George Washington contributed heavily to America's becoming and remaining conscious of itself as a nation. The British Minister underscored this contribution in a report to his Foreign Office:

> The leading men in the United States appear to be of the opinion that [public tributes to Washington] tend to elevate the spirit of the people, and contribute to the formation of a *national character,* which they consider as much wanting in this country. And assuredly, if self-opinion is (as perhaps it is) an essential ingredient in that *character* which promotes the prosperity and dignity of a nation, the Americans will be the gainers by the periodical recital of the feats of their Revolutionary War, and the repetition of their praises of Washington.[139]

The Minister's point was recognized even by those who resented Washington's overshadowing historical presence. Alexander Hamilton, though keenly aware that Washington had stolen the spotlight from others,[140] believed that "his popularity has often been essential to the safety of America, and is still of great importance to it." Although tempted at the end of the war to reveal Washington's darker side, Hamilton always kept his resentments to himself.[141] Hamilton's view was shared by Benjamin Rush:

> I once suggested to [Charles Thomson] to write memoires of the American Revolution, "No, no," said he, "I will not. I would not tell the truth without giving great offense. Let the world admire our patriots and heroes. Their supposed talents and virtues ... by commanding imitation will serve the cause of patriotism and of our country." I concur in this sentiment. ... In answer to the epithet which Washington has applied to me, I will coolly reply, "He was the highly favored instrument whose patriotism and name contributed greatly to the independence of the United States."[142]

Of course, these men were being a bit disingenuous. That Washington's reputation was hostage to Thomson's patriotism—that it would have collapsed if the former secretary of the Continental Congress had actually written his memoirs—is a hypothesis that

neither Thomson nor Rush would have been eager to test. Likewise, Hamilton's concealment of his true feelings about Washington would have struck most of his beneficiaries as a gesture
demanded more by necessity than by virtue. Nevertheless,
disingenuousness admits of psychic benefits. Detractors boosted
their own egos by identifying themselves as instrumental leaders
("We are the real leaders") and identifying Washington as a symbolic leader ("He is a mere symbol"). They portrayed him as their
tool; his reputation, as an instrument of their will. In this way,
those who were deprived by Washington of a more prominent historical reputation consoled themselves.

If George Washington had become king of America, as some of
his admirers would have liked, his remaining years of life would
have been spent in a placid glow of gratitude and affection. The
full weight of the outrage occasioned by the new government's
decisions would have fallen on the head of his prime minister. It
was fortunate that this was not the case, for if the agent of those
decisions were not also the man the people adored, the government might not have survived as well as it did. Yet, the price paid
by Washington was most dear. Although he knew that his enemies
were massively outnumbered by his friends, he was devastated by
the personal insults and charges brought against him, and he left
office a tired and wounded man. He was too close to the scene to
know that the very attacks that so injured him personally had actually strengthened his public reputation. Those attacks had drawn
attention, as perhaps nothing else could, to the suffering that
Washington endured for the nation's benefit; they transformed
the unselfish and trustworthy patriot into an Innocent One. His
eulogists would recall that Moses, too, was reviled by those he had
delivered from bondage, and that his sufferings endeared him
even more to posterity. Washington's detractors thus unwittingly
secured what the nation most needed: a symbol that not only made
unpopular but necessary policies acceptable but also gave to the
people a tangible representation of its own rising greatness.

3

Death of a
Hero

ON THURSDAY, DECEMBER 19, 1799, the clerk of the House of Representatives recorded the following entry:

> Mr. Marshall, with deep sorrow on his countenance, and in a low, pathetic tone of voice, rose and addressed the House as follows:
> The melancholy event which was yesterday announced with doubt, has been rendered but too certain. Our Washington is no more.[1]

The man defined by John Marshall as a national possession—"our Washington"—was gone. He had died five days earlier, on December 14. Immediately, a joint congressional committee was established to decide on appropriate memorial arrangements. A state funeral would not be enough. The committee resolved, and Congress agreed, to erect a marble monument in the Capitol Building and to request from Martha Washington permission to deposit her husband's remains under it. (She agreed, but more than thirty years would pass before Congress would appropriate money for the plan, and when it did the family objected, and the project was dropped.) The funeral service itself was carried out at Mount Vernon, but news accounts tell us that the hero's passing was mourned in the cities and towns of every state. The formal ceremonies (as recommended by the national government) typically involved a funeral procession which included the major groups in the local community along with an oration by one of the community's religious or political leaders.

President John Adams announced the official period of mourn-

91

ing, and in the process he made some complimentary remarks about Washington: "Malice could never blast his honor, and Envy made him a singular exception to her universal rule."[2] Adams *would* mention envy. Sixteen years later, in a letter to Jefferson, he would show it:

> The Death of Washington diffused a general Grief. The old Tories, the Hyperfederalists, the Speculators, sett up a general Howl. Orations Prayers Sermons Mock Funerals, were all employed, not that they loved Washington, but to keep in Countenance the Funding and Banking Systems; And to cast into the Background and the Shade all others who had been concerned in the Service of their Country in the Revolution.[3]

It is true that most Americans did not "love" Washington, at least not in the way they might love a close comrade or family member, nor did they grieve over his death as they would the passing of a beloved friend or relative. But public mourning, as Emile Durkheim observes, "is not a natural movement of private feelings wounded by cruel loss; it is a duty imposed by the group. One weeps, not simply because he is sad, but because he is forced to weep. It is a ritual attitude he is forced to adopt . . . but which is, in large measure, independent of his affective state."[4]

To allow the people to be indifferent to a death that had so diminished the nation would be to proclaim that that nation held no special place in the people's minds and hearts. John Adams's letter was, therefore, too cynical. It was not for the purpose of continuing the funding and banking system or of denying the services of other patriots that many ladies of Boston dressed "as if for a relative, some entirely in black," and "that black goods were scarce in shops as late as July of 1800."[5] If the audience for Gouverneur Morris's "pathetic and nervous" eulogy in New York city "listen'd even to extacy" and answered with an "involuntary burst of applause," it was to show "how warmly their feelings were interested,"[6] not to protect their interests. The double sentry placed for six months over Washington's mock grave in Philadelphia[7] did not line anyone's pockets or deny other men credit for taking part in the Revolution; nor were there ulterior motives behind the poems, hymns, and paintings inspired by Washington's death. To these rites and symbols other sources must be assigned, and other functions attributed.

A Concert of Mourning

The observances that commemorated Washington's death brought about a vivid social transformation in the communities in which they were held. Everywhere, these ceremonies melded religious, ethnic, political, and economic factions into a moral unity. In death, as in life, George Washington was to be "the man who unites all hearts."

The observances themselves varied in form from one locale to the next. The actual entombment of the hero took place at Mount Vernon. Although attended by many national, state, and local dignitaries, and carried out with appropriate religious and military ceremony, the event was relatively undramatic; it lacked massive public participation on account of Mount Vernon's distance from large population centers. In Philadelphia, on the other hand, the observance was spectacular. It would have been appropriate for the remains of the nation's first man to be honored in Philadelphia, the nation's capital, but since that was not possible, the government arranged for a symbolic reproduction of the Mount Vernon ceremony. A mock coffin, riderless horse, and burial cortege moved solemnly through the city (Fig. 21), and the effect was the same as if the hero's body had actually been in two places at once. Observances held in other cities, like Boston, featured no such displays, but they involved just as many people and were equally moving.

Boston's mourning rites began on December 26, 1799, with the first public announcement of Washington's death (Fig. 22). The timing was noteworthy: Washington's death occurred just several days before the anniversary of Jesus's birth, and the beginning of a new century. Two saviors, two new eras—the coincidence may have added something to the solemnity of the announcement in *Russell's Gazette:*

AGONIZING EVENT

"Oh Washington! Thou Hero, Patriot, Sage
"Friend of all climates, pride of every age;
"Were thine the laurels which the world could raise,
"The mighty harvest were penurious praise."

On Saturday, the 14th Dec. 1799,
DIED SUDDENLY

The Adoration of Washington

At his Seat in Virginia
GEN. GEORGE WASHINGTON
Commander
in Chief of the Armies of the United States of America,

mature in years,
covered with glory, and
rich in the affection of the
American people[8]

During the week following its announcement, Washington's death was discussed and formally recognized among the city's many groups and institutions. A eulogy was delivered at Harvard, while the Sons of the Pilgrims departed from the usually festive mood of their annual meeting to mark Washington's death through a solemn ceremony and recitation. Most businesses, including the Columbian Museum and Federal Street Theater, voluntarily closed down. The Society of the Cincinnati and the Freemasons held executive meetings to plan memorial observances of their own.[9]

During the next week to ten days, these discrete activities multiplied. The Mechanical Association, the various units of the military, and other groups held formal meetings and instructed their members on how properly to decorate and conduct themselves. At the same time, the beginnings of a city-wide observance took shape. The Columbian Museum, reopened after a week, displayed for the public an effigy of Washington in its Temple of Fame. (A real American eagle was included in the display, lest the national significance of that display be overlooked.) The Federal Street Theater also reopened with a memorial program, to which "every lover of his *country's* honor" was invited to attend [Italics mine].) The arrangements committee set up by the Boston selectmen, along with the city's independent organizations, was busy planning a massive public procession. Details of each organization's role in this procession appeared in successive issues of the *Gazette* (whose columns were now shrouded in black). The diversified population of Boston was becoming increasingly unified through attendance at public displays and logistical cooperation.[10]

Every citizen knew, as he gave expression to his personal sorrow, that he was acting in concert with others. Everyone saw, felt, and identified with the nation's grief. From the time of the death notice, massive newspaper coverage was given to celebrations held in other cities. So detailed and so prolonged was this coverage that no Bostonian who even skimmed his newspaper could fail to realize that he was witnessing events whose significance transcended the boundaries of any one community.

Bostonians also seemed to grasp the historical meaning of what was going on around them. As the story of Washington's career was retold from the podium, in the press, and in the taverns, he was becoming a part of the nation's growing martyrology. From the very beginning of hostilities with Great Britain, American poets, artists, and clergymen, along with other custodians of national morals, spoke loudly and long about the men who had died in their country's service. Among these martyrs, Joseph Warren, Richard Montgomery, and Hugh Mercer—all generals who had died in early battles—were most prominently recognized. There were others, too, like young John Laurens, killed in combat toward the war's end; General Nathaniel Greene, who died after the war; and, of course, Nathan Hale. Now Washington came to enrich the sacred heritage. This he did without delay, according to a verse published in *Russell's Gazette* (and later put to music for the religious service that would conclude the city's formal observance):

> From Mount Vernon behold the hero rise!
> Resplendent Forms attend him thro' the skies!
> The shades of war-worn veterans round him throng
> And lead, enwrapt, their honored chief along!
> A laurel wreath th' immortal *Warren* bears,
> An arch triumphal *Mercer's* hand prepares,
> Young *Laurens* erst the avenging bolt of war,
> With port majestic guides the glittering car,
> *Montgomery's* godlike form directs the way,
> And *Greene* unfolds the gates of endless day,
> While Angels, trumpet-tongued, proclaim thro' air,
> "Due honors for the First of Men prepare."[11]

By January 9, consensus on the importance and meaning of the funeral observance had been ritually and verbally affirmed, and the people assembled and cooperated in a single act of commemoration which expressed their solidarity. Awakening to the sound of cannons and bells, and finding all normal business suspended, Bostonians knew that January 9 was not an ordinary day; it was a day for sacred pursuits. The solemn procession that took place on that day began at the Statehouse and ended with a religious service at the Old South Meeting-House, thus symbolizing, through the medium of Washington's memory, the linkage of civil and religious authority. The cortege also symbolized the community's permanence and internal order. Permanence was symbolized by the male youths that led the procession. The city of Boston itself was represented in the cortege by its selectmen and procession organizing committee, its orator and chaplain, and its other political and moral leaders, and by different occupational groups. Physicians and lawyers, mostly from the elite class, were separated by two marshalls from the bourgeois "commercial and trading interests" and the proletarian "mechanic interests." The remainder of the Boston citizenry were joined together at the end of the procession.

The procession reflected Boston's affirmation of its place in the larger structure of society. County authority was represented in the procession by its sheriff, officials, and judges; the state was represented by its Lieutenant Governor, Treasurer, judges, and Council, the Speakers and Members of the House and Senate, and members of its militia; the nation was represented by the local chapters of two national associations with which Washington was closely associated—the Society of the Cincinnati and the Freemasons—and by federal military officers, who marched alongside state militia officers (as if to affirm the proper relationship between state and federal military power). Mobilized and set into motion by the death of a national figure, the local procession made visible the hierarchical integration of national and local authority, thus reiterating the structure solemnized by the ordering of the toasts that Bostonians once offered on Washington's Birthday. The medium was different, but the message was the same.

To the satisfaction of at least one observer, the event proved that "[t]he citizens of Boston can never be deficient in public gratitude," for everyone's behavior was a credit to the occasion. Even the tradesmen, whose decorum some city fathers felt could not be counted on, gave a "Testimony to Reason," according to one observer, by their massive turnout (2,500 in number) and perfect demeanor. All told, 6,000 people, or about 20 percent of the city's population, moved silently through the streets in one body. For those who watched, it was a remarkable scene: "The assemblage of all ranks in society, from venerable age to lisping infancy, to pay tribute to the virtues and services of WASHINGTON, was inexpressibly interesting."[12]

The memorial processions that took place during the early weeks of 1800 in every city of the United States had a common function: to express both the solidarity of the community and its unity with other levels of political and social organization. These events were also part of what had already become an essential tradition in American society. For a quarter-century, the American people's regard for Washington had been the clearest expression of what they had in common. In the solemn rites of mourning at Washington's death, no less than in the joyful rites of veneration that attended his life, Americans sought out one another and acted together, and so reaffirmed their attachment to their new nation.

Renewed and strengthened, the nation's unity acted back upon its human symbol. George Washington had achieved the status of a sacred object in the minds of Americans, and so his death brought multitudes together. The very process of assembling and acting in unison infused private feelings with an intensity they would not otherwise have attained. The people were carried away by mutually reinforcing transports of sorrow, moved by their own participation in the funeral ritual. In Boston and elsewhere, public mourning gave voice to the unity of society, and the consequence of that declaration was to consecrate further the image of Washington. This circularity shows how far he had come in twenty-five years. In 1775, Washington's veneration was a product of the "collective effervescence" and solidarity occasioned by war. In the early months of 1800, a similar eruption of emotion and unity was brought about by his death. At the beginning, the need for solidarity in the face of a powerful military foe led to the creation of a heroic George Washington; at the time of his death, the nation's solidarity presupposed his central, unifying role.

Varieties of Tribute

The Boston memorial observance contained a declamatory as well as a processional element. Delivered at the procession's final, destination, churchly and framed there by prayers, instrumental music, and specially prepared hymns and odes, the funeral eulogy climaxed the day's sacred event. The orator, Judge George Minot, had been selected eighteen years earlier to deliver the eulogy on the anniversary of the Boston Massacre, which was the occasion for Boston's first great funeral celebration[13] and part of the chain of events that led to the war which Washington managed and won. By headlining Minot's eulogy on the circulars announcing the memorial observance, and by giving him a special place in its procession, Bostonians prepared themselves to recognize the "soul" as well as the "body" of the occasion. Still steeped in Old World tradition, they equated the body of their solemn pageant with its tangible emblems, parades, and music; its soul, with the spiritual values expressed through its written and spoken words. In these words, the people of Boston found a "compendium of national morality."[14]

Funeral observances everywhere were capped by eulogies, and these constituted a block of material that was important in both crystallizing and to some extent forming popular conceptions of Washington.[15] For twenty-five years, event-specific versions of Washington's achievements and character had been offered from the pulpit, in the press, through holiday oratory, and along the informal grapevine, but it was not until he died that these fragments were brought together into a comprehensive and coherent story. Told across the nation in the context of sacred observances, the full story of Washington stimulated Americans' national sentiments. They linked the present to the heroic past and each individual to the state that Washington served.

The men who eulogized Washington were diverse in social background. They included lawyers, statesmen, and clergymen; Northerners and Southerners; Congregationalists and Presbyterians along with Quakers, Episcopalians, Unitarians, Deists, and Masonic grandmasters. They included Federalists and some Republicans, men who were personally acquainted with Washington and men who were not.[16] Despite this diversity, the grounds on which they praised Washington were remarkably similar.[17]

The eulogists gave voice to, and then reconciled, two important elements of republican culture: an abhorrence of hero worship and a belief in gratitude as the only proper reward for public service. Delivered to audiences that were ambivalent about great men, their words legitimated the most concentrated and ostentatious display of veneration that America had ever witnessed.

When Washington died, the danger to republican principle lay not in excessive praise but in excessive mourning. To lament too bitterly the death of a leader does not become a society of self-governing men. Yet, this excess was evident in the posture that eulogists assumed in relation to Washington. He was so far above the average man, they felt, that conventional language could not do justice to his virtues. In the presence of his memory, Henry Holcombe told his Savannah Baptist congregation, oratorical and literary giants "sink unnerved" and "tremble."[18] John Mason, a staunch Presbyterian from New York, declared: "Eulogy has mistaken her province and her powers when she assumes for her theme the glory of WASHINGTON."[19] Thomas Baldwin, a Connecticut Baptist, confessed to "a trembling diffidence in approaching a character so venerable and sacred."[20]

Washington's sanctity was to be taken literally. Americans were used to seeing him compared to Moses and other Biblical figures, but now they were presented with a new prototype, Jesus Christ himself:

> The death of Jesus will be gratefully remembered, and frequently celebrated by Christians to the latest ages of time. Any attempt to swell our present grief to a comparison with this, would be most solemn trifling. Yet our loss is great indeed. The man who was destined by Heaven to be the instrumental Saviour of his country.... Alas! we shall see his face no more.[21]

But devils, too, were needed. Just as goodness was revealed best when set in opposition to evil, so the eulogist sought out iniquitous men whose condemnations of Washington supplied the best evidence of his virtue. The intended effect of this practice was to make Washington's praise more plausible by recognizing his enemies and ridiculing the futility of their antagonism:

> [To] the disgrace of human nature, there were a few unworthy men who had the audacity and impiety to open their lips of calumny against him. Men who, from the baseness of their hearts and wickedness of their views, were unworthy even to utter the name of WASHING-TON—But men (among whom stood conspicuous the noted sot and infidel Thomas Paine) who were as unable to detract by their language of scurrility, folly and falsehood, from the merits of WASHINGTON, as would have been futile their attempt to have poisoned the Atlantic, by infusing into it the venom of a reptile; or their effort to have extinguished the sun, by ejecting their filthy saliva towards it.[22]

Reverend Ogden's oceanic and solar images expressed to his New Jersey Episcopal congregation not only the esteem in which the great man was held during his lifetime but also the grief occasioned by his death. So boundless was this grief that many of Washington's other spokesmen saw a danger of arousing the jealousy of God himself. "We humbly hope our Divine Master will not be offended with our mourning for the Man whom we so much loved," exclaimed Thomas Baldwin.[23] David Tappan of Harvard College warned against bringing down the curse of Heaven by "deifying the creature at the expense of the Creator."[24] Accordingly, Samuel Tomb, also of Connecticut, ridiculed those who attributed to Washington the new role of intercessor, or advocate of the American cause in Heaven. Nor is it proper, he said, to bypass God and make prayerful supplications to Washington alone. The first practice was "Romish"; the second, heathen. Both were contrary to republicanism.[25] Washington was taken away in the first place, in the opinion of David McClure, a Rhode Island Congregationalist, because the adulation had gotten out of hand: He was made to die, "lest perhaps we should place, too much, our hopes and affections on him, and yield to him those honors, which are due to GOD."[26]

The mourning, however, was as passionate as the earlier veneration, and so a justification consistent with republican precepts was needed. Never was the notion of gratitude put to heavier use than in the service of this justification. Since Washington refused political and monetary compensation during his lifetime, Americans could only pay their debt to him in the currency of gratitude. Too heavy a payment had its dangers, Thomas McKean of Philadelphia believed, but those who failed to acquit themselves of their debt would dishonor the nation:

> While, therefore, we avoid, in the common affliction of the government, every appearance of servility and adulation inconsistent with the independence of freemen, let us, in the respect which we pay to the singular merits of this great man, rescue republics from the proverbial stigma of ingratitude.[27]

The same rationale was adopted by others. Jonathan Sewall, a high Whig poet and ideologist, explained that "eulogy is a tribute which the ingenuous and feeling heart delights to pay—a debt of gratitude which even the basest minds can scarcely withold."[28] Fisher Ames, political leader and Biblical scholar, believed that by commemorating Washington, "man yields the homage that is due virtue" and confesses "the common debt."[29]

For those who believed that the homage paid exceeded the debt, there was the often-voiced consolation that Washington served his nation as God's agent, and that by honoring Washington one honored his Creator. That rationalization might have been the most effective of all, for it bore close affinity to prevailing opinion as to the new residence of the great man's soul, and to the conviction that if Americans had gone too far in their adoration, they were not alone:

> Here, on Angel wings, the brightening Saint ascended. . . . [V]oices more than human were heard . . . hymning the great possession. . . . At the sight of him, even these *blessed spirits* seem to feel new raptures, and to look more dazzlingly [*sic*] bright. In joyous throngs, they pour around him; they devour him with their eyes of love; they embrace him in transports of tenderness unutterable; while, from their roseate cheeks, tears of joy, such as angels weep, roll down.[30]

Parson Weems's account of Washington's entry into Heaven was plausible to most Americans; it nicely articulated the steady but vague impression they were entertaining in their own minds. To this image the republic's artists lent even greater clarity. In one of the many mourning portraits that adorned American homes at the turn of the century, Washington is lamented by a group of allegorical figures, including America, with her Liberty Pole and Liberty Cap, amid a field of national symbols. Illuminated by a divine light, the fallen leader is lifted by two angelic beings, one of whom (Father Time) signals his immortality while the other points upward to his destination (Fig. 23). In another painting, Washington is shown on his way to Heaven, mourned below by Columbia and fifteen orphaned states (Fig. 24). A third painting shows the great man seated in Heaven. Covering his breast with his right hand, he displays a characteristic humility as he is crowned with the laurel of fame in the presence of two early martyrs of the Revolution (Fig. 25).

These and similar mourning portraits were collective symbols. Displaying them within their homes, Americans could demonstrate an attachment to that national entity which the portraits represented. In at least one instance the contents of a portrait were reproduced on stage and, in concert with other forms of memorial expression, became focal points of social assembly. Thus, Akin and Harrison's illustration of *An American Lamenting Her Loss* was reproduced at the Park Avenue Theater in New York, forming the backdrop for a recitation of Charles Brockten Brown's funeral ode. The whole affair, including the poem, was put together within two weeks of Washington's death and described this way in one of the local newspapers:

> The house . . . displayed a scene calculated to impress the mind with the utmost solemnity and sorrow. The pillars supporting the boxes were encircled with black crape, the chandeliers were decorated with the insignia of woe, and the audience, particularly the female part, appeared covered with the badges of mourning. About seven o'clock the band struck up "Washington's March," after which a solemn dirge was played, when the curtain, slowly rising, discovered a tomb in the centre of the stage, in the Grecian style of architecture, supported by trusses. In the centre of it was a portrait of the general, encircled by a wreath of oak leaves; under the portrait, a sword, shield and helmet and the colours of the United States. The top was in the form of a pyramid, in the front of which appeared the American eagle, weeping tears of blood for the loss of her general, and holding in her beak a scroll, on which was inscribed, "A Nation's Tears." The sides of the stage were decorated with black banners, containing the names of the several States of the Union in golden letters, over which mourning trophies were suspended.[31]

The writer noted that the theater "was full to overflowing." What that audience saw and heard was more than a picture and a poem; that audience witnessed a sacred event, and by bearing witness in common with others, each member entered into a communion with society as a whole.

Thus, by the end of Washington's life, his cult had become an ornament of American culture, and it was through this cult that he became known. The cult publicized Washington through written and oral accounts of his origins and exploits; through graven images, like paintings, engravings, statues, and impressions on currency; through the physical sites sanctified by association with his work, travels, and achievements; through the counties, cities, streets, organizations, and people named after him; and through periodic ceremonies and holidays observed in his honor. In short, most Americans came to know Washington indirectly, through his cult, and his veneration depended on the capacity of that cult to keep him continually in the forefront of the popular imagination. It was the *total* cult, which was lived as well as conceived—or rather conceived because it was lived—that produced a unified, collective statement that incorporated sentiments and values as well as facts. Of these, the Americans had an integrated rather than a fragmentary experience. The factual record was thereby embellished by virtue and infused with affect; in turn, morality and sentiment achieved intellectual expression.

Part Two

The
Revelation
of
Washington

4

A Mirror for
Republican Culture

By joining in the common adoration of Washington, men and
women became conscious of their shared membership in the new
republic. The continuation of this adoration, however, depended
on the sustained relevance and vitality of its meaning. People cannot adore a leader unless they understand what he represents.
They cannot participate in venerational ceremonies unless they
see a reason for doing so. One such reason was America's need
to articulate and cultivate ideals that were enthusiastically accepted but not perfectly understood during the founding period.
Having only recently divested themselves of a long monarchical
tradition, many Americans longed for a tangible model of republican ideals, something that could transform them from abstrac-
tions into a dramatic and active reality.

Since images of other people are, in any age, the most vivid
parts of man's inner life, the most admired public leaders are likely
to be the most evocative symbols of patriotic ideals. These figures
not only represent emotions unleashed during the exhilaration of
great historical moments; they also incarnate the highest moral
principles of a nation, embodying them in a form that can be
understood and loved. Venerational cults therefore involve much
more than the condensing of emotion; they address, in Emile
Durkheim's words, "definite personalities who have a name, a
character, determined attributes, and a history, and they vary according to the manner in which these personalities are conceived.

The cult rendered to a divinity depends upon the character attributed to him."[1]

If we projected ourselves back to the late 1700s, we would find that many people had only an imperfect knowledge of Washington; yet, they adored him intensely and took part in well-established rites which sustained their adoration. This gap between action and belief, between rite and meaning, was a source of tension which America's moral leaders sought diligently to resolve. For these men, it was insufficient merely to venerate Washington; it was also necessary to know what he believed in—what motivated him—and to reveal this knowledge to others so that they might emulate him.

Revelation, according to certain contemporary churchmen, has a twofold aim. "First, it permits the most important naturally knowable truths of religion to be grasped by all, with full certitude, and without admixture of error. Secondly, it enables man as an intelligent creature to orient himself to the supernatural end for which God has destined him"[2] If we substitute "society" for "God," we understand better what the new republic's moralists sought to accomplish through the revelation of Washington's character: namely, clarification of the transcendent end for which America had destined itself.

That public figures set the ethical and behavioral tone of their society was taken for granted by most eighteenth-century moralists. "Facts demonstrate examples to be very forcible on human nature," explained Daniel Shute in 1768. "In some proportion then as the example of those who are in exalted stations is virtuous or vicious it may naturally be expected the character of the *whole* will be."[3] Just so, Americans were told repeatedly that although no one could duplicate Washington's public service, every citizen, even of the humblest station, could imitate his moral character. The traditional doctrine of *Ad Exemplum Regis* (The community is regulated by the example of the king), a doctrine under which many Americans were reared, was appropriated for republican ends. Although many social scientists would regard this doctrine as the basis of a socially integrative "imitative rite,"[4] such an understanding, in itself, reveals nothing of what American society was asked to imitate. Knowledge of the Washington cult's ideational content is essential, therefore, to an understanding of how and why that cult was employed as an agency of moral regulation.

And the values of American political culture can in turn be understood, in part, from the qualities ascribed to Washington—with constant reference to the cultic media (oratory, poetry, song, and icon, produced and consumed individually and in social assemblage) through which those qualities were expressed.

The Eye of the Beholder

From the time of his death in 1799 to the present, every generation of Americans has reviewed Washington's life and character in the context of its own concerns. Other nations, from different perspectives and out of different concerns, have fashioned their own image of Washington. The substance of these images is, to say the least, variable.

In 1932, United States embassies throughout the world organized special festivities as part of a massive bicentennial celebration of George Washington's birth. Representatives from host countries were invited to participate by conveying through formal address their own appreciation of Washington's achievements and character. Some spokesmen of the then fascist government of Italy described Washington as an American Mussolini. "Reconsidering every spiritual value against invading materialism," said Fani, "fascist Italy has re-established hero worship. . . . A new heroic and warlike feeling . . . brings all Italy to rally round the great name of George Washington." As Il Duce of the American Revolution, Washington was seen by Borselli as "a man of feeling and action" comparable to "the great fascist Condottiere [who] has also been able to change the course of the life of our nation." Volpi complimented America by describing its Constitutional Convention as "the dictatorship which established the United States." He reluctantly acknowledged Washington's republican sentiments, but hastened to add that "Washington's love of liberty was unfailingly linked to the conception of a strong state whose authority was supreme." Statements were drawn from Washington's own pen to prove that he appreciated the need for "the intervention of coercive power." Recognizing Washington's successful suppression of domestic rebellion, Volpi concluded that this heroic American was "always the great master of life, the achiever, never the doctrinarian [republican]." (Although these kinds of speeches were not common in the bicentennial celebrations held in pre-Nazi Germany, many German speakers did point out resemblances between Washington and Bismark and Frederick the Great—comparisons that ring strange to the American ear.[5])

Achievements and character traits praised by fascists are vigorously condemned by communists. The *Great Soviet Encyclopedia* indicates that George Washington displayed many fine qualities as the commander of America's "bourgeois revolution; but it was the struggle of the popular masses that made possible its triumph." Once the British were defeated, Washington showed his true colors. He turned against the people. He "headed the reactionary forces which crushed the democratic movement of poor farmers and artisans under the leadership of D. Shays" (Shays's Rebellion). As President, "he opposed the democratic demands of the popular masses, consolidating only those achievements of the revolution which were necessary to the bourgeoisie and the planters." In short, Washington's struggle against British imperialism earned him the reputation of a progressive, but "he remained a representative of the propertied classes, and in this lies Washington's limitation: he was a bourgeois revolutionary."[6]

These contrasting assessments of Washington and his relationship to the masses reflect the contrasts between fascist and communist ideology. Facts are selected, ignored, and bent to the service of political needs that were unfelt by Washington's own generation. One might be inclined to think that twentieth-century American observers would give a more accurate portrayal of Washington's significance to the founding generation, but in some cases they take no less liberty with the facts than do foreigners. For example, in 1976, the bicentennial of the founding of the United States, a Representative from Wyoming inserted into the *Congressional Record* a reference to John Sanford's *A More Goodly Country*. The book contains a "letter from the grave" conveying what the author surmised would be Washington's reaction to the way he is viewed in a democratic society that claims equality as its chief political virtue. Through a heavy-handed characterization of Washington's distrust of the masses, the author of this letter, along with the public official who cited it, convey an extreme egalitarian interpretation of what Washington stood for. The commentary is worth quoting at length:

> Sirs: I take my pen in Hand to correct some Misapprehensions which came into Being at my Death, & which have persisted until the present Time. I am not concerned with these erronious beliefs insofar as they

touch upon Events, for Events, under the forms of Govt known as a Republick, are suceptible of as many Interpretations as there are men to make them. But I begg leave to say that I am most deeply concernd with such Beliefs where they relate to Character. My owne Character, Sirs, has been most grievously misunderstood.

Whether willfully or otherwise, this Misunderstanding has been fostered by some of the very best people, to such an extent that I now find some of the very worst speaking my name in the same connexion as Thos Paine, Andw Jackson, & A. Lincoln, Esqs. to cite but three instances of the tortious Mingling which I have reference to. It cannot fail to be noted that I do not include the Honble Thos Jefferson, nor can my reason for the Omission be obscure: Mr. Jefferson was at least a Gentlemen. The others, whatever their Accomplishments may have been, & however great their Contributions to the power and independency of the United States, were members of the Mobility.

To put the matter flatly, Sirs, I deplored the notion of Equality all my Life, even such a fictitious Equality as the Constitution guarantees, & similarly, all my Death—especially since being joind here by Mr. Hamilton—I have deplord the constant encroachment of that fiction upon the reality. If this trend should continue without Lett of Hindrance, I make free to say that the evil day cannot be far removd when the Tresspass will have ben compleated, & the Squatter become the Soveraigne.

With so much in your favor, Sirs, nevertheless you have wrought so poorly as to fill us with Apprehention & Dismaye. You are haunted (to change a figure of Speech coind in the middle of the last Century) by the Spectre of Democracy—and well you may be. But the way in which to lay that Ghoast is not to temporize with it, but to oppose it by Force, to put it down with cold Steele and hott Ledd, as Genl Wayne did with his mutineers. But mark you, Sirs, if you wait for the Ghoast with hatt in hand, good God and God damn, you will find yourself with Alms in it! With Mr. Hamilton and the rest, Sirs, I say put this Brute the People down!

Be assured that I am, Sirs, with most unfeigned Regard, your ever obedt sevt.[7]

Although produced by men of differing political conviction— an Italian fascist, a Russian communist, and an American egalitarian—these three images bear close resemblance to one another. Each image portrays Washington as a man who appreciates the value of power, and who uses it, in a manner consistent with the interests of his own privileged class, to coerce and direct the masses. To construct such an image, the range of things Washington represented must be drastically truncated and exaggerated.

What, then, did Washington really represent? A satisfactory answer to this question is not easy to come by—not even in the current scholarly literature. From several directions at once, this literature attempts to reproduce the George Washington that Americans of the late eighteenth century beheld and knew. All these writings are partly substantiated and all disclose something of the original image, but none makes for a very comprehensive understanding. The original revelation of Washington did express, in an indirect way, his countrymen's search for perfection and stability; and also it reflected their increasingly antipatriarchal family structures, as well as the substance of their Enlightenment inheritance. In making these connotations explicit, current writers (notably Lawrence Friedman, Jay Fliegelman, and Garry Wills) reveal the subtlest aspects of the relationship between Washington's image and his society. The people they write about, however, never saw Washington in such sophisticated ways. Popular perceptions of the man were determined by, and embodied, more immediate and practical concerns.

An American Obsession: The Bane of Power

George Washington was certainly the most admired man of his generation, but he was not the master key of his culture; if he were, then an analysis of that culture would begin and end with him alone. What the public perception of Washington does provide is a vehicle for understanding how certain aspects of the political world were conceived in eighteenth-century America. In previous references to the new republic's political suspicions—its distrust of concentrated power and its apprehensions about the man in whom that power was invested—we have already seen something of the contours of this conception. It is now time for a more detailed reading.

In their struggle against crown and ministry, American dissidents of the late eighteenth century drew heavily on the ideas of British dissidents of the late seventeenth century. Whether one documents this connection through Trevor Colbourn's inventory of the libraries of the American colonies and founding fathers, or Bernard Bailyn's study of the political pamphlets distributed in the colonies during the eighteenth century, the influence of the radical social and political thought of the "Real Whigs" (like John

13

A new statue for the royal pedestal . . . *George Washington* (1792), by William Sullivan (Courtesy of the Historical Society of Delaware, Wilmington)

14

A state portrait for the new republic . . . *Washington* (The "Lansdowne," 1796), by Gilbert Stuart (National Portrait Gallery, Smithsonian Institution, Washington, D.C.)

15

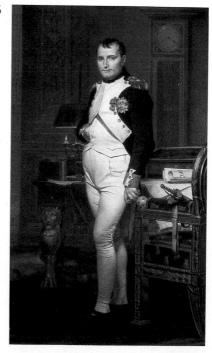

State portraiture in the imperial tradition . . . *Napoleon in His Study* (1812), by Jacques-Louis David (National Gallery of Art, Washington, D.C.; Samuel H. Kress Collection)

16

17

18

Royal Models
(Top) Portrait of Queen Elizabeth I, by an unidentified artist (The National Trust Photographic Library, London) *(Bottom left) Portrait of Philip II*, by Pantoja de la Cruz (Photograph supplied and authorized by Patrimonio Nacional, Madrid) *(Bottom right) Portrait of Charles IX*, by Francois Clouet (Kunsthistorisches Museum, Vienna)

19

20

HIGH STREET, From the Country Market-place PHILADELPHIA.

Symbolic Burial . . . *High Street from the County Market-Place, Philadelphia: with the procession in commemoration of the Death of General George Washington* (1800), by William Birch (The Library Company of Philadelphia)

(Opposite page: top) The hub of union . . . *Display of the United States of America* (1789), by Amos Doolittle (Independence National Historical Park, Philadelphia)
(Bottom) The man who unites all hearts . . . *View of the Triumphal Arch and Colonnade* (1790), by S. Hill (Courtesy of the Library of Congress, Washington, D.C.)

BOSTON, *January* 6, 1800.

THE *COMMITTEE* chosen by the TOWN to adopt such Measures as may indicate the PUBLIC SENSIBILITY on the late afflictive Event of the *DEATH* of

General GEORGE WASHINGTON,

Announce the following Arrangements, to be adopted on

THURSDAY, the Ninth Day of *January* inst.

Being the Day assigned for the Delivery of an EULOGIUM on the Occasion, at the Old South Meeting-House, by the HON. *GEORGE RICHARDS MINOT*, ESQ.

Mourning.

THE Males to wear Crape or black Riband on the left Arm, above the Elbow.

THE Females to wear black Ribands.

THIS Mourning to commence on the said 9th of January, and to be continued until the 22d Day of February next.

THE Morn to be introduced by Minute Guns and the Tolling of Bells. Both to be continued at proper Intervals, through the Day.

THE Colours of the Shipping, in the Harbour, to be hoisted at Half-Mast.

ALL Business to be suspended, and no Stores or Shops to be opened on that Day.

Order of Procession.

THE Male Youth of the Town, from Ten to Fourteen Years of Age, Eight a-breast, under the Conduct of their several Instructors.

The Uniformed Companies of Militia, with Side Arms, conducted by their respective Officers.

Military Escort.

Officers of the Militia ; of the Army and Navy.

Cincinnati.

Grand Lodge.

Committee of Arrangement and Selectmen.

Orator and Chaplain.

Sheriff of the County, with his Wand.

Lieutenant-Governor and Council.

President and Members of the Senate.

Speaker and Members of the House of Representatives.

Secretary, and Treasurer of the Commonwealth.

Judges of the Supreme and District Courts.

Reverend Clergy.

Federal Officers in the Civil Department.

Town and County Officers.

Physicians and Lawyers.

Col. JOSEPH MAY, *and Major* ANDREW CUNNINGHAM, *appointed Marshals.*

The Commercial and Trading Interests, to be arranged by the President and Officers of the Chamber of Commerce.

The Mechanic Interests, to be arranged by the President and Trustees of the Mechanic Association.

Citizens,

Not enumerated in the foregoing Classes,

Six a-breast.

THE Inhabitants are desired to meet at 11 o'Clock, A. M. at the New State House ; as the Procession will move precisely at 12 o'Clock. It will pass through Common Street, Winter Street, Summer Street, Federal Street, Milk Street, Kilby and State Streets, passing the North Side of the Town House, through Cornhill, to the Old South Meeting-House.

Appropriation of the Old South Meeting-House.

THE Wall Pews on the Floor, and the lower East Gallery, for the Ladies.

Upper East Gallery, for the Youth.

Body Pews and Aisles, for the Procession.

Centre of front Gallery, for the Singers and Musick.

West Galleries and Remainder of the front Gallery, for Citizens not otherwise accommodated.

THE *COMMITTEE* respectfully invite all Classes of their Fellow-Citizens to join in the proposed solemn Tribute to the illustrious MAN, whose Loss is so justly and universally deplored. They have taken every Measure in their Power, for the Preservation of good Order, and to promote public Convenience ; but they rely, principally, on the Sentiment and Feeling of each Individual, to enforce the Necessity of that silent, dignified and respectful Demeanour, which can alone do Justice to the Sensibility of the Inhabitants, in their Attempt to evidence their Respect for the Memory of the great, the good, and beloved *WASHINGTON.*

By Order of the Committee,

Charles Bulfinch, Chairman.

Escort to glory . . . *Announcement of Memorial Services for George Washington,* Boston (Reproduced by permission of the Huntington Library, San Marino, California)

23

Resurrection . . . *Apotheosis of Washington* (1800), by John Barralet (The Historical Society of Pennsylvania, Philadelphia)

24

Ascension . . . *The Apotheosis of Washington* (c. 1800), by H. Weishaupt after an illustration by Samuel Moore (Reproduced by permission of the Huntington Library, San Marino, California)

25

Arrival . . . *Apotheosis of Washington* (1800), by David Edwin (National Portrait Gallery, Smithsonian Institution, Washington, D.C.)

Trenchard, Thomas Gordon, Benjamin Hoadly, and Robert Molesworth) is beyond dispute. "More than any other single group of writers," observes Bailyn, these Britons "shaped the mind of the American Revolutionary generation."[8] They provided the concepts and vocabulary by means of which America's political culture articulated itself.

The writings of the Real Whigs echoed the very same sentiments that had brought on the Glorious Revolution in England in 1688. Yet, if these men were not eager to see that Revolution evolve into a British republic, their thoughts on the distribution of power went much further than most Britons were willing to follow. In America the situation was different. Elaborated by a new generation of writers, the ideals of the Real Whigs were embraced because they legitimated a decentralized political order that had already been well established. Concentration of power was limited in the colonies by the self-reliance required on the frontier and in the wilderness community, by the existence of autonomous units of government dispersed across broad territories, and by the vast distance separating these units from England. These conditions stimulated the development of aspirations that were (at least in relation to political norms in the mother country) decidedly libertarian.

As the struggle with Great Britain came to a head, the press and pulpit amplified these aspirations and solidified the consensus around them.[9] "Before the revolution," said Jefferson, "we were all good Whigs, cordial in free principles . . . jealous of the executive Magistrate."[10] During the revolution, the consensus was less perfect. Many colonists of Whig persuasion were indifferent to the American cause, and some remained loyal to the crown.[11] John Adams's statement, therefore, is the more precise: "In political theory, if not devotion to the patriot cause, nine tenths of the people are high Whigs."[12] In the heat of the war, however, "Whig" became synonymous with "republican." To understand which of George Washington's personal characteristics and achievements had the most significance for his countrymen, and to show more fully why the veneration of these qualities eventually became so intense, persistent, and widespread, we need to know what republican whiggery stood for.

The disposition of power—the cornerstone of Whig thought—was central to every political controversy in late-eighteenth-century America. Whatever his attitude toward independence, an American typically dwelt upon power "endlessly, almost compulsively," for its natural prey was liberty. He discussed the issue with passion and metaphoric elegance. Power has "an encroaching nature"; it "creeps by degrees and quick subdues the whole." Power is "elastic," ever extending itself. The hand of power is "grasping" and "tenacious"; what it seizes it retains. Power is gluttonous: "restless, aspiring, insatiable," a jaw "always open to devour," an appetite "whetted, not cloyed, by possession."[13] These concerns, as Cecilia Kenyon and Jackson Turner Main made clear, became more acute as the years passed, and they dominated political and public discourse during the Federal Convention (over which Washington himself presided).[14]

What makes power so malignant, Americans believed, was not its intrinsic force, the prudent use of which was considered quite necessary for social order, but rather the nature of man himself. On this assumption there was strong agreement. Neo-Calvinists and freethinkers alike were convinced that man was incapable of withstanding on his own the temptations of power. Corruption (defined as a lust for self-aggrandizement) was inherent in the species. "Such is the depravity of mankind," explained Samuel Adams, "that the ambition and lust of power above the law are predominant passions in the breasts of most men."[15] Likewise, Landon Carter, one of Washington's Virginia neighbors, declared: "[Of] all the failings incident to human nature, the worst disposition to be possessed in the world ... is the thirst after power ... the innate disposition to rule ... to be the sole determiner of all things."[16] From these premises flowed "the strongest suspicion of men in authority" and a fear of the institutional weapons they controlled.[17]

The Americans' concept of power, however, cannot be dissociated from their concept of virtue. Americans never tired of celebrating the merits of justice, temperance, courage, honesty, sincerity, modesty, integrity, calmness, benevolence, sobriety, piety, and rationality. Although these were classically valued virtues, the function Americans assigned to them was historically unique. Early Americans *politicized* the traditional Roman and Christian virtues, by defining them as the counterweight to man's lust for power. As

Samuel Adams put it, "Virtue and Knowledge will forever be an even Balance for Power and Riches.[18]

Given the expansive quality of power, its division and balance was assumed to be the best structural guarantee of liberty. At the same time, Americans believed that structures do not maintain themselves, but rest ultimately on the qualities of the people who occupy positions within them. As one early commentator explained, "He is the truest Friend to the Liberty of his Country, who tries most to promote its Virtue—And who so far as his Power and Influence extends, will not suffer a man to be chosen into any Office of Power and Trust, who is not a wise and virtuous Man."[19] Later, in the Virginia debate over the ratification of the Constitution, James Madison (the great proponent of the new, checked and balanced government) asserted, "No theoretical checks, no form of government can render us secure. To suppose that any form of government will secure liberty or happiness without any virtue in a people, is a chimerical idea."[20]

At a time when most Americans take for granted their government's ability to outlive its unscrupulous leaders and protect individual liberties, it is difficult to appreciate the Whiggish obsession about abuse of power, or to take seriously the conviction that government stands or falls on the virtues of its leaders and its people. But in Washington's time, these fears and these beliefs were felt with special poignancy. In particular, " 'the incantation of virtue,' " like the bane of power, "was most fervent during the uncertainties of the war and ensuing polemics over the constitution."[21]

Virtue does not speak for itself; to be known, it must be formulated in vivid, heroic images. And not any image will do—only one conceived in a recognizable way. Some of Washington's admirers may have sought to fill this need by casting him into a model of the perfection and stability they lacked in their personal lives.[22] Others may have seen in him a benevolent father, a substitute for the domestic tyrant who made them miserable as children.[23] Intellectuals may have regarded him as the champion of their philosophical preferences: the Age of Reason on horseback.[24] But these men were in a minority.[25] Most of Washington's admirers dramatized his virtues by selecting models from biblical and classical history. In the drama of the Old Testament and, to a lesser but still considerable extent, in the very popular *Plutarch's Lives* is where they found the outstanding prototypes of republican greatness. These two sources also provided many of the metaphors and models through which the veneration of Washington was expressed. From the Old Testament derived the notion of Washington as the "American Moses"; from the classics derived the images of Washington as *Pater Patriae* (Father of his Country) and "Cincinnatus."

Some contemporary scholars have taken these analogies as proof that Washington symbolized his country's classical and religious heritage,[26] but this line of argument must be qualified. Although Roman citizens did regard liberty as a cherished possession, they never believed that men were born free. They thought the protection of Roman liberty required the enslavement of others. To regard Washington as a direct incarnation of religious ideals puts him in a similar non-republican light. The internal logic of Western religion, based upon belief in an omnipotent God who demands and receives unquestioned obedience, is more consistent with monarchical than republican principles. Left to develop unhindered, the religious beliefs of most American churches might not have been institutionalized in a theocracy, but they certainly would not have led the colonies to establish republican governments.

The Americans' understanding of classical and biblical history, however, was highly selective. They perceived the past in terms of their present political preferences, and to both sanctify and rationalize the latter, they drew on the most appropriate parts of the former. As Bailyn put it, whiggery supplied the American Revolution's ideological substance; religious, classical, and other traditions, its symbols and allusions.[27] Religion and the classical past were exploited according to the political vision of a Whig culture, and it was from this culture that Americans derived their heroic ideal. They clothed Washington in religious and classical symbols in a way that satisfied their own political tastes.

Just as Plutarch and the Bible, according to the American reading, explain events as the expression of moral imperatives in the minds of great men, so Washington's admirers typically portrayed his achievements and services as being, in essence, a manifestation of his virtue. This distillation of character from conduct was their most persistent argument. Character was inferred, however, not only from the quality or magnitude of achievement but also from its "ultimate grounds" or "reasons." For Washington's contemporaries, the most important unifying element was found on this second, motivational, level. Political "motive mongering" was the point of reference for a society that refused to take its leaders' virtues at face value but insisted on probing below the surface of public action. As one observer put it, "To determine worth of character . . . we endeavor to ascertain principles and motives, as well as to notice great actions and beneficial services."[28]

Whenever people talked or wrote about Washington, they ascribed to him many such "principles and motives," but some were ascribed more regularly than others. Farmers would become prosperous and opulent, and statesmen wise and beneficent, Washington's admirers said, by cultivating his solid judgment. Citizens of the humblest station might "aspire to be great and immortal in heaven . . . by the remembrance and imitation of his industry, order, integrity and prudence, his disinterestedness and humanity, his piety and humility." Likewise, parents could teach their children "to be excited to every generous purpose by the charm of his name." Freemasons, by their memorials to Washington, were inspired "to *square* our actions by the *rules of rectitude,* persevere in the *line* of our duty and sustain our passions within the *compass* of propriety." And if slaveholders "would emulate the benevolence of Washington, [they] would abandon the savage claim of holding human beings in slavery."[29] These statements present a condensed version of both the fully developed symbol of Washington and the most pressing ideological concerns of the American people. Brooding constantly about power and its corruption, the people gave their most persistent attention to Washington's renunciation of private interests in favor of duty to the state, his immunity from political ambition, his avoidance of excess in thought, feeling, and action, his reliance on self-control and persistence rather than genius to achieve his goals, his private benevolence, and his deep religious humility.

Before 1775, these virtues were summoned to the American mind by patriots of the English Civil Wars, like John Hampden and Algernon Sydney, and by Viscount Bolingbroke, an extreme conservative whose notion of the Patriot King was appropriated by radical whigs in the service of their own interests,[30] but it was not until these virtues were enacted by Washington that their deeper, indigenous linaments would be revealed. To share in this revelation, the twentieth-century observer must put himself in the place of his predecessors. He must know about the situations in which Washington's virtues were expressed, how they were connected to other traits valued in the society, and how they stood in relation to the vices of which that society was most fearful. He must know about the consequences that were thought to flow from such virtues and how these consequences entered into the lives of the people. It was amid such conditions, and in reference to such concerns, that Washington's character became known.

5

Images of
Political Virtue

WHEN WASHINGTON AND HIS CONTEMPORARIES TALKED ABOUT "PUBLIC VIRTUE," they were thinking of an ideal that every society cultivates in its members: renunciation of self-interest for the public good. Although public virtue is everywhere instrumental to patriotism, there is no uniformity as to where its burden falls; nor is its political function constant across different societies. In authoritarian societies, public virtue implies submission to the state and its rulers. In the new republic, public virtue was required for a different, indeed, opposite, reason: to keep the state beyond the grasp of ambitious power seekers and under the control of its citizens. "To make the people's welfare—the public good—the exclusive end of government," wrote Gordon Wood, was the Americans' " 'Polar Star,' the central tenet of the Whig faith."[1] Convinced that they were the intended victims of a ministerial conspiracy to reduce and "enslave" them, revolutionary Americans regarded self-sacrifice as their first line of defense against the bane of power.

That man was born not for himself alone was indeed a cardinal assumption of the new nation—to which, in Samuel Adams's words, "a citizen owes everything."[2] Likewise, when Benjamin Rush announced in 1787 that "[e]very man in a republic is public property," and that "his time and talents—his youth—his manhood—his old age—nay, more, life, all belong to his country,"[3] he was reaffirming the belief that tyrannical designs could be resisted only in a society of selfless citizens. In George Washington, the Americans found a living symbol of this belief. The discovery infused his newly formed venerational cult with persuasive ideological content.

When Washington arrived in Cambridge in early July 1775, he was welcomed with a formal address by the Massachusetts Congress. The words of the Congress performed double duty: They not only made ritual acknowledgment of the commander's arrival but also expressed the values that presumably induced him to take up his task. In effect, the Congress had delivered a public lecture on republican duty:

> While we applaud that attention to the public good, manifested in your appointment, we equally admire that disinterested virtue and distinguished patriotism, which alone could call you from those enjoyments of domestic life, which a sublime and manly taste, joined with a most affluent fortune, can afford, to hazard your life, and to endure the fatigues of war, in defense of the rights of mankind, and the good of your country.
>
> The laudable zeal for the common cause of America, and compassion for the distress of this colony exhibited by the great dispatch made in your journey hither, fully justify the universal satisfaction we have with pleasure observed on this occasion; and are promising presages that the great expectations formed from your personal character, and military abilities, are well founded.[4]

The Massachusetts officials used a vocabulary that evoked in the American mind an immediately recognizable pattern of renunciation, a pattern that was central to the republican vision of heroic leadership. Four sacrificial elements—domesticity, wealth, life, and fame—went into the making of this pattern. The elements and the pattern proved to be enduring.

The Requirements of Public Virtue

When Washington died in December 1799, religious and civic leaders were everywhere called upon to reflect publicly on the virtues of his life. Acknowledging the belief that men are inclined by nature to selfishness, Reverend John Fitch devoted his entire eulogy to Washington's benevolence.[5] Fitch's remarks were part of a conspicuous strand of belief about George Washington's public life: to wit, that what Washington gave up as well as what he did made him great. Unlike heroes of other times and places, Washington did not seek out a position of leadership, and when it was offered he accepted it willingly, but without enthusiasm. The ar-

duous toils of camp life and of military movements and maneu-
vers, his admirers were told, were all the greater for Washington
because of the affluence and congeniality of his private situation.
Throughout, the theme of sacrifice was apparent. Sacrifice was the
process by which Washington attained communion with a sacred
entity, America, by renouncing an object of value, his domestic
comfort. Washington left affluence and ease for a life of danger
and fatigue—and nothing but duty would have induced him to do
so. Unlike many charismatic leaders who, in Max Weber's words,
"must be free of the ordinary worldly attachments and duties of
occupation and family,"[6] Washington embraced the Horatian ideal
of the good life: cultivation of the soil and tranquil repose by the
hearth. "Shedding tears," however, "he nobly abandons personal
ease and domestic felicity." Thus spoke Reverend Alexander
MacWhorter to his Newark, New Jersey, congregation.[7] A "uniform preference for the public good to private enjoyment . . . leads
him to forego the enjoyment of domestic scenes," added Washington's physician and Masonic brother, Elisha Dick.[8]

Washington's eulogists eloquently expressed what the people
had known and accepted from the very beginning of the Revolution. In 1775, John Adams had found "something charming" in
this: "A gentleman of one of the first fortunes upon the continent,
leaving his delicious retirement, his family and friends, sacrificing
his ease, and hazarding all in the cause of his country!"[9] Likewise,
Silas Deane, the once controversial statesman, saw Washington as
his "Countrys Friend—who sacrificing private Fortune and independent Ease, and every domestic pleasure, sets off at his Countrys call, to exert himself in her defence without so much as returning to bid adieu to a Fond partner & Family."[10] In spring 1776,
on the occasion of General Howe's withdrawal from Boston, Harvard College honored Washington by reiterating this theme.
"Without hesitation [he] left all the pleasure of his delightful Seat
in Virginia, and the affairs of his own Estate, that through all the
Fatigues and Dangers of Camp, without accepting a reward, he
might deliver New England from the unjust and cruel Arms of
Britain. . . . "[11] The Boston Selectmen, too, saw in Washington an
example "who, from the most affluent enjoyments, could throw
himself to the hardships of a camp to save his country uncertain
of success."[12] Nine months later, after victories at Trenton and
Princeton, his fellow Virginians "behold him abandoning the delights of peace, the enjoyment of affluence, and the pleasures of

domestic felicity and entering with ardour upon a military life again."[13]

Washington's sacrifice conformed to a model his countrymen revered: that of Cincinnatus, the Roman citizen-soldier who gave up hearth and plow at the beginning of his country's crisis and, at the end, exchanged sword and shield for what he had originally renounced. What made the Cincinnatian model so salient to the Americans was not only their devotion to the Enlightenment ideal of duty to the state, nor their disdain for professional armies, nor their belief that a community of disinterested citizens could alone safeguard liberty from tyrants, but also the sharp distinction they drew between private and public life. Since most Americans pursued their interests, satisfied their needs, and derived their status from the land, the public arena was regarded by them as a place of temporary involvement, to be entered reluctantly and left joyfully. Public service, in this pre-bureaucratic society, was synonymous with sacrifice. Thus when readers of the *Virginia Gazette* beheld Washington "abandoning the delights of peace, the enjoyment of affluence, and the pleasures of domestic felicity" when called upon to defend his country,[14] they knew from their own concrete experience, if not from abstract political ideals, what patriotism meant and cost. During the war, and afterward, that realization was given cogent, if not eloquent, poetic amplification: "The virtues which his bosom warm, / Shall force him to supreme command; / And make him quit his much lov'd farm, / To save his dearer native land." In Washington's own sense of loss, another poet told the world, inheres the magnitude of his sacrifice: "Twas thine to change the sweetest / scenes of life / For public cares—to guide / the' embattled strife." The transformation was a painful one: "Brave Washington did come to our relief: / He left his native home filled with grief." Yet he came without reluctance, for "when recall'd from Vernon's peaceful shade ... / With ready zeal the sacrifice he made."[15] Likewise, on his election to the presidency, Washington's second great sacrifice was acknowledged in a series of congratulatory addresses. Typical was the message of the government of Pennsylvania, which admired "those motives" which induced him to "relinquish the enjoyment of domestic peace."[16]

Even when undertaken for nonpolitical reasons, self-denial for the public good was heavy with political implications. To surpass others in self-denial for the public good was to place them under an obligation that could be satisfied only by gratitude and respect; such was the advantage of *noblesse oblige*. Washington must have realized this himself. As one of the most status-conscious products of his society, Washington never let pass the opportunity to re- mind his countrymen of what he had renounced for their benefit. In 1778, he told Reverend William Gordon, who just happened to be writing a history of the war, that the rewards of being Com- mander in Chief meant nothing in comparison with the cost of gaining them. And so, if "a person is found better qualified to answer [the public's] expectation, I shall quit the helm with as much content, as ever the wearied pilgrim felt upon his safe ar- rival at the holy land...."[17]

On this theme, the sanctity of his domestic life, Washington never let up. "I feel myself eased of a load of public care," he wrote at war's end to one of the state governors. "I will spend the re- mainder of my days in cultivating the affections of good Men, and in the practice of the domestic Virtues...."[18] The pause did not last long, for in a few years Washington found himself President- elect. Throughout his 1789 inaugural voyage to New York, however, he made it known at every stop that he accepted the pres- idency out of a sense of duty and in spite of a deep desire to con- tinue in retirement at Mount Vernon. In his well-publicized In- augural Address, he waxed nostalgic for the "retreat which I had chosen with fondest predilections (and in my fondest hopes) with an immutable decision, as the asylum of my declining years."[19]

Four years later, when Washington's motives were publicly ques- tioned by political opponents, his dignity did not allow a public rebuttal, but in private he let drop words that he knew would quickly get around. On one such occasion, as one of Jefferson's notes reveals, "the President was much inflamed.... [He] defied any man on earth to produce one single act of his since he had been in the govmt which was not done on the purest motives ..., that *by god* he had rather be in his grave than in his present situation. That he had rather be on his farm than to be made *em- peror of the world*...."[20] Washington's self-command was probably greater than Jefferson thought. When his desire for retirement could finally be satisfied, the words leaked by Jefferson were elab- orated in the first draft of the Farewell Address, and they reap- peared, drastically abbreviated and toned down by Alexander Hamilton, in the final version:

The acceptance of, and continuance hitherto in, the office to which your suffrages have twice called me, have been a uniform sacrifice of inclination to the opinion of duty, and to a deference for what appeared to be your desire. I constantly hoped, that it would have been much earlier in my power, consistently with motives, which I was not at liberty to disregard, to return to that retirement, from which I had been reluctantly drawn.... I rejoice, that the state of your concerns, external as well as internal, no longer renders the pursuit of inclination incompatible with the sentiment of duty or propriety; and am persuaded whatever partiality may be retained for my services, that in the present circumstances of our country, you will not disapprove my determination to retire.[21]

If the alleviation of crisis (rather than inclination alone) permitted Washington his retirement, the intensification of crisis shackled him again to duty. A year after he left the presidency, disputes with France threatened to erupt into war. The great man unselfishly accepted command of the army, but not before he made known "the determination I had consoled myself with, of closing the remnant of my days in my present peaceful abode."[22]

If Washington was an emblem of his society, he was an emblem that talked. What he represented could not be separated from his own claims. To be effective, however, those claims had to be validated, and to be validated they had to be plausible. On this score, Washington put his life where his mouth was, and every American knew it. The emptiness of Mount Vernon, above every other proof, attested to the public virtue of its owner. Mount Vernon, in fact, saw little of Washington during his last twenty-five years, and even when it did, the rooms were as full of public business as of private pleasure. This situation, the blending of public and private life, was effectively exploited in the new republic's iconography. In Edward Savage's popular portrayal (Fig. 26), Washington is found at home, but fully dressed in a military uniform and spurs; his sword and hat lie on the table at which he is seated. He is ready to depart at a moment's notice. The right arm of the General rests on the shoulder of his adopted grandson, who stands beside the pillar of state with right hand on the globe, ready to follow the path of his illustrious grandfather. On the opposite side of the table are the women and servant, all distracted from the usual domestic concerns by a map of the new capital city. Documenting graphically the subordination of private life to public demands, Savage's painting presents to the republic an allegory of public virtue.

124

The most famous capturing of Washington as a liminal figure suspended between public and domestic life is that of Jean Antoine Houdon (Fig. 27). Since Houdon executed his statue after the war, we can assume that he intended to depict his subject as a Cincinnatus returning home from battle. The disposition of Washington's hands reinforces this assumption. A walking stick, customarily carried by gentleman farmers, is held prominently in the outstretched right hand. In contrast, the sword is hung over the thirteen-columned fasces of state, partially covered by a military cape. On these objects Washington's left hand rests. The transition from left hand to right hand represents the transition from public to domestic life. Yet, when viewed in relation to the plow, which is located behind Washington, not in front of him, this symbolic opposition stands equally well for the reverse passage, from domestic to public life. This essential ambiguity in Houdon's work may or may not have been intentional, but it does convey a visual message that anticipates later eulogistic accounts, like Samuel Tomb's, which tell how Washington "alternately ascended, and descended from private to public, and from public to private life, with all the natural ease, majesty and grace which attend the revolutions of a Planet in its elliptical orbit."[23]

Yet, Washington was regarded as one who never lost sight of the boundary that demarcated the spheres into and out of which he constantly moved. Given prevailing anxieties over the restoration of monarchy, along with the attendant concern about hereditary succession, it was important for the people to know that their leader, as President, had imposed upon himself a severe rule: In any matter that involved the slightest inconsistency between private and public interest, the private inclination was always to be denied. To this rule one of the most important aspects of Washington's public virtue may be traced—namely, that he never used his influence to compensate himself for the domestic life he renounced. "His great soul was so truly *republican*, so perpetually abhorrent of everything like selfishness," explained Mason Weems, "that during the whole of his administration he was never known to advance even an individual of his own name and family."[24]

Contemplating his subject's public virtue, Weems could not help drawing parallels with ancient Rome. "Gold and silver may be easily exhausted, but public virtue and fortitude never can." When Rome was imperiled, he explained, "every citizen threw aside his own business and pressed to take up arms in defence of his country: and not only refused to receive pay, but eagerly offered for the public good, all the gold and silver in his possession.... And such through life was the patriotism of Washington."[25] No doubt Weems had hit upon a key element in the American conception of public virtue. Its salience was revealed in the new nation's earliest fantasies. No sooner had Washington been appointed commander than the rumor resurfaced in New England of his speech to the House of Burgesses: He would raise a thousand men at his own expense and lead them to battle in defense of Boston. The rumor was, of course, absurd, but John Adams believed it and (although he would later change his mind about unsalaried public service) declared Washington's statement to be "sublime, pathetic, and beautiful ... the most eloquent speech that had ever been made in Virginia, or anywhere else.... "[26] Adams was describing an illusion; but, as Freud taught us, illusions always betray our aspirations and fears. Thus if it had occurred to some members of the Massachusetts House of Representatives that Washington might someday place the army in the service of his own ambition, his refusal of salary convinced them "that a warm regard to the sacred rights of humanity, and sincere love to your country, *solely* induced you in the acceptance of [your] important trust."[27]

What made this facet of Washington's public virtue so convincing was his consistency in displaying it. When, in 1786, the Virginia legislature offered to Washington a pension and land as tokens of gratitude for his wartime services, "the donation," according to one of his acquaintances, "embarrassed him very much." Not wishing, however, to slight his home state with an ostentatious display of virtue, he declined the pension but accepted the land, on condition that it be dedicated to some public use. In like manner, he requested that his services as President be compensated for expenses only.[28] In each instance, renunciation took on significance as proof of character. "If we contemplate the motives of his actions, we are lost in admiration.... Here was no mercenary view of private emolument," exclaimed Charles Atherton, a New Hampshire lawyer. "His services were unbought. They were free will offerings at the altar of patriotism."[29]

Although George Washington's admirers believed that his services to his country went entirely uncompensated, they did not assume that everyone shared this belief; rather, they took pains to document and emphasize it. Since he refused to accept salary or gifts, the great man could not have profited materially from the war. Did personal taste—the sheer pleasure of combat—induce him to accept the command? Everyone should know that Washington's was a domesticated and not an adventurous spirit. To a man thus endowed, the course of duty was heavier with risk than reward. Reverend John Mason pointed out that Washington took the field of battle selflessly, recognizing his own and his army's limitations, knowing that he might very well lose and, in that loss, become the first victim of British vengeance.[30] What greater evidence could be given, asked Bunker Hill veteran Sammuel Macclintock, "that a pure love to his country and ardent zeal to secure her liberty and independence, were his motives?"[31]

The people convinced themselves of the genuineness of Washington's concern for the public good by relating it to another strand in the web of public virtue: the risking (and sacrifice) of life. Time and again, Washington's zeal on the battlefield was broadcast throughout the nation. During the heat of battle at Princeton, the nation learned that "General Washington came down and exposed himself very much."[32] Recalling the Battle of Yorktown, one of his soldiers reported on "a deed of personal daring and coolness . . . never before equaled." During a tremendous cannonade, Washington

> took his glass and mounted the highest, most prominent, and most exposed point of our fortifications, and there stood exposed to the enemy's fire, where shot seemed flying almost as thick as hail and were instantly demolishing portions of the embankment around him, for ten or fifteen minutes, until he had completely satisfied himself of the purposes of the enemy. During this time his aides, etc., were remonstrating with him with all their earnestness against this exposure of his person and once or twice drew him down. He severely reprimanded them and resumed his position.[33]

Washington's readiness to risk his "precious and valuable life" on the battlefield, Thomas Thacher told his Dedham, Massachusetts, congregation, was motivated by that same attitude which eventually led to his demise. A disregard for his own person was not ascribed to bravado; it was rather one more piece in the mosaic of Washington's devotion to the public good.[34] Henry ("Light-horse Harry") Lee, in his oration to Congress, was more specific: a cold, ignored by a man "habituated by his care of us to neglect himself," put an end to his life.[35]

In making these points, Washington's admirers recapitulated political values first enunciated in public addresses delivered to him at the start of the war in Massachusetts. But those addresses did not capture the entire complex of traits that defined the great man's benevolence. One aspect that could not have been apparent at the war's beginning was Washington's readiness to sacrifice fame.

Because fame was deemed by Washington's society its highest reward for public virtue, eventual military success gave to the political phase of his career special significance. In 1775, when he accepted command of the army, Washington had his life to lose, but he did stand to achieve fame, or, at the very least, a footnote in history. By war's end, however, his reputation was so exalted that he had nothing more to gain. Yet here was a man moved by duty, never profit. "Had he consulted only his personal ease and enjoyment," explained Thomas Baldwin in his funeral oration, "he would have quitted his elevated station, and returned to private life. But higher motives influenced his mind."[36]

In a society that placed great stock in personal honor, and in which the "love of fame" referred not to self-centered ambition but to pride in one's social respectability, Washington's willingness to risk his reputation in the world of politics—without even the prospect of compensating benefits—could be cited as the best proof of his public virtue. In such manner did a correspondent of Jefferson assess the extraordinary risk that Washington assumed when he agreed to preside over the Federal Convention. Failure of the Convention, he said, would bring discredit to its chief officer. Still, Washington proceeded. "In every public act he hazards, without a possibility of gaining, reputation. He already possesses everything to be derived from the love or confidence of a free people, yet it seems that it remained for himself to add a lustre to his character, by this [most] patriotic adventure of all, for his country's good alone."[37] Alexander Hamilton agreed. By sponsoring the new Constitution, Hamilton told the New York ratifying convention, Washington "came forward again and hazarded his harvest of glory."[38] James Monroe also took note of this act, and acknowledged its sublimity: "To forsake the honorable retreat to which he had retired and risque the reputation he had so deservedly acquir'd, manifested a zeal for the publick interest, that could after so many and illustrious services, and at this stage of his life, scarcely have been expected from him."[39] Likewise, on the eve of his election as President, Jefferson recognized in a letter to Washington the immensity of his sacrifice: "Your measure of fame was full to the brim: and therefore you have nothing to gain."[40]

Each reflection contains not only an affirmation of the virtue of what Washington did, but also an appraisal of his motive. This double crediting showed up in his eulogies as well. When asked to assume command of the army in the 1798 French crisis, MacWhorter revealed, the great man agreed, even though it meant taking a role that was inferior to the one he had relinquished a year before (the presidency). "For him to stoop to this inferior appointment is an instance of such strange and disinterested patriotism the world never before saw."[41]

Those who were privy to Washington's own professions of motive confirmed the public's perception. These men knew that he did not stake his reputation unwittingly, or even casually. "Certain I am," Washington wrote in a (1789) letter to Henry Lee, that "whensoever the good of my country requires my reputation to be put in risque; regard for my own fame will not come in competition with an object of so much magnitude."[42] What made Washington's selflessness even more remarkable, as Lee indicated in his widely distributed eulogy to Congress, was this: Not only did he repeatedly risk his fame, but he did whatever he could to diminish it. Always embarrassed by praise, always directing his admirers' attention to God and to other leaders of the Revolution, Washington was a reluctant hero. He did not pursue the fame that attached itself to him.[43] And so, by renouncing that one reward which the American republic reserved for its public servants, Washington showed his countrymen what the highest and purest form of public virtue looked like.

Washington's self-denial in the service of the public good reminded many Americans of one of their favorite Romans, the younger Cato, whose life and martyrdom were fashioned by Whig historians into an emblem of their own political ideals. Prominent among the media that brought the image of Cato to public attention was Joseph Addison's drama, *Cato,* one of the most popular plays in the colonies during the eighteenth century, and the unquestionable favorite of Washington himself.[44] Washington's choice was fitting, for Americans thought mainly of him when the protagonist Juba, referring to Cato, declared:

> While good, and just, and anxious for his
>   friends,
> He's still severely bent against himself;
> Renouncing sleep, and rest, and food, and
>   ease,
> He strives with thrift and hunger, toil and
>   heat;
> And when his fortune sets before him all
> The pomps and pleasures that his soul can
>   wish,
> His rigid virtue will accept of none.

And when the foil, Syphax, seeks to disparage Cato by comparing his privileged life with that of the Numidian who "[t]oils all the day, and at th' approach of night / On the first friendly bank he throws him down, / Or rests his head upon a rock 'till morn; / Then rises fresh, pursues his wonted game," Juba's reply reminded theatergoers of Washington's *voluntary* sacrifice of comfort and safety: "The prejudice, Syphax, won't discern / What virtues grow from ignorance and choice / Nor how the hero differs from the Brute."[45]

Washington's public virtue was regularly defined by his countrymen as the fulfillment of the Catonic ideal. This ideal was reaffirmed by another, closely related virtue that Americans chose to see in Washington's moral character.

Disinterested Virtue

In the vocabulary of the new republic, "public virtue" referred to the citizen's willingness to subordinate his private interests to the social good. The closely related virtue of "disinterestedness" referred to the pursuit of collective ends without regard for the personal power one attained in the process. These two virtues presupposed one another and invariably showed up together; yet they were opposed by different vices. Public virtue was undermined by selfishness, while the bane of disinterestedness was ambition. Of these vices, ambition was regarded as the more deadly. The word "ambition" appeared repeatedly in Whig discourse, and no word better expressed the nation's political fears. Most Americans believed ambition to be rooted in man's lust for power, an innate passion against which only disinterested men could prevail.

For ancient personifications of disinterestedness, Americans looked to the classics and came up with political and military leaders like Epaminondas, Timoleon, Camillus, and Fabius. Even to virtuous men such as these, Washington compared favorably. With equal frequency, however, Washington's virtues were set off in contrast to antiquity's great men of ambition, like Sylla, Crassus, Pompey, Julius Caesar, Marcus Antonius, and Diocletian. Using these tyrannical Romans as foils, America's ideologues could define more clearly the grounds for republican greatness. "The possession of power," these men believed, "exposed the ruler to temptations to which the subject, by virtue of his impotence, was immune."[46] Only by resisting the enticement of power could the sincerity of a ruler's disinterestedness be proven. From the very beginning of the war, this belief helped to shape what the public saw in Washington.

On his way to Massachusetts in June 1775, the new Commander in Chief stopped in New York to receive an address from that state's Representatives. The New York Congress wished him well, but also declared its expectation of what he should do when the hostilities ended:

> Confiding in you, sir, and in the worthy generals immediately under your command, we have the most flattering hopes of success in the glorious struggle for American liberty, and the fullest assurances that whenever this important contest shall have decided, by the fondest wish of each American soul, an accommodation with our mother country, you will cheerfully resign the important deposit committed into your hands, and re-assume the character of our worthy citizen.[47]

With no standing army yet provided for, there would have been nothing for Washington to do but retire—nothing to do, that is, within the law. The possibility that a commander might choose to retain power outside the law is what gave the Congress's words their anxious tone. To these words Washington responded reassuringly—almost apologetically:

As to the fatal, but necessary operations of war, when we assumed the soldier, we did not lay aside the citizen; and we shall most sincerely rejoice with you in that happy hour when the establishment of American liberty, on the most firm and solid foundations, shall enable us to return to our private stations, in the bosom of a free, peaceful, and happy country.[48]

The tension in public attitudes toward the war comes out very clearly in this dialogue (which appeared in every major American newspaper). Conservative New Yorkers eager for a reconciliation with Britain did not congratulate Washington for the personal sacrifices he made in favor of the war effort. The more radical members of the Massachusetts Congress, as we already know, celebrated nothing but these sacrifices, and said nothing to Washington about retirement. New York wanted to see in its commander a paragon of disinterestedness; Massachusetts, a model of public virtue. Yet both values, disinterestedness and public virtue, were deeply rooted in the political conscience of most Americans, and these values determined their understanding of what lay ahead of them.

When the victories at Boston, Trenton, and Princeton were announced in the press, the public response was passionate, verging (in the eyes of some) on idolatry. In this reaction, however, Washington's moral character received as much attention as his martial talents. After Boston, an observer declared that "Washington's Behavior has eclipsed Cicero's."[49] (Cicero was known for his scrupulous political integrity, not his military prowess.) After Trenton and Princeton, the *Pennsylvania Journal* did extol the commander's ability in the field, but then hastened to make comment on his moral worth: "Washington retreats like a general and attacks like a hero. If there are spots in his character, they are like the spots in the Sun, only discernible by the magnifying powers of a telescope."[50] Only in a nation worried about the intentions as well as the achievements of its generals would the second sentence concerning Washington's moral character fail to strike the reader as a non sequitur to the first sentence on his military skills. Intentions do reveal moral character, but how precisely were those intentions gauged?

Every hero enters a period of tribulation that tests his abilities and character.[51] British arms had tested Washington's abilities; the first test of his character took the form of a letter. In October 1777, Washington received a messenger bearing a proposition from Jacob Duché, a Philadelphia clergyman for whom he had the greatest respect. Reverend Duché had once spoken out forcefully against British injustices, but he had undergone a change of heart and wanted Washington to join him. After expostulating on the hopelessness of the American cause, he urged Washington to demand that Congress rescind the Declaration of Independence and begin negotiations for peace. Such a move would meet with approval from most Americans, Duché thought. If it should not, said the former chaplain of Congress, there is always one recourse still left: "Negotiate for America at the Head of your Army." Duché was recommending, as a last resort, a *coup d'état*.[52]

Washington immediately turned over this letter ("this ridiculous, illiberal performance," as he called it) to Congress, which took no official notice of it. However, since almost every delegate to Congress seems to have sent copies of the letter to an acquaintance, word got around quickly. "Congress have not thought it fit to publish it here," wrote one delegate, "tho it is Publick enough in everybodey's mouth In the Streets."[53] What ensued was a *cause célèbre*. For many weeks, the "Duché Letter" and Washington's reaction to it became a topic of intense public discussion. To recover the substance of that discussion requires little imagination. An ambitious man would not have reacted to the letter as quickly as Washington did; he would have instead taken time to contemplate the treasonous remarks. Duché had said that the people supported Washington, while Washington alone supported Congress. The point was grossly exaggerated, but who would deny the opportunity it implied? Would this not be the moment, then, for any son of power to make his move? For the first time, the public had concrete evidence that the disinterestedness it had ascribed to Washington was in fact his ruling motive.

How much did Washington himself participate in the fashioning of this conviction? That he was inclined toward public expressions of disinterestedness was already evident. In a letter to Congress on the requisitioning of food and supplies from civilians, for example, he confessed: "I have felt myself greatly embarrassed with respect to a vigorous exercise of Military power." Recognizing "the prevalent jealousy [suspicion] of military power," Washington indicated in other letters that he wished to avoid any act that might exacerbate it, and he distributed to all newspapers his orders requiring respect for civil magistrates and civilian inhabitants.[54] He rightly assumed that these statements would increase support for the war. In December 1781, the *Connecticut Journal* carried a letter revealing that some merchants previously indifferent or hostile to the military cause had become supporters "because General Washington did not suffer the property of the merchants at York and Gloucester to be plundered."[55] These merchants, and others like them, became not only supporters of the war but also supporters of Washington. He hoped that would be the case.

Several years after the war, Washington suggested to Henry Lee "that one should not only be conscious of the purest intentions; but ... one should also have it in his power to demonstrate the disinterestedness of his words and actions at all times, and upon all occasions."[56] Perhaps it was this penchant for "image management" that led Gouverneur Morris to declare that an *inordinate* love of fame was Washington's greatest moral weakness.[57] Although Morris may have been right, a more generous interpretation would recognize Washington's dual role as diplomat and general, and would evaluate his performance in light of his obligations, which included the mediation of competing civil and military claims. Yet, this interpretation might be a little too generous. Consider again the Duché letter. In itself that letter posed no threat to constituted authority, and a man who was not eager to demonstrate to the world the purity of his intentions would have simply destroyed it. Instead, Washington made a public spectacle of it.

Yet, Washington was not always willing to injure another in his quest for fame. When Colonel Nicola, a patriot with a distinguished record of service against the British, outlined to Washington in writing the merits of monarchy, and recommended to Washington that he allow himself to be crowned King of America, he received a fast and stinging reply. The Colonel's plan was viewed by the would-be king "with abhorrence and reprehended with severity."[58] But no mention of the letter was made to Congress, nor to any private party.

Plausible explanations exist for Washington's willingness to extend to Nicola the protection he had denied to Duché: sympathy for a fellow officer, fear of offending the other mutinous officers he was then trying to placate, the superior military and political situation of the United States in 1783, the greater security of his own reputation. To decide on any one of these explanations, however, is unnecessary. The case itself is the important thing, at least in this one respect: If Washington's image was not dependent on his own awareness of what he symbolized, neither was it independent of the public's awareness of what he did. This point must stand as a caution against a one-sided understanding of his symbolic role. Washington may well have been a screen upon which his contemporaries projected their own moral sentiments, as students of "symbolic leadership"[59] might assert, but he was a peculiar kind of screen, designed to reflect some images better than others. The content reflected depended on the stuff of which the screen itself was made. Hence the difficulty of distinguishing the qualities exposed in Washington from those projected on him by his contemporaries.

The crisis that induced Colonel Nicola to write his infamous letter proved to be the most decisive test of Washington's inner qualities. In spring 1783, the goals of the American Revolution were threatened by the prospect of mutiny. Congress's inability to collect revenue for back pay was the surface issue. Below the surface, however, was another concern: the enduring appeal of monarchy. About a year before mutiny was actively considered, many officers were convinced that the pay they had already long awaited would never be appropriated by Congress. Rumors that the long-suffering army was disposed to dissolve Congress and make Washington king were widely circulated. The number of men who were inclined to this view was probably exaggerated; yet, many prominent leaders took the matter seriously. Although they "never dared openly to avow it," wrote Thomas Jefferson, "some officers of the army, as it has always been said and believed . . . trained to monarchy by military habits, are understood to have proposed to Gen'l Washington . . . to assume himself the crown, on the assurance of their support."[60] Jefferson's fears were not unfounded, for in the unofficial and anonymous second Newburgh Address the discontented author(s) suggested that, under certain conditions, the army, "courting the auspices, and inviting direction" of their "illustrious leader," should "retire to some unsettled country" (the West) to establish a new government of their own.[61]

Everyone knew that Washington singlehandedly blocked this

plan, and that he did it not by force of arms nor by the persuasiveness of his arguments, but by the irresistible power of his direct, personal appeal. The officers remained incensed at Congress, but they laid aside their plans out of respect for him. The nation's leaders were delighted and grateful. James Madison, who originally doubted Washington's ability to put down the mutiny, declared in the end that "the steps taken by the General to avert the gathering storm, and his profession of inflexible adherence to his duty to Congress and to his Country, excited the most affectionate sentiments toward him."[62] An understatement if there ever was one. For a Congress that had just had its skin saved, and for a society acutely aware that most earlier experiments in republicanism had run the ancient cycle—anarchy, then order through tryanny—Washington's achievement was a victory over history itself. "The moderation of a single character," wrote Jefferson, "probably prevented this Revolution from being closed, as most others have been, by a subversion of that liberty it was intended to establish."[63] Even John Adams, long troubled by the singling out of Washington as the sole beneficiary of public gratitude, had to admit publicly that the General was in truth an authentically disinterested man:

> The happy turn given to the discontents of the army by the General, is consistent with his character, which, as you observe, is above all praise, as every character, whose rule and object are duty, not interest, nor glory, which I think has been strictly true with the General from the beginning, and I trust will continue to the end.[64]

And so it did. By the end of the war, Washington's disinterestedness had already become legendary. Philip Freneau had sung of it as the virtuous victor passed through Philadelphia on his way home:

> O Washington!—thrice glorious name,
> What due rewards can man decree—
> Empires are far below thine aim,
> And sceptres have no charms for thee;
> *Virtue* alone has your regard,
> And she must be your great reward.[65]

Before he reached his destination, it remained for the hero to dramatize Freneau's, and the nation's, sentiments in a solemn ritual. The time was December 1783; the place, the Annapolis Statehouse. "Never was there a more glorious display of the power which virtue possesses over the human heart, than on that memorable occasion."[66]

An American Cincinnatus

Washington's resignation of his military commission has always been compared to Cincinnatus' return to the plow; yet, the model overlooks one crucial element. Since historical details are so sketchy, it has never been known for certain whether the Roman general was actually in a position to undermine civil authority. But if the Americans knew anything for certain, it was that Washington relinquished his power by choice. He could have possessed and controlled the government from which he resigned. Twentieth-century scholars may doubt this, but Washington's contemporaries did not, and it was this certainty that determined their perception of his character. Jonathan Sewall exclaimed:

> Did he, like Caesar, after vanquishing his countrymen's foes, turn his conquering armies against that country? Far, far otherwise. Before the great Council of our Nation, the PATRIOT-HERO appeared, and in the presence of numerous, admiring spectators, resigned his victorious sword into the hands of those who gave it.
>
> AUGUST Spectacle! Glorious Example! For my own part, I never contemplate it but each fibre vibrates with rapture, and the vital current trembles through every artery of my frame![67]

In minds haunted by the specter of overweening power, such ecstacies could be, and were, induced by any form of political diffidence. Central to the Washington cult's stock of images and knowledge, therefore, was not only the spectacle of his relinquishment of military power, but also the certainty of his reluctance to convert it into political power. "WONDERFUL MAN!," exclaimed Captain Josiah Dunham before an audience of soldier-Freemasons. "Here was a sight the GODS beheld with pleasure."[68] Like a god, Washington subdued that lust for power which a Protestant nation believed to be inherent in the very makeup of man. In the words of another Freemason, George Blake: "He who had conquered the proudest nation of Europe, by a nobler achievement, had now conquered himself, had vanquished the frailties and infirmities of nature."[69]

Since most men "struggled constantly," the Whigs believed, "to secure power, and if possible to aggrandize it at the expense of others,"[70] the effortlessness of Washington's victory over the lust for power became the most celebrated theme of his legacy. As Thomas Thacher put it: "He quitted his high and exalted station with more pleasure than would have been received by the most sanguine votary of power and ambition."[71] The point was brought home as emphatically in visual art as in eulogy. On the occasion of Washington's refusal of a third presidential term, for example, the popular illustrator John Barralet reminded his patrons of Washington's earlier resignation at Annapolis (Fig. 28). The display of this mnemonic icon was a social, not an artistic, event. A life-size version of the illustration was unveiled as part of a 1797 ceremony in Philadelphia attended by "all the Foreign Ministers, many of the Members of both Houses of Congress, the Governor of the State and all the principal Merchants of the city. . . . "[72] Two years later the original illustration appeared as a frontispiece for one of the city's magazines. Both displays affirmed a cultural ideal: not the renunciation of duty but the resignation of power, the latter being a formal incarnation of disinterestedness. Each exemplification of this ideal added weight to the other. Washington's second resignation (from the presidency) was used as an occasion to commemorate his first (from the military), while the first resignation was portrayed in a manner that defined the meaning of the second. Past and present reinforced one another in one self-supporting structure, whose object was the apotheosis of resignation itself.

Consider the contents of Barralet's illustration. In the picture's foreground are placed an American eagle as well as symbols of the prosperity that comes with peace: an olive branch and cornucopia. Although still in military uniform (the actual uniform was displayed in the National Archive, as a relic, soon after his resignation), Washington appears without military power. He has removed his own epaulets. To the throne of America, situated atop marble steps (one for each state), he climbs and hands up his commission. The instruments of military power, helmet and sword, he places at his country's feet. The hero's right arm draws attention to these instruments, showing that he has turned away from every prospect of power. In the remote background are mansion and plow, symbols of awaiting domestic tranquility, toward which he extends his left arm. In the more immediate background, an altar of burning incense signifies America's gratitude, and the domed Temple of Fame makes that gratitude perpetual.

In depicting the glory of Washington's resignation, Barralet emphasizes, through the use of common symbolic devices, the greater glory of America. Unlike Gilbert Stuart's *Lansdowne* portrait (Fig. 14), which places Washington in front of his ornate executive chair (a modern variant of the feudal throne), the Barralet painting accords the seat of power to America. The supremacy of America is also reinforced by the fact that Washington appears alone before her. Powerful people use representatives and spokesmen when they choose to give an account of themselves, but no such aide represents the retiring general; he himself climbs the steps of his country's altar to return her mandate of power. It is significant, however, that he does not climb to the very top of the altar. Vertical preeminence, a familiar symbol of social power, is reserved for America. She looks down upon Washington as he gives up his power to her. Thus, an overall impression of dominance and submission is created by a dualism of action and passivity. Seated upon an elevated throne and receiving power directly from its possessor, America is the dominant and passive member of the scene. Ascending alone the steps of state to return his mandate to its higher source, Washington is the submissive and active member. The symbolism conforms to a familiar pattern: "In a very rough way, the amount of bodily displacement engaged in by each party is in inverse proportion to his status—the lower the status, the more the body movement."[73]

To the Annapolis Statehouse, then, Washington came not as a conquering hero but as a humble man. He appeared as a renderer, not a recipient, of deference. Such is the conventional view of Washington's resignation, and that view is nicely captured in Barralet's portrait. Yet, this view assigns to Congress a role that is much too passive. In fact, the Annapolis ceremony was arranged neither by Washington nor exclusively for Washington; it was an occasion contrived by Congress for reasons of its own. Although it was Washington who first raised the question of how he should resign his commission, "whether in writing or at an Audience,"[74] it was Congress that decided on the latter. And it was Congress, too, that designed the framework for that self-abnegation commonly ascribed solely to Washington's character.

The delegates fully understood that a public resignation would be a symbolic event of unprecedented importance. To bring out the full significance of this event, Congress laid two plans: first, a series of dinners and balls to honor its military commander; then, a ceremony to honor itself. In this ceremony, the great man was required to dignify Congress by transferring to it his personal glory. The transfer was dramatized by the same symbolic devices as those used in the painting that commemorated it.[75]

When the door to the Hall of Congress was opened to Washington, he saw all members of Congress seated with their hats on. The president of Congress, Thomas Mifflin, was seated on an elevated platform, above the other delegates.[76] Behind President Mifflin's chair, Washington saw the presidential secretary—the only nonelected official in the Hall, and the only official standing. When the General entered into the Hall, the secretary's messenger introduced him to Congress. The secretary himself then moved to the door, escorted Washington to his assigned chair, and bade him to be seated. Washington's aides were instructed to follow their General and to stand behind him. At this point, a clear hierarchy was expressed: the president was seated in an elevated chair, behind which stood his aide; Washington was seated at a vertically inferior station, and his aides remained standing behind him. The members of Congress were seated between President Mifflin and General Washington, their centrality denying that equality of status implied by the equivalence of spatial plane shared with the General.

Washington waited as the spectators filed into the Hall and took their places. Not until he was invited to speak by the president did he rise. Before delivering his address, Washington lowered himself—he bowed—to Congress. The members of Congress did not rise with Washington and therefore did not reciprocate his bow; they merely acknowledged his deference by doffing their hats. Washington's deference to Congress was copious and unstinted; Congress's deference to Washington, perfunctory and abridged. Thus defined as servant rather than master of his government, Washington read his resignation speech. Having finished, he walked forward, then *up* the steps of the seated president's platform, and submitted to him a written copy of his speech along with his commission. President Mifflin was the passive, superordinate member of the ceremony; Washington was the active, subordinate member.

The first draft of the protocol required Washington to deliver his papers indirectly. Specifically, "he is to deliver a copy of his Address [and Commission] to his Aid to be presented to the Secretary" (who would then pass it on to the President). This original passage was revised by President Mifflin. By substituting the words "to the president" for "to his Aid to be presented to the Secretary,"[77] Mifflin underscored the symbolic importance of a gesture of delegation, an importance that no one understood better than Washington himself. Two years earlier, at the surrender ceremony at Yorktown, Washington was in a position similar to Mifflin's. As the victorious commander, he was entitled to receive the sword of surrender directly from Cornwallis, his vanquished counterpart. Cornwallis never showed up; instead, he delivered his sword to Washington through an aide. Refusing to accept the instrument himself, Washington instructed Cornwallis's aide to present it to his own aide, General Lincoln. Thus by surrendering his commission directly into the hands of the president, Washington ritually humbled himself in the same way Cornwallis was expected to, but did not.

In the next phase of the ceremony, Washington returned to his chair but remained standing in deference to the president, who rose at his elevated station and, looking down upon the General, responded to his address. At this point in the ceremony, Mifflin had thought of another way to diminish Washington's status. In the draft he had received from the committee, Mifflin had recommended a pause, "a proper interval," before the delivery of his own address, but he crossed out the entry.[78] Mifflin decided against using the ancient tactic of subordinating another by keeping him waiting.[79] The ceremony had already communicated a clear message of congressional authority; better not to undermine that authority, Mifflin must have thought, by pushing it too far. Besides, another symbolic putdown remained. Having read his response to the resignation address, the president delivered a copy of it to Washington indirectly, through his secretary. The president, then, communicates to the General through a mediator, while the General's communication to the president must be direct—another instance of the superordinate's privilege of energy conservation.

Finally, Washington retired from the Hall, but not before bowing to Congress. As before, the delegates acknowledged his submission by removing their hats; they did not reciprocate his bow. From the beginning of the ceremony to the end, then, Washington is the most active, and therefore subordinate, participant.

The image of a victorious general humbly returning his sword to the hands that gave it was thus created by Congress. The humility was not so much in the man as in the script prepared for him. Yet, the authors of that script could have found few men who would have enacted it better than Washington. If the character he assumed at Annapolis was not of his own making, it was still he who brought that character to life.

This spectacle of Washington, vanquisher of the most powerful nation on earth, submitting himself to that body which depended on him, at one point, for its very security, and doing so with utter sincerity, was deeply moving—perhaps more moving than anyone had expected. The further the ceremony progressed, the more its carefully devised framework became saturated with affect. Only the president of Congress, a former conspirator against Washington, maintained his composure. For everyone else, the resignation became a rapture wherein ceremonial form was enlivened by passion, and passion ennobled by form. In a letter to his fiancée, one of the men who devised that form, James McHenry, captured the quality of Washington's performance and the resulting texture of the occasion:

> To day my love the General at a public audience made a deposit of his commission and in a very pathetic manner took leave of Congress. It was a solemn and affecting spectacle; such an one as history does not present. The spectators all wept, and there was hardly a member of Congress who did not drop tears. The General's hand which held the address shook as he read it. When he spoke of the officers who had composed his family, and recomended those who had continued in it to the present moment to the favorable notice of Congress he was obliged to support the paper with both hands. But when he commended the interests of his dearest country to almighty God, and those who had the superintendence of them to his holy keeping, his voice faultered and sunk, and the whole house felt his agitations.[80]

Mr. McHenry went on to tell of how the great man paused to recover himself. Then the final, glorious, words: "Having now finished the work assigned me I retire from the great theatre of action, and bidding an affectionate farewell to this august body under whose orders I have so long acted I here offer my commission and take leave of all the employments of public life."[81]

As Margaret Caldwell came to the end of the letter, she knew that the plan her fiancé helped to design had backfired. The producers only wanted a *show* of humility, but the actor was serious.

By so earnestly yielding himself to Congress, Washington rose above it. His humility eclipsed the body it was supposed to elevate.

The Annapolis ceremony was not witnessed by the general public; but it was quickly and fully broadcast in the press, and the people at once grasped its significance. "Thus he who Rome's proud legions swayed / Return'd and sought his sylvan shade."[82] The image lingered, and settled, in the collective consciousness.

The Second Call to Duty

In his Annapolis address, Washington had pledged a second time never to return to public life. The first pledge had been made six months earlier, in his "Circular Letter" to the nation's governors. What engages our interest in this letter is not only its sensitive diagnosis of national problems (the lack of an effective political center, the endurance of local and provincial attachments, the accumulation of unpaid debts [especially to military officers], the failure to provide for a national military establishment), but also the lengths to which that letter goes to convey its author's intention to retire. Anticipating that some might regard his preference for a more powerful government as part of a hidden agenda for self-enhancement, Washington's prefatory remarks expressed the hope that

> the determination I have formed, of not taking any share in public business hereafter, the ardent desire I feel, and shall continue to manifest, of quietly enjoying in private life, after all the toils of War, the benefits of a wise and liberal Government, will, I flatter myself, sooner or later convince my Countrymen, that I have no sinister views in delivering with so little reserve, the opinions contained in this Address.

His letter concludes on the same note—"a last farewell to the cares of office, and all the imployments of public life."[83]

Given the firmness of this announcement, it is no surprise that when Washington was called by Virginia's delegation to lead it to the Federal Convention in Philadelphia, he found himself in a ticklish situation. If he even attended the convention, let alone accepted its presidency, his *disinterestedness* would be open to question. His earlier professions of desire for private life would be seen as a screen for political appetite, about which many suspicious critics warned the public as his wartime fame grew. "The world and posterity," he feared, "might probably accuse me [of]

143

inconsistency and *ambition*."[84] He announced therefore, that he would not go to Philadelphia.

"A thought however has lately run through my mind, which is attended with embarrassment. It is wheather my non-attendance in this Convention will not be considered a deriliction to republicanism, nay more, whether other motives may not (however injuriously) be ascribed to me for not exerting myself on this occasion in support of it."[85] In short, if Washington had not gone to Philadelphia, if he had refused to participate in an assembly seeking reforms that he himself had endorsed, he would have stood open to charges that he valued his own fame more than the public good. That would have made for an intolerable questioning of his *public virtue.*

At length Washington decided to attend. "As I have yielded ... to what appeared to be the earnest wishes of my friends, I will hope for the best. . . . "[86] His aspiration was realized. The convention succeeded, without cost to his reputation. Indeed, he emerged from that convention as a unanimous choice for the new government's presidential office. Again, Washington found himself torn between the imperatives of disinterestedness and public virtue, and he resolved this new dilemma by means of the same reasoning he publicly applied to the old. "[N]othing in this world can ever draw me from retirement," he told Benjamin Lincoln, "unless it be a *conviction* that the partiality of my countrymen had made my services absolutely necessary, joined to a *fear* that my refusal might induce a belief that I preferred the conservation of my own reputation and private ease to the good of my country."[87]

Paradoxically, Washington's reappearance in an office of influence strengthened the public's belief in his disinterestedness. The manner rather than the fact of reappearance made the difference. For most Americans, the best indicator of ambition was the deliberate seeking of power. Ambitious men *strive* for high public office; virtuous men *accept* such office when called to it by others. A politically suspicious people, then, expects its leaders to accept power with reluctance, and reluctance was precisely what Washington displayed.

Was this display genuine? Did Washington put on a show of reluctance in order to conceal his real desires?[88] If it were a show, it certainly was not a very coherent one. Spanning a period of five months, Washington's letters prior to the Federal Convention vacillate widely. Today he is going; tomorrow, he is not. In one letter he worries about offending the Society of the Cincinnati, whose presidency he had just declined; in another, he broods over his public declaration of retirement; in a third, he complains of his rheumatism and bad health. But, then, it is his duty to go. He asks his friends for advice on what to do.[89] A similar, although more consistent, performance is occasioned by the prospect of the national presidency. In his letters, he stressed that he could not commit himself without presumption to an acceptance or rejection of this office until it is officially offered to him, and if it should be offered, he would accept it only if there were no way, consistent with his conscience, to refuse. These letters, better than any other documents, express Washington's dread of a return to public life. Yet, he knew all along, from correspondents privately pleading that he accept the office and from public declarations expecting him to, that he was its only candidate.[90] A show? Who can say for sure? But one can say how Washington's professions were viewed by two important groups of contemporaries: his fellow statesmen, and the eulogists and publicists who summed up his character and motives for posterity.

When Washington arrived in Philadelphia to preside over the Federal Convention, Madison noted the enthusiasm with which he was received, and "the affection and veneration which continues to be felt for his character."[91] The many letters that passed among the delegates reveal their awareness of Washington's reluctance to return to the national scene. And if anyone believed he was acting out a script in order to preserve his image or to prepare groundwork for a power play, they did not let on. Even more convincing, to many a mind, was his hesitation to take on the new presidency. "The opinion seems to be universal that Genl. Washington will be elected President," said friend and former military aide, David Humphreys in a November 1788 letter. "His inclinations," the letter went on to say, "will certainly lead him to refuse. Should circumstances overcome his inclinations, I know it will occasion more distress to him, than any other event in his life."[92] Several months passed, but the perception of Washington's preferences did not change. Jefferson told a correspondent that "Genl. Washington . . . will undertake the presidency if asked . . . tho' with vast reluctance."[93]

Eulogists gave the most abundant testimony of faith in Washington's disinterestedness. From the beginning of his career to the end, explained one of them, Washington assumed public office not because of ambition but as one "obsequious to the will of his country."[94] The American people believed this. They believed that Washington saw himself as their servant rather than their master, and in this conviction they rested secure. In 1797, this man would confirm his admirers' convictions by declining a third term in office. Although few would have complained if Washington had chosen to retain and exploit his influence, this second retirement brought to Washington's eulogists the full realization that his greatness lay in rejection rather than use of opportunity. A third term would have been an opportunity for aggrandizement, and had there been no such opportunity, there would have been no way for him to demonstrate his virtue. "However his long and familiar intercourse with the world might have exposed him to temptation," declared Timothy Bigelow, "he preserved his morals not only pure but even unsullied by the breath of suspicion."[95] Washington having allowed himself to be twice elected to the presidency, Henry Lee added, only "the promulgation of his fixed resolution stopped the anxious wishes of an affectionate people from adding a third unanimous testimony of their unabated confidence."[96] This voluntary retirement from the presidency, for Unitarian minister Aaron Bancroft, "is the consummation of character; the last evidence of the greatness of the man."[97] And so it would be remembered. The date of Washington's retirement was reverently marked on many of the nation's new coins and on granite monuments that commemorated his death.

On these points, the publicists were as emphatic as the eulogists. Thus, shortly after Washington died, a Boston newspaper announced the preparation of a book containing a selection of his public addresses. The selection itself revealed what was considered most significant in his career: the speech accompanying his acceptance of a military commission from Congress, the Circular Letter to state governors on the occasion of his return to civilian life, his farewell address to the army, his speech on the surrender of his military commission to Congress, his first Inaugural Address, his Farewell Address on the completion of his presidency, and his formal acceptance (in 1798) of a second military commission.[98] The focus is exclusively on induction and resignation—the acceptance and relinquishment of public duty. Sacrifice is made and temptation resisted both by leaving private life and by returning to it, both by taking power and by giving it up. This contradiction carries its own resolution: Washington's disinterested commitment to public duty allows him to be called to power without seeking it, and to relinquish power without being asked. As Mason explained, "It was for him to set as great an example in the relinquishment, as in the acceptance, of power."[99] No better summation of a century of Whig discourse on political virtue could be conceived.

Greatness from Goodness

Conceptions of heroic leadership which emphasize talent and deed have little affinity with the grounds on which Washington was praised; these revolved around public virtue and disinterestedness, not great exploits. Washington's achievements were celebrated mainly because they helped his countrymen gauge his character, and it was this *inner* merit that defined his greatness. In the words of Reverend Henry Holcombe: "He would have been equalled by several, if he had not shone in the mild majesty of morals."[100] On this point most of the eulogists were emphatic. Fisher Ames explained:

> [It] requires thought and study to understand the true ground of the superiority of his character over many others, whom he resembled in the principles of action, and even in the manner of acting. But perhaps he excels all the greatness that ever lived, in the steadiness of his adherence to his maxims of life, and in the uniformity of all his conduct to these same maxims. . . . [If] there were any errors in his judgment, we know of no blemishes in his virtue. . . . Mankind [thus] perceived some change in their ideas of greatness.[101]

Considering the uniqueness of the republican ideals made animate by Washington, Samuel West, a Unitarian minister, former soldier, and one of the most ardent of revolutionary Whigs, agreed with Ames. "How widely different," West proclaimed, "is this from what the world has been used to estimate as greatness."[102]

Washington was "great" because he was "good." Indeed, some eulogists believed that the traditional distinction between greatness (genius or extraordinary achievement), and goodness (superiority of moral virtue) had been rendered obsolete by Washington's example. "We now almost instinctively apply the epithet GREAT," declared David Tappan, the Harvard theologian, "to high moral excellence, rather than to superiority of intellect or fortune" (achievement).[103]

To dramatize the nature of this contrast, Washington's eulogists looked for negative counterparts among history's great leaders and founders of states. (This tactic also served nationalistic interests by demonstrating the superiority of America's founding hero over the heroes of other states, present and past.) The most recurrent comparisons were drawn between Washington and Alexander, Julius Caesar, Cromwell, Peter the Great, Marlborough, and Napoleon. Washington compared favorably to these figures not because of his genius, which was in fact no match for theirs, but because every one of them was blemished by a fatal moral weakness: for Alexander, self-indulgence and intemperance; for Caesar and Cromwell, a willingness to compromise the liberties of their countrymen; for Peter the Great, fiendishness and criminality; for Frederick the Great, ostentation and perversion; for Marlborough, shameless fraudulence; for Napoleon, a thirst for domestic dictatorship and foreign conquest. These men and their assembled exploits, said Samuel West embodied the established formula for heroism "to which the aspiring son of pride has waded."[104] Among such men, "greatness and guilt have too often been allied," added Baldwin.[105] In distinct contrast, Bancroft concluded, Washington's achievements were "not erected upon the agonies of the human heart."[106]

Against the traditional criteria of stunning military and political accomplishment, Washington distinguished himself as hero by total disregard of self and spotlessness of motive. But the great man's admirers went deep into his character; they revealed not only its essential benevolence and disinterestedness but also the matrix from which these virtues derived.

6

The Foundational Virtues

AFTER THE WAR, when Americans reached into their pockets to make a purchase, one of the coins they pulled out bore George Washington's profile under the inscription *Non vi virtute vici:* "I prevailed not by might, but by virtue." Pressed to define the meaning of virtue, they would have thought of a complex set of attributes that included not only self-sacrifice and disinterestedness but also temperateness. Washington embodied all three attributes. He renounced his own interests for the public good; he resisted the temptations of power; and he overcame the natural tendency to excess in feeling and conduct.

Too much feeling—or any line of conduct pushed too far, Washington's countrymen believed—was odious. For them, as for Aristotle, virtue implies "a kind of mean, since . . . it aims at what is intermediate."[1] In politics, the application of the Aristotelian mean was straightforward. Seventeenth-century Americans regarded the best men as "mediocre." In the eighteenth century, too, the middling state, defined in Samuel Johnson's (1755) dictionary as "the forebearance of extremity" and the "state of keeping a due mean betwixt extremes," was most valued. Likewise, the main assumption of the "Whig science of politics" was that extremes in anything were bad; the main goal was to make moderation prevail over excess. And the virtue of moderation was commonly attributed to Washington. It was on characteristics such as diffidence, frugality, and evenly balanced traits of character and intellect that the great man's public virtue and disinterestedness were thought to depend.

Diffidence

George Washington was able to maintain a sober and restrained conception of himself, a "mean betwixt extremes," despite the extreme adulation that engulfed him. His countrymen certainly expected him to be self-reliant and forceful, but in an age of suspicion as well as defiance, they regarded Washington's diffidence as an essential counterbalance to his assertiveness. Diffidence could manifest itself in an unwillingness to actively seek positions of power and a reluctance to accept them when offered, and also in an avoidance of ostentation in appearance and manner. From the very beginning of the war, Washington satisfied the public taste on both scores. He had to be coaxed to accept military power, and his modest mien was a counterpoint to the arrogance and haughtiness attributed to the British foe in almost every pamphlet, sermon, poem, and song.

Washington's demure and unassuming character was established locally well before the revolution. When the Virginia House of Burgesses in 1758 passed a resolution commending him for his military expeditions, everyone present—and, through the grapevine, all the best families in Virginia—discovered that modesty was one of the young colonel's distinguishing traits. An eyewitness recalled:

> He rose to express his acknowledgement for the honor, but such was his trepidation and confusion, that he could not give distinct utterance to a single syllable. He blushed, stammered, and trembled, for a second; when the speaker relieved him. . . . "Sit down, Mr. Washington," said he with a conciliating smile, "your modesty is equal to your valor, and that surpasses the power of any language that I possess."[2]

Modesty proved to be an enduring feature of Washington's personal makeup. Even when chosen Commander in Chief in 1775, he expressed to Congress, publically and in private, sincere doubt of his ability to succeed in the "momentous duty" assigned him. Nor did he labor under illusions of what others thought of his ability. In his public letter to the Virginia militia, Washington acknowledged that his lack of experience induced him to avoid a major appointment, but "the partiality of Congress . . . assisted by a political motive [the need for a Southern commander] rendered my reasons unavailing." The Boston newspaper in which this statement appeared may have been the real source of Abigail Adams's conviction (expressed after seeing Washington for the first time) that "Modesty marks every line and feature of his face."[3]

Since republican culture placed a premium on humility, many military men were given to public self-depreciation. "You may depend ... on my zeal and integrity," Charles Lee assured the Massachusetts House of Representatives at the beginning of the war, but "I can promise you nothing from my abilities."[4] When Lee made this statement, he was considered to be the colonies' most able, if not most trustworthy, general. As it turned out, neither Lee's morals nor his abilities could be depended upon. But that was his contemporaries' verdict; of his contempt for that verdict the haughty Englishman made no secret. As a native-born republican, Washington knew better than Lee, the foreign-born aristocrat, what kind of demeanor the public expected of its leaders. As Washington's reputation grew, he became more, not less, responsive to this expectation, and so enhanced his reputation further.

When the war ended, Washington went to Annapolis to "resign with satisfaction the Appointment I accepted with diffidence. A diffidence in my abilities to accomplish so arduous a task.... "[5] Six years later, the public gained further proof of his modesty. On the way to his first inauguration as President of the new government, Washington spent the night in Philadelphia. He left unexpectedly early the next morning, and though disappointed at not being able to see him off, everyone "knew" the reason for his sudden departure. When the President-elect saw the city cavalry preparing itself to escort him to Trenton, he left before the appointed hour, according to a local newspaper, "from a desire to avoid even the appearance of pomp and vain parade." As to the pomp and parade of his entry into Philadelphia, that was something "he could not possibly elude," since it "necessarily must attend manifestations of joy and affection." And if he could not avoid the show that awaited him in New York, he could at least express personal misgivings about the whole affair. He could also remind his admirers in the Inaugural Address itself that they were welcoming to office a man of "inferior endowments." The people loved what they heard, for it confirmed their belief that in Washington they had a first magistrate who would not imitate those rulers of Europe who "assume the titles of gods and treat their subjects like an inferior race of animals. Our beloved magistrate delights to shew, upon all occasions that he is a man—and instead of assuming the pomp of master, acts as if he considered himself the father—the friend—and the servant of the people."[6]

As father, friend, and servant, Washington was a personification of that complex standard to which Americans held their leaders. To be in certain respects superior to the people, in other respects their equal, and in yet another way subordinate to them, was the combination that unlocked the people's hearts. But if Washington became the paragon of this combination, it was the sincerity of his actions, not the persuasiveness of his words, that made him so.

Duly sworn in as first magistrate, Washington rose to deliver his inaugural speech to Congress. He did not move his audience by dominance and certainty of bearing. Quite the contrary: The man's demeanor lent weight to the modest tone and substance of his words. He seemed to be in the grip of stage fright. His gestures were awkward; his voice barely audible; his delivery flawed by an apparent inability to make out the words of his own prepared speech. These defects, however, were precisely what captivated his audience. Fisher Ames, the greatest orator in Congress, was there, and he recounted the performance and its effect:

> [I]t was a very touching scene and quite of the solemn kind. [Washington's] aspect grave, almost to sadness; his modesty, actually shaking; his voice deep, a little tremulous, and so low as to call for close attention; added to the series of objects presented to the mind, and overwhelming it, produced emotions of the most affecting kind upon the members. I . . . sat entranced. It seemed to me an allegory in which virtue was personified. . . . [7]

Ineptitude and self-depreciation do not in themselves lead to admiration, much less veneration; they merely intensify existing positive feelings and facilitate their expression. Washington's flawed performance in New York was captivating because the weaknesses to which it called attention mitigated apprehension over the strengths he had already demonstrated. Those strengths, which had made him so admired, had also aroused feelings of envy and fears of dependence among his colleagues and followers, but Washington's stammering inaugural performance made him seem vulnerable, and so less threatening. Far from endangering his authority, this awkward modesty, by revealing the common side of him, complemented the respect his uncommon achievements commanded and so increased the appeal of his leadership.

As we recognize that Washington typically appeared both imposing and modest, and that some of his least impressive qualities were those which most impressed his admirers, we are reminded of the maxim that "the modesty of those who attain the highest eminence is due to a desire to appear even greater than their position."[8] That Washington, a man so concerned with reputation, might try to elevate himself by such a public show of humility is not implausible. His audience, however, was not a naive one; it was very sensitive to the use and consequences of false modesty. In sermons and political addresses, the people were warned repeatedly about the wolf in sheep's clothing—the man who feigned modesty in order to ingratiate himself with the people, only to reveal himself the tyrant when his position became secure. "Men upon their first promotion, commonly act and speak with an air of meekness and diffidence," cautioned Phillips Payson. "The practice of power is apt to dissipate these humble airs."[9] Beneath Washington's meekness and diffidence, however, the people sensed a virtue that would not be so corrupted.

John Adams never accused Washington of tyrannical motives, but he was one of the few who insisted on attributing his hold on public audiences to a "Shakespearean and Garrickal excellence in Dramatic Exhibitions." He was the "best actor of the Presidency we have ever had."[10] Few besides Benjamin Rush, the man to whom these words were addressed, would have agreed. Anyone in a position to know would have denied that Washington was much of an actor. Adams had confused effect with motive. Had he been with Washington at Newburgh, he would have known that his influence lay in the failure, not the success, of his histrionics.

The scheme devised in Newburgh during the last year of the war would have turned a glorious victory into tragic defeat. At the very time the British delegates in Paris were prepared to accept the independence of the colonies and recognize their confederated government, American officers, rightfully indignant at Congress's failure to make good on months of back pay, determined to take justice into their own hands. An anonymous proposal was circulated, urging the officer corps to take one of two courses of action. If the peace talks failed, the officers would withdraw from the warfront and leave the country unprotected; if the talks succeeded, they would move against Congress itself. In either case, the American army would by one swift stroke bring about the fall of the government—something the British army had not been able to do in eight years. Only one voice, Washington's, could have dissuaded the officers from acting on their proposal. So compelling was that voice, and so total its effect, that not even a rumor of insurrection was ever heard again. However, the point at which Washington thwarted the designs of his mutinous officers came not at the conclusion of his carefully prepared address but during a moment of utter confusion, when his eyes failed him and he drew from his pocket something few had ever seen him wear: a pair of spectacles. The simple admission that he had "not only grown gray but almost blind" in the service of his country produced the effect he sought from the persuasive logic of his speech. The sight of their glorious commander as a weakened, bespectacled suppliant set the hardiest veterans, and most dedicated mutineers, to open weeping.[11]

Nine months later, with the war officially over, Washington went to Fraunces Tavern to bid farewell to his officers. His self-possession failed him again. When "his excellency entered the room," recalled Colonel Benjamin Tallmadge, "his emotion was too strong to be concealed," and this failure of concealment, Tallmadge went on to say, "seemed to be reciprocated by every officer." The result was "a scene of sorrow and weeping I had never before witnessed, and fondly hope I may never be called upon to witness again."[12] Fortunately, Colonel Tallmadge was not present at Annapolis three weeks later, when Washington resigned his commission and the scene was repeated.

Clearly, Washington's Inauguration Day was not the first time he had failed to exhibit the self-possession that successful acting requires. The deeper meaning of his failure on that day, however, derived not only from its spontaneity but also from the situation in which it occurred. Washington, a self-controlled and resolute military commander, had lost his composure during a rite of passage to induct him into his nation's highest and most powerful civil office. The flaw in his performance at this ritual, as the audience saw it, betokened not stage fright or embarrassment but awe—and the revelation of this sentiment induced the audience to recognize in Washington its own respect for the sanctity of the station he was about to assume.

Not polish, but sincerity; not boldness, but diffidence, is what Americans found appealing in Washington's Inaugural performance. Eight years later, in his Farewell Address (which was never read, but rather distributed for public consumption through the newspapers), these qualities were revealed again as the chief magistrate both reasserted "the inferiority of my qualifications," which had "strengthened the motives to diffidence of myself," and recognized those "situations in which not infrequently want of success has countenanced [justified] the spirit of criticism."[13] Eulogy would later reaffirm the humility to which these statements gave voice. Washington's traits were "superior to the inflations of vanity; and they furnish a model of humility," Reverend Abiel Holmes told his Boston congregation. Meekness is a virtue he shared with Moses, Alexander MacWhorter asserted before his listeners. Henry Lee told Congress that the man's modesty was "innate," and therefore useless as a screen for vice.[14]

Frugality and Industry

Ostentation was not the only type of excess disdained by the new republic. Even more widely discussed and more vigorously condemned was luxury. Severe admonitions against sensual pleasure were part of puritanical tradition, but it was on political as well as religious grounds that luxury was reporved. Luxury was a condition of material comfort that interfered with public duty. Knowing that many men did not renounce their ease, as Washington did, when their country needed them, "Mentor" warned readers of a Boston newspaper that "the love of pleasure swallows up all those resources, from which we should pay our honest debts, and refund the monies borrowed for the defence of our liberties."[15] To "wallow in luxury," especially during national crisis, was to be distracted, enervated, "effeminate"—and unqualified for positions of public trust. Almost twenty years earlier, "Tribune's" letter to a Charleston newspaper drove the same point home: "That luxury creates want, and that want, whether artificial or real, has a tendency to make men venal, are truths that are too evident to be disputed. Luxury therefore leads to corruption." By extension, corruption is the first step to tyranny, a prospect that only moderate men can avert: "To men who are superior to the baits of luxury there can be no temptations to become corrupt, either as electors or representatives; and therefore it must be on the virtues of such men only that public freedom, justice and security can ever rest. . . . "[16]

Tribune's words, written almost ten years before the start of the war, were prophetic of the way a critical dilemma of his culture, the contradiction between privilege and virtue, would resolve in the image of Washington. In Washington's time, public virtue was assumed to be monopolized by the privileged class, for it was wealth that gave men a stake in society. Yet, wealth was itself an agent of potential corruption. "The exorbitant wealth of individuals," explained Phillips Payson, "has a most baneful influence on public virtue, and therefore should be carefully guarded against."[17] For this warning the manners of society gave ample cause. "A notion from the land of lies," Mason Weems revealed in his life of Washington, "has taken too deep root among some that labor is a low lived thing, fit for none but Negro-slaves! and that dress and pleasure are the only accomplishments for a gentleman!"[18] Enjoyed in limited amounts, however, wealth always betokened social merit. The key was self-restraint: Since the rich must be ascetic by *choice,* theirs must be the superior morality. Joseph Lathrop, a Congregationalist minister widely known in New England, explained:

> While the poor are frugal from necessity, and the common farmers and mechanics are frugal from prudence, let the opulent be frugal from patriotism: and if they would make their patriotism a still more excellent virtue, let the savings of extraordinary frugality be applied to some charitable purpose. For the rich no certain rules can be prescribed; their frugality must be voluntary and discretionary.[19]

For the public at large, Lathrop's principle was animated in the career of Washington. His moderation was apparent in early youth, when he forsook the comforts of the plantation for the harsh outdoor life of surveyor and wilderness fighter. Even when at home, he eschewed leisure and engaged in studies and household duties—all in preparation for more important events. "While each effeminate son of peace was revelling in luxury," declared a correspondent to the *Virginia Gazette,* Washington's "active mind was employed in preparing for scenes equally glorious to himself and terrible to his enemies."[20] As these difficult scenes were acted out, Washington allowed himself few indulgences. Recognizing the nation's "happy and glorious Necessity": to strengthen itself against the British "by renouncing all luxuries and by a severe Oeconomy," John Adams admitted that "General Washington sets a fine example. He has banished Wine from his Table and entertains his friends with Rum and Water. . . . [T]he Example must be followed."[21] General Washington was to set other examples. When he visited Philadelphia in 1779, General Nathaniel Greene told his correspondent, "[E]very exertion was made to show him respect and make his time agreeable; but the exhibition was such a scene of luxury and profusion they gave him more pain than pleasure."[22]

Although the extent of Washington's private wealth was well known, that wealth was never converted, in the people's eyes, to sensual pleasure, and so never undermined the people's conviction that he was really one of them. According to Mason Weems, everyone knew that Washington sought to make money "not meanly to hoard, but generously to lend to any worthy object that asked it." Washington's industry, on the other hand, was an end in itself. Great wealth, said Weems, incites many to "sloth, high living, and the gout. But in Washington, whose industry was founded on principle," it incited gratitude to heaven and "a wish to be useful." On his industry this man allowed no pleasure to impinge. His dearest friends, in this respect, took second place:

> Gentlemen: he would often say to his friends who visited him, "I must beg leave of absence a few hours in the forenoon; here is plenty of amusements, books, music . . . and consider yourselves at home, and be happy." He came about 12 o'clock, and then, as if animated by the consciousness of having done his duty, and that all was going on right, he would give himself up to his friends and to decent mirth the rest of the evening.[23]

Guests at leisure accentuate, by counterpoint, the host at work. Lest readers come to the conclusion that their hero worked only half a day, however, Weems pointed out that Washington's early mornings as well as forenoons were "his own." The possessive conveys the moral lesson. To industry Washington laid rightful claim; to mirth he "gave himself" out of regard for others. Work, he felt, was his entitlement; leisure, his obligation. His priorities were contagious. "Long before the sun had peeped into the chambers of the sluggard, WASHINGTON was on horseback and out among his overseers and servants and neither himself nor any about him were allowed to eat the bread of idleness. . . ."[24]

Americans loved to talk about frugality and industry, and in

Washington's daily routine they found these. Between work and leisure he had built an impenetrable wall, which his countrymen used as a model for the moral architecture of their own lives.

"The Balance of All ... Qualities"

Whereas Washington's frugality and industry made him immune to the temptations of wealth, his evenly developed talents and moral inclinations enabled him to overcome the bane of political ambition. Washington's countrymen, good Whigs that they were, believed that any one source of individual power, cultivated at the expense of other traits, could dominate the rest of the personality, suiting a man perhaps for private gain, but not for public trust. Well-rounded competence, not specialized genius, was the desideratum in their heroic ideal. Washington reflected this taste for symmetry and balance; his merit inhered not in his possession of one extraordinary quality, such as political or military genius, but in a combination of moderately developed talents and strong but temperate moral dispositions. Each talent and each disposition was cultivated only so far as to prevent others from exceeding their proper boundaries. In Washington, then, was found a man who was competent but rarely brilliant; virtuous but never fanatic.

To communicate that discovery, people invoked a favored geometric metaphor. Washington's character, they said, was reminiscent of that most perfect of all forms, the circle, which has no salient points or angles to spoil its symmetry. As a metaphor of character, the circle represents a *coincidentia oppositorum,* an agency that blunts exorbitance and so unifies otherwise separate traits. The poet could sing of "Patience, serene, as ills and injuries tried, / Meek without meanness, noble without pride, / Frank yet imperious [dignified], manly yet refined, / As the sun watchful, and as angels kind."[25] The eulogist could speak of firmness counterposed by mildness; courage by prudence; passion by composure; public duty by private affection; dedication to progress by love of tradition; vigor and force by grace and compassion. The great masculine endowments were seen to be joined in Washington with the gentle, feminine qualities, and this balance enabled him to perform well the contradictory roles of audacious general and prudent statesman, dominating leader and submissive citizen.

In oration after oration, listeners were told that their hero possessed not only a set of bold, heroic traits but also a second set of self-abnegating, common traits, equally desirable but nevertheless inconsistent with the first. Washington thereby became the incarnation of a moral miracle. Beside such a man, all other heroes, ancient as well as modern, shrank in fame and stature:

> Other Generals have been equally brave in the field, conducted equally difficult enterprises, and made more splendid conquests; other Patriots and sages have had an equal affection for their country, and have been ready to preserve, or die to defend its liberties; and other private citizens have equalled him in moral and social duties: Yet where is the man (the inspired characters recorded in the holy scripture excepted) who hath united in himself such measure of military, political, and moral excellence?[26]

The striking parallel between what eulogists said about Washington and how artists depicted him was that both emphasized the combination of qualities that set him apart from other men. Artists recognized that none of Washington's physical features, taken separately, was particularly outstanding; it was their harmonious integration that engaged the viewer. This sublime physical symmetry was regarded as an external mark of the internal moral equilibrium that defined Washington's character. On this correspondence of appearance and character, Henry Tuckerman, a Washington scholar and art critic, wrote at length. Although Tuckerman lived in the mid-nineteenth century, his essay on Washington's character closely resembles those of his predecessors—perhaps because he grew up at a time when the veneration of Washington was still intense—and his perception of Washington's life portraits was probably just as similar:

> [Washington's] appearance and his character left an impression harmonious rather than original; like all that is truly grand in nature, in life, and in humanity, it was the balance of all and not the predominance of a few qualities that rendered him illustrious. In vain the observer sought to carry from his presence a single extraordinary feature whereby to identify the man; in vain the painter watched for effective attitudes, melodramatic situations, or a characteristic phase of dress, manner, or look; Washington was too complete, too accordant, too humanly representative, too evenly as well as largely gifted with the elements of our commoner nature, to serve a theatrical purpose either for the historian, the dramatist, or the limner. . . . [T]he portrait of Washington, like his character, boasts no speciality to catch the eye, is without an extraordinary single feature.[27]

Nothing better attests to Washington's lack of distinguishing features than the diversity of his portraiture. So unlike were the many versions of his appearance, even among life portraits executed at approximately the same period of time, that the National Academy of Fine Arts, in 1824, set up a committee to determine which actually resembled him. But there is one painting, Gilbert Stuart's *Athenaeum*, that was always believed by the people, if not the experts, to depict Washington's character—so "humanly representative" and "gifted with the elements of our commoner nature"—better than any other (Fig. 29). This portrait (named for the Boston Athenaeum, which owned it for over a century) is totally lacking in heroic dimension; yet, when reproductions of it first appeared they were bought up immediately, and neither the artist nor the engravers could keep up with the subsequent demand. The *Athenaeum* became, by every account, the favorite Washington portrait in 1798 and eventually dominated America's visual conception of Washington.[28]

What made this particular portrait so appealing? Existing accounts provide no useful answers. Depicting Washington in his advanced years, the portrait is said by one authority to possess a "patriarchal" air. Another expert describes it as "avuncular."[29] The trouble with these accounts is that they treat the *Athenaeum* as an individual rather than cultural production. The painting itself depicts Washington as an undistinguished man, without uniform and against an empty background: There are no pillars of state, no massive drapery, no symbols of political authority. Like the works of his predecessors, such as Christian Gullager, Edward Savage, and Adolph Wertmuller (Figs. 30–32), Stuart's painting expresses a mode of state portraiture, and a perception of Washington, preferred by and familiar to all. The painting did not suggest a head of state or former general, let alone a great man. Rather, it projected the image of a plain citizen, an image that impresses by its commonality and not its uniqueness. Though the *Athenaeum* portrait of George Washington did possess a distinguishing aesthetic quality, aesthetics alone do not explain its vast appeal. It became America's most cherished icon because it did credit to its subject by reducing rather than enlarging him, by placing him among the people rather than above them. The new republic's admiration for restraint and its disdain for ostentation were captured in this most popular image of its representative man.

26

A visitor in his own home . . . *The Washington Family* (1796), by Edward Savage (National Gallery of Art, Washington, D.C.: Andrew W. Mellon Collection)

27

The transitional man . . . *George Washington*, by Jean-Antoine Houdon (State Capitol Building, Virginia State Library, Richmond)

GENERAL WASHINGTON'S

RESIGNATION.

Published by B. Davies Philada 1st Feby 1799.

A new conception of human greatness . . . *General Washington's Resignation* (1799), by Alexander Lawson after a design by John Barralet (Historical Society of Pennsylvania, Philadelphia)

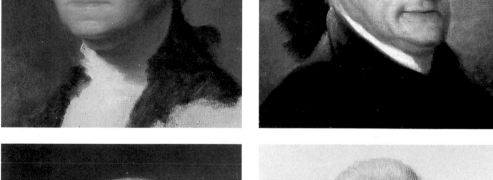

Republican Simplicity

(Top left) George Washington (The "Athenaeum," 1796), by Gilbert Stuart (National Portrait Gallery, Smithsonian Institution, Washington, D.C.) *(Top right) George Washington* (1789), by Christian Gullager (Courtesy Massachusetts Historical Society, Boston) *(Bottom left)* George Washington (c. 1796, replica of 1793 portrait) by Edward Savage (National Gallery of Art, Washington, D.C.: Gift of Henry Prather Fletcher) *(Bottom right) George Washington* (c. 1794), by Adolph Ulrich Wertmuller (The Historical Society of Pennsylvania, Philadelphia)

33

34

Civil Magistrate in Epaulets

(Top) General Washington, President of the United States of America (c. 1796–1798), by H. Houston after design by John Barralet (McAlpin Collection, Print Collection, The New York Public Library, Astor, Lenox and Tilden Foundations) *(Bottom) Washington at Dorchester Heights* (1806), by Gilbert Stuart (Courtesy, Museum of Fine Arts, Boston)

35

36

Triumph of Virtue

(Top) His Excellency George Washington (1783), by an unidentified artist after John Trumbull (The Historical Society of Pennsylvania, Philadelphia *(Bottom) His Excellency General Washington* (1779), by John Norman after Charles Willson Peale (McAlpin Collection, Print Collection, The New York Public Library, Astor, Lenox and Tilden Foundations)

37

38

(Top) An omen of justice . . . *The Early Days of Washington*, by Henry Inman (From *The Gift*, Philadelphia, 1844, opposite p. 139)

(Middle) Beyond public view . . . *General Washington at Prayer at Valley Forge* (1854), by Lambert Sachs (Courtesy of the Valley Forge Historical Society, Valley Forge, Pennsylvania)

(Bottom) Private benefaction . . . *The Benevolence of Washington*, by Peter F. Rothermel (From *The Eclectic Magazine*, January, 1855, frontispiece)

39

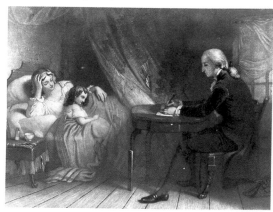

40

Entered, according to Act of Congress, in the year 1865, by J. A. Arthur, in the
Clerk's Office of the District Court for the Eastern District of Pennsylvania.
WASHINGTON & LINCOLN. (APOTHEOSIS.)

The heavenly host . . . *Washington and Lincoln Apotheosis*, by an unidentified artist (Lincoln Picture Studio, Dayton, Ohio)

41

In the company of Washington . . . *President Carter and President-Elect Reagan*, photograph by Wide World Photos, Inc.

Firm in purpose . . . *Washington Crossing the Delaware* (1851), by Emanuel Leutze (Metropolitan Museum of Art, New York)

The ship of state adrift . . . *Nixon Crossing the Delaware*, by Edward Sorel (Courtesy of Ira D. Rothfeld, M.D., New York, N.Y.)

Wisdom and Genius

In an age that saw commanding genius as a potential threat to liberty, an age that shunned every form of extravagance and excess, Washington's balance of attributes represented a stunning model. But the Americans' relatively low regard for genius as a requirement for high social position did not imply a rejection of the intellect; it implied a preference for one type of intellect over another. Thus a list of qualifications for leadership in the new republic would include, in the words of one observer, "sufficient abilities; gravity, wisdom, and sound judgement; decision, close attention and perseverance; a great command of ... passions, and steady attendance."[30] Not *extraordinary* abilities, but *sufficient* abilities, coupled with a willful yet virtuous character, equip men best for positions of power and trust.

In this light, we can see why the detractors of Washington's intellect never got very far. Genius was suspect, because it was beyond the masses' grasp, while wisdom, an attribute cultivated in most men amid the difficulties and challenges of life itself, was rooted in common experience. In the public mind, Washington's evenly balanced virtues and talents made him understandable, predictable, and safe. They were also correlated with his ability to see all sides of an issue—"the big picture"—and to act in ways at once successful and morally proper. Not specialized knowledge and skill, Samuel Mead maintained in his funeral eulogy, but "[e]xtensive views of things ... form the great man."[31] Time and again, the people were told that genius was the corruption of this higher intelligence. "General Washington was great," according to the poet and Yale University President Timothy Dwight, "not by means of that brilliancy of mind often appropriately termed genius and usually coveted for ourselves and our children; and almost as usually attended with qualities, which preclude wisdom. ..."[32]

If the authentically wise man inherits no genius himself, he succeeds in harnessing the genius of others to purposes higher than they might themselves contemplate. To this noble end, Washington's strength of judgment was essential: "Leaving to feebler minds the splendor of genius, which, while it enlightens others, too often dazzles the possessor—he knew how best to use the rays which genius might emit, and carry into act its best conception."[33] As

Gouverneur Morris made this statement, he was probably thinking of Washington's use of the brilliant minds of Jefferson and Hamilton, as well as his moderation of their sometimes extravagant views. Morris's observation was typical. Almost everyone who spoke approvingly of Washington's intellect made reference to its wisdom and judiciousness, and declared these attributes to be of greater value to the nation than the glittering intelligence of its more naturally gifted leaders.[34]

Such was the mind of Washington in the eyes of his countrymen: not a learned or brilliant mind, indeed a mind not unlike that possessed by most men. But in that mind, with its varied and well-balanced qualities, Americans discerned the intellectual basis for their hero's other, invaluable attributes.

Self-Defense Through Self-Control

Of the many virtues imputed to George Washington, none were more ardently celebrated than his solid judgment and serene courage on the battlefield. No aspect of the original perception of the man, however, is more frequently misunderstood today. When Americans look back at the way Washington's own generation beheld him, the image they come up with often underestimates these martial qualities; the original image has been demilitarized. "People did not admire a conquering Caesar in him," observed Garry Wills, "but a Cincinnatus resigning. He embodied the ideal of limited power, restrained and checked, but with a dignified authority."[35] It was indeed the restrained use and the relinquishing of military power that set Washington apart from the other great men his countrymen knew. But it would be a mistake to ignore the fact that Washington was regarded as a real war hero.

From the very beginning of the Revolutionary War, as the poet Philip Freneau reminds us, Washington was the focal symbol of martial ardor. "See Washington New Albion's [New England's] freedom owns, / And moves to war with half Virginia's sons, / Bold in the fight, whose actions might have aw'd / A Roman Hero, or a Grecian God."[36] In everyday prose, too, Americans learned that a great warrior stood in their midst. On January 17, 1777, Virginians picked up their paper and read that the hero of Trenton and Princeton was "one of the greatest generals the world ever saw."[37]

The war ended, but the martial encomiums continued. True, Congress elected Washington President largely because of its trust in his moral character; but many citizens saw the election as an appropriate token of gratitude for his military accomplishments.[38] After assuming the presidency, he was usually referred to as *General* Washington, and sometimes welcomed into cities to the tune of "Hail the Conquering Hero Come." The warrior archetype was also preserved in the portraits and engravings that dressed President Washington in military attire (Fig. 33). Even Gilbert Stuart's decidedly unmilitary *Athenaeum* portrait of Washington, although embraced as soon as it appeared, never replaced the earlier, heroic portraits that showed him in uniform, with sword drawn, or on horseback; the later image was instead added to the earlier one. Expressed in these two variant icons are two different layers of the collective consciousness—one embracing political passion and military zeal; the other, self-restraint and civil moderation. Gilbert Stuart himself reconciled these two tendencies by attaching a presidential head to the body of a military officer presiding over an operation that had occurred twenty years earlier (Fig. 34).

Even at his death, eulogists almost invariably dedicated their works to "General Washington." The very men who celebrated the hero's moral qualities—his public virtue, his disinterestedness, his moderation—also told their listeners of his combative exploits. "He was stronger than a LION," said Jonathan Sewall, "comparable to Samson in his manly prowess."[39] Samuel Macclintock regarded him as "The General and Hero who has slain his thousands, and ten thousands."[40] A "man of war from his youth," Samuel MacWhorter exclaimed; he is "the most eminent, the most prosperous, and the most honored general in modern times."[41] John Brooks, a former aide to Washington, recalled that his victories "thrilled through the hearts and renovated the courage of dejected millions."[42] He was a savior who brought deliverance by the sword. The mythical story about Frederick the Great, the Prussian warlord, sending Washington his own sword and declaring him to be the best general in the world further verified the popular assessment of Washington's martial virtues.

Although presidential achievements were spoken of by every admirer, they were rarely discussed in as much detail as military achievements. The difference in emphasis was partly a matter of expediency, for the military phase of Washington's career was much less controversial than his presidency. Yet, even if the latter had been less stormy, his military virtues would have remained important, for the eighteenth-century American saw in military and moral virtuosity two aspects of the same paragon. Since Washington's military ventures were viewed in a moral as well as technical light, Americans could acknowledge the hero's lack of training and experience without depreciating his soldierly merit. Indeed, Washington's innocence of advanced military technique rendered his achievements, and his reputation as a warrior, all the more stunning.

In its list of the most remarkable events of 1776, the *Boston Gazette* included the spectacle of a "Virginia Farmer" forcing a professional army to evacuate Boston.[43] In doing so, it touched on the essential element in Washington's military reputation—that he was a David facing the British Goliath. Washington's success, however, did not reside in his fighting ability; he succeeded instead by strength of will. On occasion, Washington did outgeneral, even mortify, his enemies; but never did he annihilate them. On the contrary, he was determined to avoid decisive confrontations. Condemning those who criticized Washington for this reason, his admirers set forth the glowing precedent of Fabius, the Roman general who successfully defended his country against Hannibal. Like his predecessor, the "American Fabius," as Washington was called, prevailed against a superior enemy by a prudent campaign of attrition, not by the reckless measures urged upon him by advisors. Dramatic assaults might win temporary acclaim, but they would surely lose the war. Washington won that war by being undramatic:

> Through varying dangers with unequal force,
>   The godlike hero guides the dubious day,
> Faces the proud Howe and checks his haughty course,
>   With Fabian art, victorious by delay.[44]

Washington's victory, in the eyes of America, was a victory of humility over arrogance, perseverance over strategy, will over strength.

On this matter, artists left nothing to the imagination. In one engraving, originally published in a Dublin magazine (Fig. 35), Washington is laureled by an allegory of Fame. At his feet lie the hated documents of British oppression; in his right hand, a scroll setting forth the virtues by which he and his countrymen prevailed. The scroll says nothing of military genius or prowess, but rather tells of "American Freedom established by Valour and Perseverance." Another portrait of Washington (Fig. 36), originally published in Philadelphia, is embellished by symbols of war—cannon, sword, and drum—and supported by a pedestal on which is inscribed a list of his winning qualities: "Temperance," "Prudence," "Fortitude," and "Justice." Here again, no mention is made of military brilliance.

Triumph of Will

Great Britain lost the war, the Americans believed, because it failed to measure up to George Washington's indomitable will. As conceived in the eighteenth century, "will" was a complex notion, but its two main aspects were clearly expressed in classical and religious terms. Through the Stoic tradition, Americans articulated Washington's capacity to persist alone in the face of pain and defeat. Through the Protestant tradition, they articulated the rational, calculated, and systematic quality of his perseverence. Neo-Calvinists saw in Washington "an example of successful control of passion by reason, exemplifying worth of time and method in its distribution, diligence, punctuality and perseverance."[45] This perception goes some way toward explaining why Washington's austere reserve, which makes him appear so cold to us, was admired by so many of his contemporaries and considered by them the very foundation of his military achievements. As Reverend Tomb explained: "His zeal for the public good was eminently tempered with that perfect self-possession, that manly deliberation, that rational coolness which enabled him to conduct all his operations with such order and effect as are the result of a premeditated plan."[46] Viewed in the light of his Stoic-Protestant character, Washington's achievements could be defined as the most dazzling exemplification of strength of will.

As the essence of character, will presupposes something to be overcome, but in the new republic it presupposed no exceptional aptitudes. If Washington led an army to victory, if he brought stability and unity to a new and untried government, it was not because of his talents but in spite of his shortcomings. Weakness, based on natural limitations and inexperience, became a necessary element in the display of heroic resolve. "Had he been neither deflated nor repulsed," John Mason explained, "we have never seen all the grandeur of his soul."[47] Defeats entail adversity, and the belief in redemption through adversity—a belief that was central not only to the Puritan element in American culture but

also to the Stoic values that culture derived from classical learn-
ing—was shared by most of Washington's contemporaries. The
Stoic theme was expressed most artfully, and most famously, in
Addison's *Cato:*

> But grant that others could with equal glory
> Look down on pleasures, and the baits of sense;
> Where shall we find the man that bears affliction,
> Great and majestic in his griefs, like Cato?
> Heavens, with what strength, what steadiness of mind,
> He triumphs in the midst of all his suff'rings!
> How does he rise against a load of woes,
> And thank the gods that throw the weight upon him![48]

Cato's preseverence against misfortune engaged the American
reader because it reinforced his own vision of "the good ruler"
and his corresponding admiration for those whose "firmness and
fortitude of soul . . . enable them to comport with personal incon-
veniences, and stand firm amidst the severest trials, in executing
the duties of their office."[49] Such was the new republic's version
of the political strongman.

Concerned that all men are "exposed to temptations" and that
"human nature at best is very imperfect," Americans believed that
their leaders' resoluteness of will must be sufficient to "[s]uppress
every undue sally" of their own ambitions as well as their enemies'.[50] Counterpoised against the innate lust to power, the will is
in this light always a defensive, never an offensive, agency, and the
greatest triumph of will inheres in self-control and resistance to
superior strength rather than in domination of others. Washington's triumph was thus disclosed. Here was a man who could not
only master events; he could also master himself. His "passions,
by nature strong and irritable, were brought by discipline, into
complete subjugation."[51] Everyone knew he possessed this virtue—or, more precisely, everyone could find some reason to attribute it to him. One observer, for example, wrote about the time
(1798) he saw Washington being escorted from Georgetown to Virginia. During the parade, he recalled, "something at a distance
suddenly attracted [Washington's] attention; his eye was instan-
taneously lighted up as with the lightning's flash. At this moment

I see its marvellous animation, its glowing fire, exhibiting strong passion, controlled by deliberate reason."[52] A more seasoned observer, Gilbert Stuart, projected this same virtue of self-control onto Washington's countenance when he first saw him:

> There were features in his face totally different from what I had observed in any other human being; the sockets of his eyes were larger than whatever I met with before, and the upper part of his nose broader. All his features were indicative of the strongest passions; yet like Socrates his judgement and self-command made him appear a man of different cast in the eyes of the world.[53]

Washington's self-control was deemed essential to his military success, but little was said about it during the war itself. It was "discovered" after America had shifted from a revolutionary to an institutional mood. Sensitive observers could see that the passion for liberty which animated American resistance in the 1770s had become less appropriate during the search for a new order in the late 1780s. Earlier, the libertarian attitude had "produced a fierce and independent spirit, without which the revolution could not have been effected; but it has also in too many created a licentiousness, at present very detrimental, and incompatible with good Government." Self-control alone protected liberty from this kind of licentiousness. Believing that "man is naturally an unruly animal little capable of governing himself, and very averse to control from others," and that such unruliness made one an undutiful subject of any government,[54] many Americans were quick to focus on Washington's self-control and to find in it the very keystone of his character.

Self-mastery was a virtue that could be nicely expressed through astronomical metaphor. If the perfect symmetry of the circle evoked Washington's well-balanced attitudes and talents, the immutability of the planetary orbit (in contrast to the glittering yet self-consuming meteor) compelled recognition of his steadiness in a universe of tumult. Like a heavenly body, Washington traveled a fixed route, neither elated by success nor disheartened by failure, unaffected by the ragings upon which he threw his own heat and light. "Moving in his own orbit," Henry Lee observed, "he took his course, commiserating folly, disdaining vice, dismaying treason, and invigorating despondency."[55]

Occasions for the application of this metaphor were many. Washington's was the steady movement amid seething and flux—

the constant in both the revolutionary and establishmentarian equation. In battle, pervasive sentiments of apprehension and danger were never evident in his bearing and conduct. "When surrounded by the greatest dangers," Caleb Alexander told his Presbyterian congregation, "he never disclosed to those near his person, by a look or change of voice, nor rash action, his own apprehensions.... A rare instance of bravery and self-command."[56] Similarly, in political life Washington resented unwarranted criticisms and intrigues, but he never expressed this resentment publicly. His actions were uniformly calculated and deliberate, never the result of fear or antagonism. Jeremiah Smith, a New Hampshire statesman, recalled in another sermon how Washington "stood collected in himself, like a rock in a tempestuous sea, unmoved by the storms of popular fury that beat upon him."[57] Thus restrained, he exhibited "those noble exertions of mind" which, according to longstanding Whig tradition, all civil rulers require:

> The art of self-denial must be learned and frequently practised by them;—a prevailing attachment to their own private interests and gratifications be given up to the public—angry resentments be tempered down to the standard of right action.... [58]

The vast social consequences of this one man's self-possession were made plain. Military victory was due to Washington alone. When all other sources of inspiration failed, the army's bravery and determination were sustained by his example. Commitment to the military cause was faltering everywhere, but in the midst of treason, astonishment, fear, irresoluteness, and despondency, Washington remained erect and unmoved. His was "a spirit unbroken by adversity," Jeremiah Smith declared—"a spirit, which not only enabled him to sustain the weight of cares, which devolved on him, but served to revive and animate his fainting troops."[59]

The long years that followed the war were also "big with prodigies and monsters—when the elements of social connection seemed in a state of separation, when the moral world was fast falling into chaos." Old traditions of deference and privilege that had previously restrained the vulgar were losing their grip, and as the respectable classes' inveterate dread of licentiousness and mobocracy became acute, Washington reacted strongly against domestic uprising. As he left his presidential desk to take personal

command of the military expedition against the whisky tax rebellion, the New England Federalist cadence, inspired by a yearning
for stability and order, grew especially audible. By moving against
popular insurrection, Washington preserved order, checked the
excesses of democracy, and saved America from the fate of post-
revolutionary France.[60]

Commitment to the political cause—the cause of national union
and the national interest—was even less secure and less understood. Assailed mercilessly by demands for action against the British on France's behalf, Washington, as President, served this union
and defended this interest in spite of the confusion and passionate criticism that raged about him. Again Washington opposed his
will to the great deluge and, again, he saved the republic. And so
Washington, as military commander, delivered his countrymen
from their enemy; as chief magistrate, he saved them from themselves.

To a people motivated by the virtue of moderation, Washington's soft side made attractive the more severe aspects of his inflexible will. No one, therefore, failed to mention the great man's
compassion and generosity. If this man could distinguish himself
as the instrument of his nation's vengeance, he could also set himself apart by his benevolence. Fearful blows against the enemy any
commander is duty-bound to inflict, but forbearance is discre-
tionary and stems from personal sympathy and mercy.[61] In the
stories of young Washington's Virginia militia days, this virtue
found vivid illustration. On one occasion, the young colonel and
his companion were led through the forest by an Indian guide.
Suddenly, the Indian whirled and took aim with his rifle. The shot
missed. Washington seized the betrayer, only to set him free later.
A magnanimous gesture—and grist for the poetic mill: "And mark
his nobleness of soul / In one so young and warm / Although the
savage he did take, / He done to him no harm."[62]

Several months later, Washington put on a similar display. He
and a certain William Payne met at the Fairfax Courthouse and
discussed the merits of different candidates for the Virginia assembly. Out of affection for his favorite, who differed from Payne's,
Washington provoked an argument and offended Payne, who
knocked him to the ground. Immediately, Washington's friends

prepared to punish his assailant, but Washington dissuaded them from doing so. Instead, the humiliated young colonel conceded his fault and offered Payne an apology. "In what history ancient or modern, sacred or profane," Mason Weems asked, could a more moving instance of heroic valour be found? "Joseph forgiving his brethren in the land of Egypt; David sparing that inveterate seeker of his life, Saul; Sir Walter Raleigh pardoning the young man who spat in his face; afford, it is true, charming specimens of the sublime and the beautiful in action.... But yet none of them have gone beyond WASHINGTON in the affair of Payne."[63] Never mind that Joseph, David, and Raleigh did little or nothing to provoke their offenders; the parallel is accurate enough—for all practical purposes. It provides yet another example of Washington's unwillingness to exploit his powers to full use. His "forgiveness" was a prophetic instance of the resignation of power. More than twenty-five years later, this same theme, exemplified in Washington's humane treatment of British prisoners (including the immediate release of Cornwallis and his soldiers after their surrender at Yorktown), was noted and celebrated by many. "As you have seen his fortitude under the severest shocks of fortune, so have you known his humanity after success. The vanquished found in him, not an implacable victor, but a generous and sympathizing friend."[64] Thus if Washington reconciled the Puritan belief in strength through adversity to the Roman virtues of *gravitas* (seriousness), *pietas* (regard for discipline and authority), and *integritas* (serene stoicism), he also stood for the milder virtues of compassion and mercy. Finding in Washington the strength and determination of the noble Roman and the understanding and charity of the Christian, the people also found in him something, they hoped, of themselves.

Piety: The Ultimate Virtue

George Washington's conduct convinced most Americans that he was a good Christian, but those possessing first-hand knowledge of his religious convictions had reasons for doubt. Shortly after his retirement from the presidency, for example, Washington was presented with a congratulatory address signed by twenty-four Philadelphia clergymen. The address was deliberately composed with a view to eliciting from Washington a public affirmation of his Christian faith—something he had never issued before. But on this occasion, too, he was reticent. His reply was polite, but devoid of any reference to his own religious beliefs. Bishop White, the man who read the address to Washington, was certain of the reason for his failure to testify. "I do not believe," he confessed many years after Washington's death, "that any degree of recollection will bring to my mind any fact which would prove General Washington to have been a believer in the Christian revelations; further than as may be hoped from his constant attendance on Christian worship...." Reverend Ashbel Green, who wrote the address, entertained a more charitable view, ascribing Washington's reserve to "the proprieties of his station."[65] Few Americans knew about this little episode, but if it had been publicized, most would have subscribed to the opinion of Reverend Green.

Few things were taken more seriously in the new republic than religion, and few things created more dissension. Conflicts among the churches were correlated with, and intensified, conflicts among regional and economic interests. Yet, there was consensus on a number of fundamental points. The vast majority of the population shared a belief in the existence of God and the soul, worried about salvation, and was committed to the moral principles that God handed down through his agents. In every discussion about the qualifications of good leaders, therefore, an unwavering religiosity was deemed essential. Thus Phillips Payson announced in his Boston Election Day sermon that

> political knowledge, a sense of honor, an open and generous mind, it is confessed, will direct and urge a ruler to actions and exertions, beneficial to the State. And if added to these, he has a principle of religion, and the fear of God, it will, in the best manner, fit him for the whole course of allotted duty. The greatest restraints, the noblest motives, and the best supports arise from our holy religion. The pious ruler, is by far, the most likely to promote the public good.[66]

Few would have argued with Payson. Reading and quoting the Bible more widely than any other book,[67] most Americans believed that the virtues required of a republic were the products of religion. Religious messages were therefore molded to the prevailing political temper. Appealing to anxieties associated with that temper, David Tappan stated that "[t]he religion, which we teach and promote is emphatically the guardian angel" of liberty.[68] Two years later, in his funeral oration, Thaddeus Fiske added: "Without religious principle, great abilities and peculiar opportunities are always liable to be perverted to the purposes of mischief."[69]

In Washington's religious piety Americans found a balm for their political worries. Washington, they said, acknowledged that the moral standards embodied in religion were superior to his personal accomplishments. Did not the prayers he ordered after every military victory prove that he wished no credit for himself? In the hands of such a man, a man humbled by the thought of God, a man dedicated to the advancement of His glory alone, the scepter of civil power could be confidently placed. Even after that scepter was given him, Washington proved the authenticity of his piety by exploiting every opportunity, from his first Inaugural Address to his Farewell Address, to venerate publicly his Creator. In a way that everyone could understand, Washington's submissiveness to God restated, on a different level, his submissiveness to popular will. His political and religious virtues were deemed two aspects of the same thing.

Washington's piety was articulated not only by men who believed in the God of the Bible but also by nonbelievers whose views on religion were strictly utilitarian. The true intentions of these "immoral philosophists" or "atheists" were, of course, questioned by many. "[T]hough their talents may be brilliant," warned David McClure, "their motives are despicable and dangerous."[70] Eager to divest themselves of this image and to affirm their good will toward traditional religion, many secular-minded men claimed Washington as one of their own. Abraham Clarke made this claim in an address to his Masonic brothers:

> The superstitious bigot, guided by an unenlightened zeal, [shall no longer] asperse our order, or dare to assert, that there is any thing in Masonry repugnant to genuine piety, or the tenets of the Christian religion—To silence calumnies like these, we need only say, that the "first of all men, first of heroes, and first of statesmen" presided in our lodges.[71]

Mr. Clarke's defense was convincing to his audience; but more importantly, it revealed the continuing strength of religious forces in a society that had been deeply influenced by the Enlightenment. Indeed, the burden of accommodation in America between religious morality and secular morality fell almost exclusively on proponents of the latter. The secular moralist had to show that his views were consistent with those of the religious majority, not the other way around. Thus, if the freethinking Masons regarded Washington as a soul brother, they made no attempt to secularize his image; nor would they have seen in such a venture any useful consequence. Following a tradition transmitted from Cicero, through Machiavelli, to their own contemporaries like Paine and Jefferson, the less pious men of the time saw in religion a necessary and assured support of civil society. Although guided in their own conduct by secular traditions, they felt that only religion could unite the masses and induce their submission to custom and law. So they joined their orthodox countrymen in attributing to the hero a deep religious devotion.

Nonbelievers, proponents of natural religion, and religious moderates did not go so far as to portray Washington as an instrument of divine intervention, but they were effusive in their praise of his piety. Toward religion as well as politics, they said, his attitudes were balanced and temperate. He pursued "the happy mean between the extremes of levity and gloominess, indifference and austerity."[72] His regular attendance at a house of God was never overlooked, nor were his public addresses, in which he acknowledged the assistance of the Deity in establishing the new republic and recommended religion as a secure foundation for public morals. He sought aid from "the source of Light and Being," and to this Creator he gave credit in the day of his success," Moses Cleaveland maintained in his Masonic eulogy.[73] Even for the most "liberated" of his countrymen, then, Washington's regard for religion constituted a notable part of his character.

In contrast, Americans of neo-Calvinist and neorevivalist persuasions saw Washington as the executor of God's plan. God had made him childless so that he could be the father of all. He was a "Gift from God," raised up from youth "for the salvation of his country"; a deliverer who presided over the Revolution, itself "fixed in the divine mind long before it took place."[74] As the youthful Ralph Waldo Emerson, in 1814, conceived it: "The God of Israel heard our groans and cries / And bade to life a WASHINGTON arise."[75] On this point the New Englanders were most insistent, but many Southerners, too, could agree that Washington was "the man designed by heaven" to see through the cause.[76]

Washington's many narrow escapes as a Virginia colonel reinforced the belief that he was under God's special protection. The people knew that many French and Indian rifle balls had whistled past him rather than through him, and like the legendary Indian who had taken seventeen good shots at him without effect, they believed that Washington was not born to die at the hands of an enemy. Reverend Samuel Davies' famous prophecy, pronounced in 1755, had become the touchstone of American confidence in their hero's divine sponsorship: "I may point out to the public that heroic youth, Colonel Washington, whom I cannot but hope Providence has hitherto preserved in so signal a manner, for some important service to his country."[77] But if God blessed the nation with a savior as a reward for its righteousness, He would also take him away in retaliation for its iniquity. Washington's death was seen by neo-Calvinists as God's way of inciting a return to the true path.[78] Through both acts—the giving and the reclaiming of a deliverer—the doctrine of divine intervention and the virtue of piety were reaffirmed.

In what the pious American believed to be an age of infidelity, Washington was a symbol of faith. Time and again, orthodox spokesmen made the point that he "was not ashamed" of his religious convictions and "did not disdain to acknowledge and adore a GREATER SAVIOR whom Infidels and Deists affect to slight and despise."[79] For this same reason—that Washington was "no less eminent for his Christian piety than his other virtues"—the Charleston (South Carolina) City Council recommended at the time of his death that all the city's pulpits as well as its civic offices be draped in black.[80] Thus, for the religious people of America, who made up the vast majority, Washington embodied and reinforced sacred values challenged by the wave of secularism that swept through the country in the late eighteenth century.

As President, Washington regularly attended Christian services, and he was friendly in his attitude toward Christian values. However, he repeatedly declined the church's sacraments. Never did he take communion, and when his wife, Martha, did, he waited for her outside the sanctuary. Noticing this, Reverend James Abercrombie of Philadelphia once looked directly at Washington and wondered publicly when the President might choose to set a good example by presenting himself before the Holy Altar. The President politely shook the minister's hand after the service, and never showed up in his church on a Sacrament Sunday again.[81] Even on his deathbed Washington asked for no ritual, uttered no prayer to Christ, and expressed no wish to be attended by His representative.

George Washington's practice of Christianity was limited and superficial because he was not himself a Christian. In the enlightened tradition of his day, he was a devout Deist—just as many of the clergymen who knew him suspected.[82] Thus, Mason Weems could tell his readers that Washington's life and death "furnish glorious proof of the infinite importance of religion," but his account of Washington's piety was partly expressed in Deist terms: Washington believed in a "particular providence," in the "everpresent parent and preserver of men," in "the Great Governor of the world." Weems made reference to Washington's role as a Masonic Grandmaster, and as if to recognize Freemasonry as the institutional seat of Deism, he listed the virtues it extolled.[83]

Weems never criticized the secular premises of Deism, but he felt contempt for Deist critics of Christianity and used Washington as a vehicle to express that feeling. Weems might have privately regarded Washington himself as a Deist, but he never said so publicly. In the midst of all his allusions to Deism, he told his readers in no uncertain terms that Washington was a Christian and that he derived all his virtues from his Christian upbringing and beliefs. In this respect, Weems's message was emphatically antisecular. Condemning Thomas Paine's *Age of Reason*, for example, he asked:

> Can you reject so innocent a person as Christ, and court for your guide to heaven such a blind slave to his lusts as Mr. Paine who (if common report be true) has no other church but the ale-house, and whose palsied legs can scarce bear him tottering to that sink of vomiting and filth?.... Embrace the religion of Christ.... This was the religion of your fathers. This was the religion of your WASHINGTON.[84]

Although Weems made much of Washington's belief in Christ, and of his attendance at Christian worship, he said little of Washington's relationship to the distinguishing concepts of Christianity. Weems never portrayed him as a redeemed sinner, and rarely as a man whose life was directed by the Christian virtues of faith, hope, and love. Often, in fact, he compared him with the pagan heroes of ancient Greece and Rome. On the other hand, Weems saw no incongruity in likening Washington's virtues to Christ's as well as to those of classical antiquity, and his readers seemed to be engaged rather than repelled by the combination. Thus, Weems's use of classical allusions did not, as one writer has recently suggested, reflect his countrymen's new, secularized image of Washington.[85] Indeed, Weems's first edition was completed before Washington's death, and the very audience that responded so favorably to his classical models also responded favorably to the funeral eulogies, which were saturated with Mosaic imagery and published the same year as the Weems biography.

The Moses-Washington analogy was not invoked because of religious sentiment alone; it was also an allusion that articulated the nation's changing political situation in familiar religious terms. During the Revolutionary War, Mosaic allusions legitimated the American cause and clarified the moral significance of Washington's role as military leader. Regarding themselves as heirs to a promised land, Americans saw in their declaration of political independence a fulfillment of the ancient covenant and, in their new leader, a reincarnation of the faithful Hebrew deliverer. The parallels had special relevance in Puritan New England, but they were drawn thickly, and with conviction, everywhere. To Egypt and its Pharoah were likened Britain and its King, the latter being the most recent in a long line of liberty's enemies. But "kind heaven, pitying the abject and servile condition of our American Israel, gave us a second Moses, who should, (under God) be our future deliverer from the bondage and tyranny of haughty Britain."[86]

At the end of the eighteenth century, Mosaic allusions infused religious meaning into the building of a new government and articulated the significance of Washington's role as chief magistrate. Now a more comprehensive analogy could be drawn. As Americans became convinced more than ever that their country was the New Israel, the whole story of Washington's life was merged with that of the savior of ancient Israel. Washington, like Moses, was called to his mission from domestic ease and tranquility. Moses and Washington were of nearly the same age when they undertook their missions. Both men led an approximately equal number of people to emancipation from foreign rule. Moses faced a superior foe with little likelihood of success; so did Washington. Moses suffered detractors among his own following; Washington did, too. The leader of the New Israel, like the leader of the Old, placed no relatives in positions of power. Just as Moses died at the point of bringing his nation to Canaan, Washington succumbed just before his nation's government was settled in its new capital. And if Moses left his followers "sage legislation" (Deuteronomy), Washington's Farewell Address was regarded by his people as his most enduring legacy.[87]

That most of these parallels are far-fetched, that they could link Washington to many other great men, is necessarily so, and signal proof that the Moses-Washington analogy was *created* (in the context of political crisis) rather than *discovered* in the careers of the men in question. In its main aspect, the creation was retrospective; it involved a selective rendition of Old Testament history, a harnessing of the past to the Whig heroic ideal. Thus, if Washington were to be regarded as the American Moses, Moses had to become the Jewish Washington. The values that Washington represented— public virtue, disinterestedness, moderation, resoluteness and self-control, and religious piety—had to be projected backward in time. And so they were.

Washington's selfless public virtue was prefigured in Moses, who "endured unintermitted and unparallel toils and hardships," yet was moved by "no consideration in comparison with the public good." Moses, like Washington, was ready to sacrifice his fame and become a man of "no reputation." Like Washington, Moses was disinterested. He "appears to have been a stranger to ambition. He sought none of the high offices which he filled." Only "the command of GOD, and assurances of His presence and aid, could have forced him from his calm and delightful retreat." In Moses, as in Washington, Americans could find clear evidence of moderation. Moses' extraordinary humility revealed itself as soon as he was called to his mission. ("Who am I, that I should go unto Pharoah and that I should bring forth the children of Israel out of Egypt?" [Exodus iii:11]) As to the compass and balance of Moses' abilities, "No human character probably ever combined greater, more numerous, or more useful talents. . . . " Was Washington resolute and self-controlled? So was Moses. He endured with "dignity and calmness" the hardships of his mission and the complaints and ingratitude of his followers. And he was "so great a master of his passions, that he lived as though he had none. . . . " Was Washington pious and submissive to the will of God? So was Moses. God chose him out of all men and "sanctified him in his faithfulness."[88]

This many-faceted parallel, which assimilates Old Testament history to Whig political aspirations and ideals, amplified the American people's conception of Washington and of themselves. It invested both with a meaning, a power, and a sense of destiny that neither would have otherwise possessed.

7

The Image Enhanced

STANDING FAR ABOVE the nation's other founders in public affection, George Washington had become the object of a national religion whose chief precept was the sacredness of republicanism. This is essentially what John Adams meant by his reluctant but sincere admission: "I glory in the character of Washington because I know him to be an exemplification of the American character."[1] To see Washington in this way is to see him as a symbol of the values and tendencies of his society, and not as an innovative, charismatic hero who was the source of such values and tendencies. Indeed, Washington did not merely deviate from this more traditional conception of heroic leadership; he was its very antithesis. Great charismatic leaders like Cromwell and Napoleon exuded confidence in their extraordinary abilities, loved power, and used it to bring about radical change. Washington, in contrast, was diffident, uncomfortable with power, and committed to the traditions of his society. If the American Revolution is viewed as an essentially conservative uprising—a struggle not to create a new order but to restore and maintain ancient liberties and rights—then it found its perfect symbolic expression in the image of Washington. Expressing the new republic's first conception of heroic leadership, that image revealed the virtues which Americans wished to live up to. It also depicted, by implication, the vices they wished to avoid:

Self-sacrifice	Self-indulgence
Disinterestedness	Ambition
Moderation	Excess
Resoluteness and Self-control	Licentiousness
Piety	Religious Indifference

Toward the self-centered, ambitious, and impious leaders of both present and past the Americans expressed disdain or, at best, suspicion. Toward the simpler, more modest qualities attributed to George Washington—public-mindedness, moderation, firmness, piety—they expressed reverence. In doing so, Washington's admirers reinvigorated their dual heritage of moral restraint and political liberty.

Since the qualities of Washington worth thinking about were those associated with concerns already present in the collective consciousness, the statements made about him may be taken as neither valid nor invalid but as more or less appropriate. But are we then to regard Washington as a tabula rasa, a blank slate on which any message can be written, any value expressed? For the purpose of abstracting the man's symbolic significance from his actual motives and conduct, this assumption may be justifiable, but it ignores something important: the relationship between the man as he really was and the man the public knew. Because they suspected the true character of any man in whom they invested power, this relationship was a matter of great concern to eighteenth-century Americans. Their desire to know the real Washington was motivated by political qualms, not biographical curiosity.

The Public and Private Washington

Every man takes pains to conceal his vices from public view. For this reason the revelation of the real Washington, most Americans believed, had to be based on a consideration of his private life. Parson Weems acknowledged this belief in the first editions of his biography, whose long subtitle told the reader that it would contain "many curious and valuable ANECDOTES tending to throw much light on the *private* as well as *public* life and character" of the hero. In the introduction to his sixth edition, Weems elaborated the rationale for this emphasis. Although Washington was regarded by his countrymen as a great man, he noted, they had based their judgment on "greatness of public character, which is no evidence of *true greatness*, for a public character is often an artificial one." Take a man like Hannibal, or the Duke of Marlborough. "[L]et him be thrust back into the shade of private life, and you will see how soon, like a plant robbed of its hot bed, he will drop his false foliage and fruit, and stand forth confessed in . . . sterility and worthlessness. . . . It is not then in the glare of *public* but in the shade of *private life*, that we are to look for the man."[2]

The questions that Americans asked themselves about Washington, then, revolved around the issue of his "real" self. What if he were motivated by the desire for personal profit rather than collective well-being? What if he were merely using history to his own advantage? What if below a surface of patriotic magnanimity lurked a spirit of vanity and ambition? To a generation whose greatest fear was not the flagrant violator of public trust but "the patriot who would contribute to the welfare of the whole with external diligence and activity and would perform such duties out of motives of self-interest,"[3] these questions came naturally. Had not Washington been accused repeatedly in the Republican press of moral turpitude? Had not Thomas Paine, darling of Republican publicists, registered the same charge in his open letter? Against such charges, strong defenses had to be, and were, mobilized. First, defenders disparaged the motives of Washington's opponents. The Republicans, they said, were playing politics in order to win more power for themselves. Thomas Paine might appear to be an objective observer, but he could not be taken seriously because his personal grievances were trumpeted, never examined, by Republicans. Besides, he was an infidel. The cornerstone of the defense, however, was a convincing positive demonstration that Washington's good deeds were essential, not incidental (let alone contrived), manifestations of his character.

If Washington's greatness were authentic, its omens would be found in childhood, a period in life when deception is not possible. Thus Samuel Tomb inquired into the hero's youth and discovered that "[t]he principle of true patriotism, and of every heroic and humane virtue were congenial with his infant constitution."[4] Likewise, Thomas Thacher told his listeners that Washington attended to studies and household duties "at an age when young gentlemen of fortune are too apt to be rioting in luxury and dissipation."[5] The hero's future sacrifices on behalf of the public were presaged by his youthful sacrifices on behalf of his family, as when he renounced a desired naval career at the solicitation of his mother. He also gave signs, as a youth, that he would be the man whose wise and good policies would one day unite his contentious countrymen. "While yet at school," explained Elisha Dick, "his deportment was such as to procure him the confidence and respect of his younger companions: He was the common arbiter of their juvenile disputations, and his decisions were conclusive and satisfactory."[6] In this biography, newly reconstructed, the republic gained assurance for what it already believed. Through life, as Mason Weems put it, "the admirable harmony of his virtues . . . were the same *yesterday and today*"[7] Washington was "in essence," "in the first place," "all along," and "in the final analysis," a moral hero.

As Washington's essential virtue had its roots in his childhood, it could also be confirmed by inspecting the comportment of his domestic life. Vividly did he distinguish himself in this setting. "First in war—first in peace—first in the hearts of his countrymen, he was second to none in the humble and endearing scenes of private life. . . . his example was as edifying to all around him, as were the effects of that example lasting. . . . [T]he purity of his private character," Henry Lee added, "gave effulgence to his public virtues."[8] In the midst of his family, far from the view of even his closest neighbor, he displayed all the tender aspects of human character. There especially were witnessed his profound humanity and beneficence. The more intimately he was known, the more he was loved, for beneath the polished image of public perfection no private blemishes could be found. Washington was the perfect husband, and he was devoted to his wife's children and grandchildren. In the eyes of other family members, his virtues were such that not so much as a harsh word was ever uttered against him.[9]

Even the unfortunate stranger felt Washington's benevolence. Throughout the war, he gave instruction to his Mount Vernon steward to maintain hospitality to the poor, and when present himself, as one of Mason Weems's "anecdotes" revealed, he never degraded his suppliants by keeping them waiting "like a Negro slave," as was customary among his privileged neighbors. "Knowing the great value of time and of good tempers to them," Weems explained, "he could not bear that they should lose these by long waiting, and shuffling, and blowing their fingers at his lordly door. ... [Even] if he was in company with the greatest characters on the Continent when his servant informed him that a poor man wished to speak to him, he would instantly beg them to excuse him for a moment and go and wait on him."[10] This story is fabricated out of familiar material. From Washington's well-known public gestures, like the voluntary resignation of military and political power, as from his lesser-known private gestures, like magnanimity toward enemies and reluctance to cause lesser men to wait for his charity, one draws out a common element: the refusal to exercise power at the expense of others. Each gesture—the big and the small, the famous and the obscure—restates and amplifies the virtue of political restraint.

Even though much was known about Washington's youth and private life, much was left to the imagination. While Washington lived, formal portraits of his family could be reproduced and distributed (and, in eulogy, his private life could be discussed); but "candid" portraits, like those depicting him as a child, or as an adult engaged in strictly personal pursuits (see Figs. 37–39), would have violated the existing canons of social distance. These kinds of paintings did not appear until the mid-nineteenth-century, but they are nevertheless useful to our understanding of the eighteenth-century mind, for they depict mental images that, though not then iconically representable, must have been evoked by verbal recitations of the hero's private virtues. Thus Figure 37 shows the youthful Washington mediating a dispute between two boys of different social background: the son of a backwoodsman and the privileged son of a gentleman. Young Washington looks at neither contestant as he separates them. He looks straight ahead, in a way that prefigured his just nonpartisanship as President. Figure 38 depicts Mason Weems's anecdote about Washington's praying at Valley Forge. To demonstrate that his piety was genuine, not merely contrived for public consumption, the artist added foliage to the naked trees of winter in order to conceal from Washington an observer (upper right in the picture) who accidently passes by.[11] In Figure 39 the great man is shown in the home of an afflicted widow and her daughter. Beyond public view, he writes out a check to help relieve the family's burden. The artists' interpretations of Washington's private virtues thus reiterated the virtues his public life was already known to embody.

At a time when the people were not entitled to pry freely into the intimate lives of their leaders, the most private of all Washington's documents, his last will and testament, was open to public inspection. It is difficult to imagine the will's having being published without Washington's expressed desire (which would follow from his lifelong concern for his reputation) or without his family's consent. Whatever the motivation, the appearance of this document in the public press enlarged the people's knowledge of Washington's benevolence. Everyone now knew that he had provided generous sums for education. Everyone now knew that the slaves he kept during his lifetime (because of unspecified "conditions" in the Southern states) were not only granted freedom at his wife's death but also prepared for freedom by money set aside for their training and instruction, or for sustenance in old age. In these acts of domestic benevolence, political values were reaffirmed. "Thus uniform in all his conduct was this FRIEND of the Rights of Mankind—thus consistent were his Republican principles."[12] To this revelation Mrs. Washington lent weight when she emancipated all her slaves the year after her husband's death.

In the matter of moderation as well as beneficence, Washington's "private character as well as his public one will bear the strictest scrutiny. He was punctual in all his engagements—upright and honest in his dealings—temperate in his enjoyments—liberal and hospitable to an eminent degree—a lover of order—systematical and methodical in all his arrangements."[13] This exactness and regularity were extended to his family as well as his business contacts. Even on his deathbed, Washington's doctors told their readers, "he economized his time in arranging his affairs and anticipated his death with every demonstration of equanimity, for which his whole life has been so uniformly and singularly conspicuous."[14]

The panegyric did not end there. So authentic and sincere a man was Washington that he displayed his characteristic virtues in the face of death itself. His doctors' account of his very last moments, which appeared in every major newspaper (and reappeared, highly embellished, in eulogies and in Mason Weems's biography), reiterated the continuity of his moral character. Just as Washington silently endured military defeat and, later, the harangues of vile and ill-meaning critics, so at the end, though in extreme pain, not a groan or even a sigh escaped him. He faced the end with supreme dignity, accepting medications and treatment only to oblige his wife. At the point of death, he bade his physicians not to trouble themselves further and, just before he expired, closed his own eyes.[15] And so, Washington died a "rational death," a death awaited and accepted with self-control and presence of mind. This death was also a feat of self-affirmation, for by evincing in the secrecy of his final moments those qualities publicly displayed during two decades of national service, Washington abolished the last doubts of a suspicious society.

The Real Washington—and the "Washington Myth"

Many of Washington's contemporaries recognized that a great man's admirers often deceive themselves by ignoring his vices and conjuring up only praiseworthy attributes and deeds. Yet, most of them believed that Washington's virtues were unmarred by human failings, that no discrepancy lay between the public man and the real man. Hardly anyone today would believe such human perfection to be possible, and their doubts, if applied to Washington, would be well founded. In the daily management of his affairs, national and domestic, he was a flesh-and-blood man who did not always live up to the people's conception of private virtue.

Praised publicly for his self-possession and even temper, Washington often revealed his passions and moodiness in private. He was pessimistic and given to brooding. In his social relations he was correct, but rarely warm. There was a distinct crankiness, even meanness, about him. At Mount Vernon, "under my vine and fig tree," as he was fond of saying, Washington was a hard taskmaster. He supervised his employees and slaves closely, and no one, it seemed, was industrious enough for him. When advised during his presidency of the lengthy illness of one of his slaves, he wrote back in a fury: "[F]or every day Betty Davis works she is laid up two. —If she is indulged in this idleness she will grow worse and worse. . . . " A month passed, and still the woman had not recovered. What was to be done with this "lazy, deceitful and impudent huzzy . . . ?" Washington fumed: "If pretended ailments, without apparent causes, or visible effects, will screen her from work, I shall get no service at all from her."

Poor Betty Davis was not the only servant to incur Washington's wrath. "What sort of lameness is Dick's," the President asked, "that he should have been confined with it for so many weeks?" And "what is the matter with Ruth and Ben ... that week after week they are returned sick?" Had Carpenter James injured himself? "He is a very worthless fellow; indeed I have sometimes suspected that he cuts himself on purpose to lay up."[16] And so it went. Behind every physical ailment and every slowdown in work Washington saw the likelihood of malingering. Residing in Philadelphia, he may have had some doubts about his presidential judgment, but he rarely extended the benefit of any doubt to those at Mount Vernon. Occasionally, a slave gave Washington something certain to complain about by running away from the estate. The President would bear the expense of capture, but added, hypocritically, "I would not have my name appear in any advertisement, or any measure, leading to it."[17] The master's hand was not only strong but also invisible.

Other leaders of the Revolution, when called to public service, retained responsibility for the conduct of their estates, but none so compulsively as Washington, and none, probably, with as much prodding and scolding. This was especially true in business and money matters. Whoever made the mistake of sending him the wrong merchandise, whoever failed to repay a loan, received a biting and often insulting reprimand. What caused this otherwise polite and self-possessed man to express himself so coarsely? Whether it was moral outrage or extreme fondness for money is difficult to say. Washington was the man who refused a salary for public service, but he was also the man who made several thousand dollars in stud fees from the donkey he received as a gift from the King of Spain. Clearly, his private motives in financial matters differed from those which ruled his public conduct.

Intolerance was an equally conspicuous part of Washington's makeup. He may not have been a cruel man, but as a General he did not hesitate to declare insufficient the number of lashes that Congress had allotted for his soldiers' ordinary offenses.[18] As for extraordinary offenses, like the 1781 mutiny in New Jersey, Washington had greater powers, and he made full use of them. "You will instantly execute a few of the most active and incendiary leaders,"[19] he instructed his officers. Such was Washington's military justice. Example, not due process, was his ruling principle. That principle may have been shared by other American officers, but Washington's inflexible adherence to it was not. It is hard to believe, for example, that these officers would not have extended to their own men the compassion they felt for Major John André, a young British officer caught behind American lines with information in his possession that would have assisted the British army in capturing West Point. The serene courage and dignity with which this man faced death softened the hearts of many, and they wished to see the letter of the law bent in his favor. But Washington, in what was unquestionably his most unpopular decision of the war, remained unmoved. Knowing that his fate had been determined, André requested that he be executed with dignity, by firing squad. Washington hanged him. Alexander Hamilton, already convinced that his commander had a "heart of stone," complained that "some people are only sensitive to the motives of policy."[20]

Washington's sensitivity to criticism was another trait that his countrymen would have found displeasing. No one knew this better than General Nathaniel Greene, who was censured by Washington on account of the capture of a fort that Washington himself should have ordered vacated.[21] The incident was typical. Washington was more than willing to share with others the public congratulation that followed his successes, but he was also inclined to make others responsible for tragedies that resulted from his mistakes.

Enough disparaging things have been said about George Washington to permit the raising of a question about his contemporaries. Why did people who were so doubtful about human perfection attribute it so readily to this one man? Lack of biographical information is one plausible reason. The private documents that now prompt even the most sympathetic scholars to set forth the flaws in Washington's character were simply not available to his own countrymen. And while it is true that many men knew Washington personally and were aware of his imperfections, the sheer force of his reputation inhibited them from making their knowledge public. But perhaps the single most convincing reason why Washington was seriously regarded as a flawless man is that his reputation was based on virtues that were demonstrable and above suspicion. Whatever his private failings, in the matter of political conviction there was little in the way of criticism to assert. Over the past two hundred years, every indicator of his inner thoughts, from public and private conduct to letters and reading habits, has been scrutinized by hundreds of scholars, and not one has ever doubted his patriotic dedication.[22] Given his own countrymen's will to believe in his total perfection, it was easy for them to project, by means of a kind of "halo effect," the visible merits of Washington's public career to the invisible realm of his private life.

The brightness of Washington's halo, however, was intensified by the fact that his personal affairs were actually less private than most people believed. His last days of life, spent in the seclusion of his own bedroom, suggest as much. Since so much was actually known about them, those final moments could not have been secret, although the public probably assumed that Washington thought they were. Having been in the national spotlight for twenty-five years, however, Washington must have realized that his dying words and gestures would be reported in the press by his secretary and doctors. He must have realized that lithographs of himself on his deathbed would be widely distributed. Washington's last moments were public moments, and his awareness of this fact probably affected the way he used them.

Washington had always worked earnestly to cultivate a favorable impression of himself. That this effort stemmed from a deep yearning for public recognition is amply attested to in letters that go back to his Virginia militia days. In the most vehement of these letters, written long before independence from Great Britain was even conceived, the young Colonel announced his desire for a commission in the regular British army. So earnestly did Washington pursue this appointment that critics who knew about the letters wondered publicly during his presidency whether he might have turned his sword against his own country rather than against Britain if his wish had been fulfilled. On that interesting question no one can argue, one way or the other, with conviction. However, Washington's letters do show that he was not content to be a mere colonial militia officer. His desire for a higher, more prestigious station was symptomatic of what his biographers, almost to a man, take to be the main flaw in his character, namely, an intense and deep-seated vanity.

It remains for the psychohistorian to reveal the childhood sources of Washington's egotism. But, whatever those sources may have been, they will not allow us to separate Washington's adult egotism from his commitment to his country's ideals. Both traits, egotism and patriotism, fed off yet reinforced the other; they were inextricable in the man and his life. The egotistical side of Washington, however, was concealed from the public at large because it was expressed in a socially acceptable way: through the pursuit of fame.

In the late eighteenth century, vanity was understood, as it is understood today, as a form of self-love, but fame was not. Instead, fame was regarded as a kind of moral brass, minted to drive out the immoral currency of ambition. A love of fame, and a readiness to bestow it, were necessary safeguards against tyranny. True, men who "panted for glory" *too* earnestly were charged with common conceit (a criticism to which Washington himself was by no means immune), but the aspiration was not in itself a cause for reproach. On the contrary, by accepting the praise of their countrymen as sufficient compensation for public service, patriotic leaders demonstrated their indifference to power. Accordingly, when Alexander Hamilton considered the faults of Aaron Burr, he observed that "Mr. Burr has never appeared solicitous of fame, and that great ambition unchecked by principle, or [by] the love of Glory, is an unruly Tyrant who never can keep long in a course which good men will approve." Conversely, when Washington announced to the world that he was motivated solely by the desire for "reputation," he was not only confessing to his egotism but also conforming to his culture's code of honor.[23]

If this were not the case, Washington would have never expressed so candidly, in private and public correspondence, his pleasure at gaining in reputation. After the siege of Boston, for example, he told his brother of his delight "to hear from different Quarters, that my reputation stands fair, that my conduct hitherto has given universal satisfaction. The addresses which I have received, and which I suppose will be published . . . will afford many comfortable reflections."[24] Likewise, after the war's end, in his own address to the South Carolina legislature, he declared: "To meet the plaudits of my countrymen for the part I have acted in the Revolution, more than compensates for the toils I have undergone in the course of an arduous contest; and to have them expressed in such indulgent, and flattering terms . . . is not more honorable than it is pleasing."[25] By proclaiming publicly his contentment in the role of national idol, Washington expressed regard for his countrymen's opinions, and he defined those opinions as the primary source of his motivation and reward.

Few had reason to doubt Washington's statements. If he had not conducted himself in terms of national interests, if he had given in to rather than resisted political temptation, if he had been extreme rather than moderate in word and deed—in short, if his actions had been inconsistent with national values—then his emergence as a national hero would have been improbable. The people's belief in the sincerity of his sense of duty and honor were essential to their perception of him. It is therefore ironic that twentieth-century writers should refer to "the Washington myth" when discussing his eighteenth-century image. In fact, there is nothing mythical about that image. Flaws in Washington's character were certainly overlooked by his admirers, and many "incidents" in his life were consciously fabricated by biographers in order to dramatize what he stood for, but the accounts of his conduct as military commander and President are essentially correct. He really did renounce affluence and comfort for the hardships of war. He really was incorruptible. To invoke "the Washington myth," implying that a baser conception of the man is the truer one, is itself a fabrication—the product of a cynical rather than a suspicious age, an age whose basic assumptions induce many to deny the social value of heroic actions by reducing them to ignoble motives. This view, itself a remnant of America's early-twentieth-century fascination with debunkery, was not and could not have been the prevailing view of Washington's time. Without substantial correspondence between the people's Washington and the real Washington (however imperfect the real Washington might have been), the cult of hero worship would have collapsed.

Even on the public level, however, the correspondence between the man and his image was imperfect. A venerational cult began to form around Washington not after but before he demonstrated his military and political virtues. And while many of the virtues that he eventually demonstrated might have been expressed out of conviction, as most Americans believed, the actions themselves were also guided by external pressures. In particular, those who praised Washington for his deference to public opinion and civil authority were, in hindsight at least, making a virtue of necessity, for if there was anything the people and their representatives would not have tolerated, even in their most vulnerable moments, it was a power-hungry general or president. The popular image of Washington's life, then, was neither mythical nor a simple reflection of his conduct and character. It was the result of the people's attempt to understand, by selective emphasis and deemphasis of factual information, the quality of their own ideals.

The development of the Washington image did not take place in a vacuum. That the praise accorded Washington often outstripped his achievement, and that the bitterness of his condemnation exceeded the magnitude of his sins, are facts that make sense only when restored to the social context in which they arose. Washington's public identity was formed not only by his own words and deeds, nor solely by the concerns and needs of his society, but by the way words and concerns, deeds and needs, reverberated upon each other. That identity was formed, and secured, insofar as he appropriated for himself and enacted publicly the same moral values that others, under the pressure of definite social circumstances, were induced to attribute to him.

Since most Americans did not know the private Washington, they could imagine him to be more saintly than he really was. The people's willingness to give this man so much of the benefit of their doubt was based on the quality of the social relationship they had established with him. This relationship, however, had been secured before, not after, anyone began to wonder about his personal affairs. From the very beginning of the war, Washington was sacred to the people, and so he and they had always expressed their conceptions of each other in a dramatic and hierarchical ritual environment. Take away the official addresses read to and by Washington in all the places he visited as military commander and President; take away the public ritual attending his movement into and out of positions of power; take away the exuberant gatherings and festivities on the anniversaries of his birth; take away the massive funeral rites following his death; take away his image from coins, public statuary, engravings, and everyday housewares; take away his name from counties, cities, and streets—in short, retain the man's actions but divest him of his cult—and we see a man whose biography and virtues stand intact but cease to be representative of anything but the man himself; we see mere congeries of "information" with no power to bring other men together or move them to action.

Such ritual occasions and ritual objects are more than expressions of personal perception and belief. They are, indeed, forms through which individuals act and think in common. Different people may have entertained their own conceptions of what Washington really stood for, but when they came together, or acted together, the consensus and credibility of their beliefs became more concentrated, more secure. And as these people declared what they held in common, their consciousness of themselves as a society was reaffirmed. What the cult and its ritual enactment did, then, was to express what could not be expressed by the individual alone. Through them, personal conceptions of Washington became a medium for sanctifying the collective life.

Since the new republic's citizens were not given to unexamined adulation, their conceptions of Washington were arrived at self-consciously. What they saw in Washington was determined by his impeccable public conduct: his self-sacrifice on the nation's behalf, his immunity to political ambition, his moderation, his fortitude and self-control, his religious piety. Inferring from this public conduct an absolute purity of private life, the Americans idealized their conception of the man. They also sanctified, through that idealization, the virtues to which they themselves aspired.

Coda

A Man for Posterity

IN THE EUROPEAN ROMANTIC TRADITION, a leader's greatness is revealed through his stunning use of power. By declaring that "Jarge Washington was no' a great man,"[1] Thomas Carlyle gave clear voice to that tradition. Many years later, the German scholar Johannes Kuhn explained, "It is not easy for Europeans to comprehend the significance of a man like Washington. We are too accustomed to seek human greatness in unusual talents and gifts of an individual nature."[2] Drawing from this same intellectual tradition, Max Weber found in the leader's "specific gifts of the body and mind" the basis of his followers' "duty" to submit to his commands. Against this conception, with its emphasis on entitlement, privilege, and strength, the ideal of heroic leadership that took root in eighteenth-century America stressed the republican virtues of obligation, sacrifice, and disinterestedness. This ideal was important not only for its practical political significance but also because it embodied a solution to one of political philosophy's most enduring dilemmas: the reconciliation of democratic structures with the veneration of individual leaders.[3] Washington was the first and most dramatic personification of this ideal. By worshipping Washington, citizens of the new republic could worship themselves. By commemorating Washington, every succeeding generation of Americans could continue to do so.

The veneration of George Washington was most remarkable for its endurance. Without the massive propaganda apparatus of a totalitarian state, Washington remained "first in the hearts of his countrymen" long after his death. To relate the ebb and flow of Washington's reputation to America'a changing conditions over the last 185 years is beyond the scope of this book. But something can be said about the magnitude and trend of that reputation among succeeding generations, including our own. George Washington was not a symbol for his age alone; his image represents something deep and permanent in American society.

Washington's image, however, has not endured by itself; it has been kept alive by commemoration. The act of commemoration, as Emile Durkheim tells us, serves not only to identify for the present the most important men and events of the past but also to "revivify these most essential aspects of the collective consciousness. . . . The glorious souvenirs which are made to live again, and with which [people] feel that they have a kinship, give them a feeling of strength and confidence: a man is surer of his faith when he sees to how distant a past it goes back and what great things it has inspired."[4]

In the present case, the past does not go back very far, but Americans have made up in scriptural and ritual intensity what they lack in antiquity. Between 1800 and 1860 alone, American writers produced at least four hundred books, essays, and articles on Washington's life.[5] During this time, Washington's image was not that of a mere celebrity; it was sacred. The pronoun "Him" was capitalized in many biographies, and the comparison with Jesus, which first appeared in the eulogies, was pushed further than ever. Writers noted that the mothers of both men were named Mary and that the births of both were the only two celebrated nationally. The comparison was belabored in much detail. In 1812, John Adams observed:

> Among the national sins of our country . . . [is] the idolatrous worship paid to the name of George Washington by all classes and *nearly* all parties of our citizens, manifested in the impious applications of names and epithets to him which are ascribed in scripture only to God and to Jesus Christ. The following is a part of them: "our Savior," "our Redeemer," "our cloud by day and our pillar of fire by night," "our star in the east," to us a Son is born," and "our guide on earth, our advocate in heaven."[6]

At about the same time, in 1815, a Russian traveler observed that "[E]very American considers it his sacred duty to have a likeness of Washington in his home, just as we have the images of

God's saints."[7] During his visit to America with Tocqueville in the early 1830s, Gustav de Beaumont wrote: "In America . . . do not look . . . for monuments raised to the memory of illustrious men. I know that this people has its heroes; but nowhere have I seen their statues. To Washington alone are there busts, inscriptions, columns; this is because Washington, in America, *is not a man but a God*"[8] (italics in original). Attitudes such as these were to be expressed for thirty more years. During this period, known in hindsight as the antebellum era, the image of Washington was celebrated in history, biography, belles lettres, drama, and the arts.[9] Its veneration was no less intense at the end of the era than at the beginning. In 1854, for example, *Graham's Magazine* began its serial of Headley's biography of Washington and immediately received a flood of new subscriptions. In 1856, seven thousand people waited inside New York city's Academy of Music to listen to one of Edward Everett's speeches on "The Character of Washington." Infuriated that tickets to the reading had been sold out, the crowd that had gathered outside overpowered the doorkeepers and filled the aisles and part of the stage so as to share in the great event. In 1858, Walt Whitman described the feeling behind this and similar demonstrations. "The name of Washington," he said, "is constantly on our lips. . . . His portrait hangs on every wall and he is almost canonized in the affections of our people."[10]

During the Civil War, Mount Vernon was declared neutral territory, as both sides, North and South, claimed Washington as a symbol of their cause. In the North, Washington stood for union; in the South, whose President was sworn in on his Birthday and under his statue, Washington stood for resistance to tyranny.[11] As the war drew to a close, the North sanctified its achievements by drawing on his memory (just as the English once drew, in crisis, on the spirit of their own Saint George):

> Ever since WASHINGTON'S day, secession has been trying to show its head, but has always been put down in his name. WASHINGTON is completing his second cycle. He was with JACKSON in 1832, when he suppressed treason, and he also sailed with WINFIELD SCOTT into the harbor of Charleston; stood by Anderson in 1861, and was with GILLMORE, last Saturday, when he put that good old flag on Fort Sumter once more. He has been with ABRAHAM LINCOLN, and has gone with us through the war, teaching us to bear reverses patiently. He was with GRANT at the taking of Vicksburgh, and will go with him to Richmond. He went with PORTER to Wilmington; with SHERMAN

to Atlanta and Charleston, and will go with him to Richmond. His spirit leads us in this second war of the Constitution, and if the rebellion should cease, he would still guide us in peaceful enterprises.[12]

After Lincoln

Less than two months after this statement appeared, Abraham Lincoln was assassinated and the American people made of him their second national deity. Lincoln's cult would grow to a level comparable to Washington's, but it would not replace it. Indeed, it was the image of Washington that was most often invoked to legitimate Lincoln's apotheosis. As Lincoln's body lay in state in the Capital Rotunda, every statue but one, Washington's, was covered with a black drape. The joining of the two men was expressed poetically as well:

> Heroes and Saints with fadeless stars have crowned him—
> And WASHINGTON'S dear arms are clasped around him.[13]

The scene was vividly illustrated in popular portraits depicting the Founder of the Union welcoming the Preserver of the Union into Glory (Fig. 40). Similarly, when eulogists contemplated the life of Lincoln, they projected onto it the same virtues they had come to associate with Washington. Thus, if Washington, out of a sense of duty, sacrificed comfort and affluence for the public good, Lincoln, out of feelings of love, sacrificed his life. He regarded himself as the servant of the people, and "he fell, if any man did, fighting their battles." In his disinterestedness as well as in his public virtue, Lincoln incarnated the glory of the great founder. Although fully exposed during his presidency to the temptations of money and influence, Lincoln remained "uncorrupted by position; unspoiled by power." Here was a man who "had no ambition for high place." Lincoln was also the moderate man. His mind was not revered for its "intellectual grandeur"; he was, rather, moral and wise, and his "mistakes were redeemed by his honest purpose." In his character were also displayed, in balanced proportion, every human virtue. Although a kindly and gentle man, his refusal to move on matters of principle revealed great resoluteness and self-control. Beneath this upright public image, the eulogists went on to say, lay no private vices. He was a dutiful son and kind husband. From youth to maturity, his personal life, like Washington's, was one of "unblemished purity." In Lincoln's special relationship to God was found the basis of his authentic good-ness. He was compared to God's agent, Moses, as often as Washington was, and it was said that "no president since George Washington ever brought in so eminent a degree to his official work a deep religious faith."[14]

If Lincoln was chosen to be savior of his country "to affirm and reassert the principles of Washington," he also broke Washington's unique hold on the nation's affections. "Mt. Vernon and Springfield will henceforth be kindred shrines," one eulogist declared. Another, noting that Lincoln's portrait had been placed below Washington's in the public hall in which he spoke, promised that in "coming days their portraits shall hang side by side. . . . "[15] No words could have been more prophetic. In the 1850s, the *Bibliotheca Washingtoniana* shows, ninety-eight books and articles on Washington were published, while only thrity-nine were published in the 1860s. In the 1870s and 1880s, the number of entries dropped further to thirty-two and thirty-one, respectively. Yet, the public's fascination with Washington was not eclipsed by its reverence for Lincoln. In 1902, schoolchildren in at least one (Pennsylvania) town chose him as an exemplar over Lincoln by a substantial margin.[16] The periodical literature displays a similar, though less pronounced, pattern. Between 1870 and 1900, the *New York Times* published sixty-two articles about Lincoln and ninety-six articles about Washington. During the last decade of the century, according to the *Readers' Guide,* about ten articles were written about Washington for every nine on Lincoln. And when the Hall of Fame was established in Brooklyn, New York, in 1899, Washington received the most first-place votes. Lincoln came in a close second—one vote behind him.[17]

As the United States evolved from a rural republic to an industrial democracy, and as "equality" replaced "liberty" as its major political concern, the dignified restraint and aloofness of Washington's image began to undermine its popularity. By the early years of the twentieth century, in fact, the popularity of his cult was surpassed by Lincoln's. Popular media indexes, at least, show Lincoln to be the pre-twentieth-century figure most often written about (i.e., in magazines and newspapers) during the past eighty-five years; Washington ranks second. National opinion polls, too, place Lincoln above Washington, largely because "he was a greater humanitarian, more down to earth, more of a people's President."[18] The passage of time has not altered this (1945) assessment.

In 1958, Americans chose Lincoln as the famous man in history they would most like to invite to dinner.[19] And in the most recent polls of expert opinion, Lincoln is rated as the nation's greatest President. Washington usually ranks second.[20]

But the trend admits of sharp fluctuations. Lincoln's leading place was lost from 1925 to 1935 as the nation planned for, carried out, and reflected upon its year-long bicentennial (1932) celebration of Washington's birth—the most extensive celebration ever held for a national leader. And since 1970, it has been Washington, not Lincoln, who appears most often in the popular media. It would be a mistake, then, to conclude that Lincoln has replaced Washington in the nation's historical consciousness; rather, Lincoln's cult has been superimposed upon Washington's. Washington remains an object of profound attachment.

"Profound attachment"? Would not "superficial attachment" be the more appropriate characterization? Every year, the newspapers tell of towns and cities that have abandoned or cancelled their traditional celebration of Washington's birth because of a lack of public interest. Every year, we are reminded that the United States House and Senate no longer assemble for the annual reading of Washington's Farewell Address. Every year, editorial pages and commentators lament the commercialization of the Washington holiday, which is itself no longer observed on February 22, the actual date of Washington's birth, but on the third Monday in February. Historical significance seems to have become the pretext for a long weekend.[21]

From such ritual erosion many observers infer a fading of Washington's image from the collective memory. That inference presumes that the anniversary of Washington's birth is the chief method of his commemoration and that the anniversary was celebrated more enthusiastically in the past than at present. Neither assumption, however, can be supported by evidence. On the contrary, we know from the diffusion of portraits, the production and reading of biographical essays, and the movement to establish monuments and shrines that reverence for Washington's memory reached its peak in the 1850s. But the very commentaries that describe these developments, and this mood, also tell us that few people paid much attention to the Birthday observance. In 1858, for example, Walt Whitman bore witness to the great man's place in the people's affections, but in the same breath made note of the "singular anomaly that we allow the day that presented him

to the Western World to pass with the most chilling indifference."[22]

Commemoration adheres to no settled forms; it is a living thing
that adapts itself to the changing conditions of a society. As the
years go by, the past becomes more crowded; heroes and events
accumulate and compete with one another for the present generation's attention. Memorial sentiments and ritual energies, ap-
portioned among more, and increasingly remote, objects, become
cooler, less intense. The older cults lose their capacity to arouse
and their function becomes more specialized: viz., to *remind*.

The transformation is inevitable. To expect that a nation should
turn out, year after year, in heartfelt veneration for a man who
died many generations ago is to make unrealistic demands on its
capacity for emotional attachment. Intellectual and moral recognition, on the other hand, prove more durable. If Washington's
memory is no longer the object of annual parades, feasts, and balls,
it continues to be evoked by his portrait, in front of which Presidents still pose in order to identify themselves with America's
past (Fig. 41). Iconic reminders also represent Washington on city
landscapes, appear on the most frequently printed currency and
stamps, and continue to saturate the capital city and Capitol building (in both places overwhelming, by volume, every other figure
in American history).[23] But icons are not the only media that remind the nation of its most prominent founder. The memory of
Washington is honored by the places named for him: the one state,
eight streams, nine colleges and universities, ten lakes, seven
mountains, thirty-three counties, and one hundred twenty-one cities and towns[24]—not to mention the thousands of streets and businesses, and the hundreds of thousands of people that still carry
his name. His historic importance is underlined annually by massive visitation to his shrines, including the Washington Monument, Mount Vernon, the Wakefield birthplace, and the many
places between Boston and Savannah that the great man himself
visited. And, too, the continuing annual observance of his birth,
though no longer the occasion for effervescent ceremonial display, occasions a nationwide cessation of activities in many public
institutions.

Smaller gestures command little national attention but indicate,
in their totality, the regard for Washington hidden by the erosion
of the traditional commemorative rituals: the naming after him
of a plaza outside a new federal building; the scattering of the

ashes of loved ones upon the grounds of Mount Vernon; the delivery of Washington's Farewell Address to an empty House or Senate chamber by a faithful congressman who has braved wind and snow; the passage through these same chambers of a bill to give Washington a posthumous military promotion so that no American commander can be said to have held a higher rank than he.[25] The sheer numerical weight of these kinds of markers and gestures indicates a commemorative cult of enduring vitality.

Washington's present significance cannot be measured solely by the frequency with which symbols of his memory appear before the public. If frequency of appearance were crucial, then we would be compelled to assign to "celebrities," such as entertainers and sports heroes, more cultural significance than we assign to him. What gives meaning to cult markers is not their volume but the way in which they are assembled. The articles written about Washington, for example, are concentrated around specific dates, like the anniversary of his birth (in connection with which 43 percent of all *New York Times* articles on Washington appeared) and the anniversary of America's founding events. Read in the context of national commemorative celebrations, these articles achieve a significance they would not have if they were scattered throughout the year. The arrangement of monuments in the central parts of cities, near central buildings like city halls and capitols, also conveys an importance that could not be inferred from numbers alone. The Washington Monument, visual center of the capital city, is carefully aligned with the dome of the United State Capitol Building (the seat of popular rather than executive sovereignty) and so helps to fix the significance of the Lincoln Memorial, which rests upon the very same plane; the symbolic unity of these three structures is affirmed by the straight line that runs through their centers. Likewise, the walls of the Vietnam War Memorial jut out at angles that lead directly to the Lincoln Memorial, on the one side, and to the Washington Monument on the other. Like antennae, the walls are picking up messages from these two sacred sites, messages about great men, messages that add luster to the war dead they commemorate.

The Enduring Values

George Washington remains a prominent object of commemoration because the values he stood for in the late eighteenth century remain central to the political culture of the late twentieth century. Few contemporary leaders actually live up to these values. Selfishness, lack of moral standards, and corruption may be no more common today than they were in the past, but given the size and complexity of the modern state, it would be surprising if they were less so. Yet it is precisely these vices that give the moral example of Washington its significance. Amid the imperfections of the present, the memory of Washington's character keeps alive the ideals of the past. For the mature American, that memory embodies a clear standard for political judgment; for the young, an effective tool of moral instruction.

Renunciation of personal comfort for the public good, a value that so engaged Washington's own generation, remains fundamental to the nation's political morality. Thus, no one can read a recent juvenile life of Washington without being reminded, as by the following scene, of his public virtue:

> "I could never understand why he [Washington] became a soldier," said a woman. "He was a surveyor and was making money."
>
> "He is also the richest planter in Virginia," said another woman. "He was only twenty when Lawrence died and left him Mount Vernon. His wife, Martha, is very wealthy, too."
>
> "Then I am more puzzled than ever," said the first woman. "Why would he leave that lovely place for the hardships of a soldier's life?"
>
> "I can tell you why," said the officer. "In the Indian wars he felt he must go to the aid of the poor settlers in the borderlands. He knew the wilderness better than anyone. So he thought it was his duty to go."
>
> "It was the same thing in the War of the Revolution," said another officer. "He felt again that it was his duty to fight. No one knew better the terrible hardships of war. But he loved his country so much he was willing to suffer them."[26]

Today's children are still taught to understand Washington's love of country in the context of an alternative sentiment: the love of power. And it is still the avoidance and abdication of power that distinguishes him, in the juvenile readers, from history's cast of dictators. "Some were afraid the [first] President would turn into a king," Stewart Graff explains to his young audience. "But people soon stopped worrying. Washington did not act like a king. He did not try to run the country alone. He asked other leaders for their ideas. He chose the best people in the country to help him. He took trips North and South. He wanted to find out what the people were thinking."[27] For adult audiences the same theme is played out. James Flexner, one of the foremost Washington scholars, explains in *Reader's Digest* that Washington's determination to oppose rather than lead the Newburgh conspiracy against Congress has had a continuing effect. "Never again, although many nations around us have succumbed to dictatorships, has there emerged in the United States any serious danger."[28]

In matters of presidential as well as military power, Washington's name continues to be evoked. When President Nixon, in 1973, tried to deny Congress its right to appropriate funds with the assurance that they would be spent as directed, a *New York Times* editor recalled President Washington's unwillingness to impose his own powers against those of Congress, lest such encroachment lead, in Washington's own words, to "despotism." Nixon might disregard such a principle when it was expressed by his opponents in the Senate, the *Times* editorial went on to say, but "he might honor it with grave consideration as a memo from the first President to the 37th."[29]

At no time has Washington's disinterestedness—his immunity to political ambition—been more salient than during the Watergate crisis. The reasons for which President Richard Nixon was condemned—abuse and corruption of public power, converting the government itself into an instrument for private use—seem to be the obverse of those for which Washington was praised. And Washington's virtues were brought directly to bear on this condemnation. Consider one of a series of vignettes by columnist Russell Baker attempting to answer the question "Why was Washington a great man?"

> One day in the 1790's word spread through the capital that George Washington was sick and tired of Thomas Jefferson's constant bickering with Alexander Hamilton. That afternoon a man named J. Edgar Hoover was admitted to George Washington's office.
>
> "I have been keeping an eye on this Jefferson," said the visitor, "and have here ye goods to justify giving him ye heave ho from ye Cabinet." He offered George Washington a dossier.
>
> George Washington recoiled and asked what was in it. "Ye transcripts of Jefferson's activities while wenching," said Hoover, "as well as recordings of his dinner-table criticism of ye Government." George Washington took the dossier and deposited it in his fireplace where it burned to ashes while he was having Hoover thrown into the street.
>
> "It would have been unworthy of my office," he told Martha Washington afterwards, "to do ye throwing myself."[30]

The use of executive power to injure political enemies was foremost in the mind of Representative Peter Rodino as he contemplated Washington's disinterestedness. He "denied the temptations of power as few other men in history."[31] President Nixon (whom Rodino's House Judiciary Committee impeached) is not often counted among these few men, and the consequences of his shortcomings inspire comparative artistic comment. If Washington's victory over the temptations of power made him an emblem of national purpose and an effective master of the ship of state, as Emanuel Leutze's *Washington Crossing the Delaware* (Fig. 42) suggests, the ambition of his successor, as portrayed in Edward Sorel's *Nixon Crossing the Delaware* (Fig. 43), brought the state to aimlessness and internal strife.

Moderation, along with public virtue and disinterestedness, remains a cardinal virtue in American politics. Remarks by succeeding generations of Congressmen on Washington's "genuine modesty" and "frugality" remind us of this. Congress's attention has also been called to those evenly balanced qualities that Washington's contemporaries celebrated:

> What is Washington's rank among the world's greatest heroes? He was a successful commander of armies and he displayed much genius, but among the world's great captains he cannot be placed in the very first rank. As a statesman he must again take a second place. Wherein lay Washington's greatness? ... [He] was exactly fitted for the position in which Providence placed him. Had he been a greater genius, he might have misused his power; had he been a weaker man, he could not have succeeded.[32]

Accounts of Washington's moderation are accompanied now, as in his own time, by accounts of his resoluteness and strength of will. Today's children receive early exposure to the latter virtues through a legend of Washington's youth—one of the favorites in the juvenile literature:

> With his free hand, George clutched a hank of mane and swung himself onto the colt's back.... Firebrand squealed.... George was jerked forward. He sailed over the colt's head and struck the ground. Firebrand dragged him by the braided rein looped around his wrist. George heard his mother cry, "Let him go. You'll be hurt." He knew the danger, but such a strong feeling rose in him not to give up, that he couldn't let go. He rolled over onto his stomach and pulled on the rein with both hands. He bumped along over the grass until his weight slowed the colt, then stopped him. George got to his feet and reached Firebrand's quivering side. He caught the mane and jumped astride again.[33]

That same resoluteness and strength of will that contributed to Washington's victories are recognized in his conduct in the face of misfortune. This recognition is made explicit in the enshrinement of Valley Forge, where Washington's defeated army withdrew and recovered to fight again, and where hundreds of thousands of tourists annually enter into communion with the stoic ideal which animated that recovery. The same ideal is expressed in the Washington's Birthday editorials. "The miracle was not that he won," *New York Times* readers were told in 1965, "but that he endured.... We don't know how he would treat the menacing problems that face us, but the qualities that made him unbeatable—steadfastness, patience and enormous resolve—are no less valuable today than when he practiced them."[34] Washington's contemporaries convinced themselves that he derived these qualities from his self-control, and so have we. A Bicentennial commentary on Washington's legacy tells us: "He was always engaged in the unending process of trying to know and to master himself."[35] After years of research, James Flexner noticed the same thing: "My labors have persuaded me that he became one of the noblest and greatest men who ever lived. He was not born that way.... He perfected himself gradually through the exercise of his own will and skill."[36]

Self-mastery depends upon the recognition of one's own defects, and perhaps nothing better attests to America's regard for this attribute than the continuing popularity of the cherry tree story. Many of the Mason Weems tales portray Washington's exemplary boyhood conduct and relate it to his achievements as a man. But when we remember that President Washington conceded readily in his Farewell Address to both personal limitations and errors of judgment, we are also reminded of the more complex aspect of the youthful Washington: notably, his simultaneous inclination toward waywardness and repentence. Owning up to the destruction of the beautiful tree, the young hero provides an example of self-redemption that many generations of American youth have sought to emulate.

Americans have always regarded self-mastery as a necessary component of private virtue. A recent (April 1984) television miniseries that depicts Washington renouncing his desire for another man's wife (the presumably coquettish Sally Fairfax) is an allegory of this moral principle, and is in turn reminiscent of Barry Goldwater's comment on "the home life of this extraordinary man, [which] like so many other phases of his distinguished career, stands out with glowing radiance across the decades as an example to the Nation."[37] And since many Americans still find in Washington's religious piety the foundation of his greatness, they want to ensure that "[e]very school child knows that Washington knelt in the snow at Valley Forge," and that this attitude was characteristic of the private man.[38] The children's book writers have certainly gone about their work with that end in view.[39]

The Washington image, along with the ideals associated with it, has maintained its hold on American society for more than two hundred years. It has been evoked and reinforced by periodic commentaries in schools and the mass media, and by the material signs of the Washington cult—its icons, shrines, place names, and observances. By their common exposure to these media, millions of people are drawn into a moral communion, and through this relationship the continuity of their political tradition is reinforced. The commemoration of Washington thus provides a continuous American interpretation of American life.

Although the memory of Washington remains part of America's tradition of liberty, it obviously does not in itself restrain the forces that might undermine liberty. Contemplation of Washington only evokes ideas and feelings about the issue of political power; it only renders these ideas and feelings intelligible by expressing them in symbolic terms that allow for a more forceful rendition of their meaning. The commemoration of Washington is the retention of an image, and its function is not to influence directly the disposition of power but to make the issue of power itself visible and understandable. It focuses attention on those underlying ideals in American life that might otherwise be less visible and less salient. The commemoration of Washington is in this sense more a way of understanding the present than of understanding the past. It is also an instrument for articulating the continuity of present and past. The men of the past, at least, would see it that way. Beholding the continued admiration of Washington, our forebears, were they alive today, would rest content in the knowledge that their highest ideals had been preserved. Washington, they would find, symbolizes our age as well as their own.

Yet, few symbols carry permanent significance; their impact and resonance vary as conditions change. George Washington emerged as a national hero when the centralized power needed to achieve an independent and stable government was the very thing the people most feared. The present political climate is different. The powers placed in the hands of today's leaders are far greater than those placed in the hands of Washington, and few worry about these men turning into tyrants. This trend must give pause to those who contemplate Washington's future place in the national consciousness. America's drift toward centrism and a devotion to order is not in itself conducive to the commemoration of a man who has always stood for restrained power and liberty.

A lessening regard for Washington among future generations, however, is improbable—at least so long as Americans remain committed to their political heritage. Given this commitment, it would make no sense to separate the strong power now granted to national leaders from the political tradition that governs its use, for it is precisely this tradition of liberty that allows such power to be granted in the first place. Americans can now assign mandates to their leaders because of their certainty that at the appropriate time these will be returned and applied to other leaders and other purposes. Far from being inconsistent with George Washington's legacy, therefore, the American people's tolerance of dominating leadership presupposes its continued vitality. No longer a model for the way Presidents and generals conduct themselves, Washington still endures as a symbol of the values that keep power within proper bounds, and that distinguish America, despite its strong national government, as the least centralized of all the Western democracies.

Imagine, then, a future America without Washington. Think him out of existence and estimate the consequences. In this strange new world, Washington's Birthday passes without comment in the public media. Schools, banks, and post offices remain open. In the capital city, which now bears a new name, the familiar monuments remain, but the place on which the Washington Monument stands is an empty knoll. Inside the Capitol building, the places formerly occupied by statues and paintings of Washington are now filled with icons of other men. Across the Potomac, in Virginia, a riverside suburban development has replaced Mount Vernon. The site of Washington's birthplace, farther south, is no longer enshrined. The entire cult is gone. Bills and coins bear the images of men who were not on them before. No biographies are listed under Washington's name. Children's books make no mention of him. Historical chronicles tell of the war for independence, but give no indication of a Washington taking part in it. The success of the Federal Convention, the endurance of the new government, owed nothing to his efforts.

Suddenly the lights of the past go out altogether. All the great men—from Adams and Jefferson to Jackson and Lincoln—are forgotten. The chronicles of the past remain, but they no longer make sense to us. Heroic achievements are now indistinguishable from mundane ones. No golden age inspires us; no dark age dismays us. The high points are confounded with the low. Uninformed by a morally differentiated past, the affairs of the present become pointless.

Just as suddenly as they left, the great men reappear—all but Washington. Now the significance of his loss comes into sharper focus. It does not radically transform the political climate, but the difference it makes is discernible. Although abuses by men in power still elicit stern reaction, the tradition that evokes that reaction articulates itself less dramatically. The good leader is more difficult to visualize; the norms of power lose some of their clarity; the meaning of liberty becomes less understandable. People recognize what the nation stands for, but not quite as well as before. Withal, they have the nagging sense of knowing something, and feeling something, they cannot put their finger on.

Abruptly, like the restoration of light after a blackout, the Washington cult returns to us. The icons, place names, and shrines repossess the landscape; biographies return to the bookshelves; holidays and ceremonies resume their traditional course. Recovering the memory of Washington, we regain part of ourselves and feel more complete. Recovering the memory of Washington, we regain fuller possession of that heritage of liberty that has tamed the growing power of America. On the permanence of that heritage, we now more surely realize, depends the meaning of George Washington for posterity.

Notes

Works frequently cited have been identified by the following abbreviations:

Biographies

GW   Douglas S. Freeman. *George Washington: A Biography.* 7 vols. New York: Scribners, 1948–57.

HGW   Mason L. Weems. *A History of the Life and Death, Virtues and Exploits, of General George Washington.* Georgetown, D.C.: Green and English, 1800.

Books

CIN   Garry Wills. *Cincinnatus: George Washington and the Enlightenment.* New York: Doubleday, 1984.

EF   Emile Durkheim. *The Elementary Forms of the Religious Life.* New York: The Free Press, 1965.

IO   Bernard Bailyn. *The Ideological Origins of the American Revolution.* Cambridge: Harvard University Press, 1967.

Letters

AFC   L. H. Butterfield, ed. *Adams Family Correspondence.* 4 vols. Cambridge: Harvard University Press, 1963–73.

LBR   L. H. Butterfield, ed. *Letters of Benjamin Rush.* 2 vols. Princeton: Princeton University Press, 1951.

Notes

LDC Paul H. Smith, ed. *Letters of Delegates to Congress, 1774–1789.* 10 vols. Washington, D.C.: Library of Congress, 1976–83.

PAH Harold C. Syrett, ed. *The Papers of Alexander Hamilton.* 26 vols. New York: Columbia University Press, 1961–79.

PTJ Julian P. Boyd, ed. *The Papers of Thomas Jefferson.* 20 vols. Princeton: Princeton University Press, 1950–82.

WGW John C. Fitzpatrick, ed. *The Writings of George Washington.* 39 vols. Washington, D.C.: United States Government Printing Office, 1931–44.

Newspapers

ARA (Philadelphia) *Aurora*

BG *Boston Gazette*

GUS (Philadelphia) *Gazette of the United States*

NG (Philadelphia) *National Gazette*

PG (Philadelphia) *Pennsylvania Gazette*

VG (Williamsburg) *Virginia Gazette*

INTRODUCTION

1. *Debates in Congress,* 22nd Congress, 1st Session, Vol. 8, Pt. 1, February 7, 1832, p. 297; Vol. 8, Pt. 2, February 13, 1832, p. 1782.

2. *Ibid.,* Vol. 8, Pt. 2, February 13, p. 1787.

3. *Ibid.,* p. 1797.

4. *Ibid.,* Vol. 8, Pt. 1, February 13, pp. 367–77; Vol. 8, Pt. 2, February 13–14, 16, pp. 1782–1813 for full debate.

5. *HGW.*

6. Washington Irving, *Life of George Washington,* 5 vols. (New York: G. P. Putnam, 1856–1859); Jared Sparks, *The Life of Washington* (New York: Perkins, [1837] 190?); James K. Paulding, *A Life of Washington,* 2 vols. (New York: Harper, 1836); Joel T. Headley, *The Life of George Washington* (New York: Scribner, 1856); Henry Cabot Lodge, *George Washington,* 2 vols. (Boston: Houghton, Mifflin, 1896); Woodrow Wilson, *George Washington* (New York: Harper and Brothers, 1896); Paul Leicester Ford, *The True Washington* (Philadelphia: J. B. Lippincott, 1896); Rupert Hughes, *George Washington,* 3 vols. (New York: Morrow, 1926–30); William E. Woodward, *George Washington: The Image and the Man* (New York: Boni and Liveright, 1926); *WGW;* John C. Fitzpatrick, *George Washington Himself* (Westport, Conn.: Greenwood Press, [1933] 1975); *GW;* Marcus Cunliffe, *George Washington, Man and Monument* (Boston: Little, Brown, 1958); James T. Flexner, *George Wash-*

210

ington, 4 vols. (Boston: Little, Brown, 1965–72). Only a small sample of the most prominent full-length and multivolume biographical works is included in this inventory, for scores of Washington biographies have been written. The periodic literature is even more voluminous: Approximately 850 articles on Washington have been published since 1900. For a partial inventory of the nineteenth-century literature, see William S. Baker, *Bibliotheca Washingtoniana* (Philadelphia: R. M. Lindsay, 1889).

7. Robert P. Hay, "George Washington: American Moses," *American Quarterly* 21 (1969):780–91.

8. Michael Kammen, *A Season of Youth* (New York: Knopf, 1978); George B. Forgie, *Patricide in the House Divided* (New York: W. W. Norton, 1979); Lawrence J. Friedman, "The Flawless American," in *Inventors of the Promised Land* (New York: Knopf, 1975), pp. 44–78; Jay Fliegelman, "George Washington and the Reconstituted Family," in *Prodigals and Pilgrims: The American Revolution against Patriarchal Authority, 1750–1800* (Cambridge: Cambridge University Press, 1982), pp. 197–226; Catherine L. Albanese, "Our Father, Our Washington," in *Sons of the Fathers: The Civil Religion of the American Revolution* (Philadelphia: Temple University Press, 1976), pp. 143–181; James H. Smylie, "The President as Republican Prophet and King: Clerical Reflections on the Death of Washington," *Journal of Church and State* 18 (1976):233–52; *CIN.*

9. Dyer to Trumbull, June 17, 1775, *LDC,* 1:499–500.

10. Washington to Congress, June 16, 1775, *WGW,* 3:292.

11. Reported by Patrick Henry to Benjamin Rush. See Benjamin Rush, *The Autobiography of Benjamin Rush,* ed. George W. Corner (Princeton: Princeton University Press, 1948), p. 113.

12. Rush to Patrick Henry, January 12, 1778, *LBR,* 1:183.

13. John W. Daniel, "Oration," *Dedication of the Washington Monument* (1876), Senate Document 21, no. 224 (Washington, D.C.: U.S. Government Printing Office, 1903), p. 274.

14. Jefferson to Walter Jones, January 2, 1814, *The Writings of Thomas Jefferson,* ed. Paul Leicester Ford, 12 vols. (New York: G. P. Putnam's Sons, 1904–5), 11:375.

15. Adams to Rush, March 19, 1912; April 22, 1812, *Old Family Letters,* 2 vols. (Philadelphia: J. B. Lippincott, 1892), 1:372–73, 377.

16. Rush, *Autobiography,* p. 180.

17. Joseph Charles, *The Origins of the American Party System* (Williamsburg, Va.: Institute of Early American History and Culture, 1956), p. 40.

18. Jefferson to Walter Jones, January 2, 1814, *Writings of Thomas Jefferson,* 11:375.

19. John M. Mason, *A Funeral Oration Delivered in the Brick Presbyterian Church in the City of New York* (New York: G. F. Hopkins, 1800), p. 12.

20. Albanese, *Sons of the Fathers*, p. 145.

21. Charles, *Origins of the American Party System*, p. 38.

22. Albanese, *Sons of the Fathers*, p. 144.

23. *EF*, p. 236.

24. *Ibid.*, pp. 243–44. See also Durkheim., *Sociology and Philosophy*, ed. J. G. Peristiany (New York: The Free Press, 1974), pp. 58–59.

25. Adams to Rush, February 25, 1808, *The Spur of Fame: Dialogues of John Adams and Benjamin Rush, 1805–1813*, ed. John A. Schutz and Douglass Adair (San Marino, CA.: The Huntington Library, 1966), p. 104.

26. For a more general statement, see *EF*, especially pp. 463–66, and A. R. Radcliffe-Brown, "Religion and Society," in *Structure and Function in Primitive Society* (New York: The Free Press, 1968), pp. 153–77.

CHAPTER 1

1. *GW*, 3:xiii.

2. Max Weber, *Economy and Society*, ed. Guenter Roth and Claus Wittich, 3 vols. (Berkeley: University of California Press, 1968), 1:241; 3:1111–17.

3. *EF*, pp. 243–44.

4. Victor Turner, *Dramas, Fields, and Metaphors; Symbolic Action in Human Society* (Ithaca, N.Y.: Cornell University Press, 1974), p. 111. Turner's discussion includes an analogy between feelings involved in political insurrection and Freud's "primary process."

5. Gordon S. Wood, "Rhetoric and Reality in the American Revolution," in *American Themes: Essays in Historigraphy*, ed. Frank O. Gatell and Allen Weinstein (New York: Oxford University Press, 1968), pp. 70, 73.

6. *IO*, pp. 94–143.

7. Philip Davidson, *Propaganda and the American Revolution, 1763–83* (New York: W. W. Norton, 1973); Harry P. Kerr, "The Character of Political Sermons Preached at the Time of the American Revolution" (Ph.D. diss., Cornell University, 1962), pp. 106–7.

8. For a discussion of the Freemasons' contribution to the nation's founding, see Bernard Faÿ, *Revolution and Freemasonry* (Boston: Little, Brown and Co., 1935), pp. 226–61.

9. Stephen E. Lucas, *Portents of Rebellion: Rhetoric and Revolution in Philadelphia, 1765–76* (Philadelphia: Temple University Press, 1976), p. 163.

10. *Ibid.*, p. 162.

Notes

11. John Adams to Abigail Adams, June 10, 1775, *AFC,* 1:214.

12. Margaret Willard, ed., *Letters on the American Revolution, 1774–76* (Port Washington, N.Y.: Kennikat Press, 1968), p. 102.

13. John Adams to Abigail Adams, May 29, 1775, *AFC,* 1:207.

14. *EF,* p. 241.

15. Abigail Adams to John Adams, March 2, 1776, *AFC,* 1:353.

16. *Georgia Gazette,* May 31, 1775.

17. Davidson, *Propaganda and the American Revolution,* p. 206.

18. Sullivan and Langdon to Thornton, June 20, 1775, *LDC,* 1:524. See also Charles Royster, *A Revolutionary People at War: The Continental Army and American Character, 1775–83* (Chapel Hill: University of North Carolina Press, 1979), p. 25; Albanese, *Sons of the Fathers,* p. 101; *Georgia Gazette,* May 31, 1775; August 23, 1775. For additional description of the 1775 "war psychosis," see Richard Buel, Jr., *Dear Liberty: Connecticut's Mobilization for the Revolutionary War* (Middleton, Conn.: Wesleyan University Press, 1980), pp. 36–38; George F. Schur and Hugh F. Rankin, *Rebels and Redcoats* (Cleveland: World Publishing Company, 1957), pp. 65–66.

19. James Flexner, *George Washington,* 1:339.

20. *Georgia Gazette,* July 12, 1775.

21. EF, p. 251.

22. John Adams to Abigail Adams, June 17, 1775, *The Works of John Adams,* ed. Charles Francis Adams, 10 vols. (Boston: Little, Brown and Company, 1856), 1:175–76.

23. John Frederick Schroeder and Benson John Lossing, *Life and Times of Washington,* 4 vols. (Albany, N.Y.: M. M. Belcher, 1903), 4:1654.

24. Albanese, *Sons of the Fathers,* p. 149. See also Schroeder and Lossing, *Life and Times,* 2:784.

25. Rush to Thomas Ruston, October 29, 1775, *LBR,* 1:92.

26. Lydia Minturn Post, *Personal Recollections of the American Revolution, 1774–1776,* ed. Margaret W. Willard (Port Washington, N.Y.: Kennikat Press, 1968), p. 228.

27. *BG,* October 30, 1775; January 29, 1776; March 4, 18, 1776; April 1, 1776; *VG,* October 7, 1775; *PG,* August 7, 14, 1776.

28. Rush to Thomas Ruston, October 29, 1775; Rush to Julia Rush, April 14, 1777, *LBR,* 1:92, 138–39; *VG,* August 3, 1776.

29. *WGW,* 4:488–90; *BG,* April 8, 15, 1776.

30. Royster, *A Revolutionary People at War,* p. 31.

31. *VG,* February 24, 1776.

32. *VG,* January 12, 1775. For a more sustained but equally passionate statement, see Philip Freneau's "American Liberty" (1775) in Fred

213

L. Pattee, ed., *The Poems of Philip Freneau*, 3 vols. (Princeton: University Library, 1902–7), 1:142–52.

33. *PG*, September 4, 1776. See also *VG*, January 24, 1777.

34. Hooper to Morris, February 1, 1777, *LDC*, 6:191.

35. *Pennsylvania Journal*, February 19, 1777, reprinted in Frank Moore, ed., *Diary of the American Revolution*, 2 vols. (New York: Charles Scribner, 1860), I:397.

36. Rush, *Autobiography*, p. 141.

37. John Adams to Abigail Adams, June 23, 1775, *AFC*, 1:226; Adams, *Works of John Adams*, 2:415–18; 3:38.

38. Adams to Greene, April 13, 1777, *Papers of John Adams*, ed. Robert J. Taylor, 6 vols. (Cambridge: Harvard University Press, 1977–83), 5:150–52.

39. *LBR*, 1:1xii, 1xv, 193; *Autobiography of Benjamin Rush*, pp. 6–7.

40. Adams, *Works of John Adams*, 3:93. On Adams's supposed support for the cabal, see Madison to Jefferson, October 10, 1788, *PTJ*, 14:17. See also Hamilton to Sedgewick, October 9, 1788, *PAH*, 5:225.

41. Gilbert Chinard, *George Washington as the French Knew Him* (New York: Greenwood Press, 1969), p. 69.

42. This entire discussion of Washington's military and civil duties is indebted to Don Higgenbotham, *George Washington and the American Military Tradition* (Athens, Ga.: University of Georgia Press, 1985).

43. *VG*, July 14, 1775.

44. *VG*, July 1, 1775.

45. Laurens to Lafayette, January 12, 1778, *LDC*, 8:572. For an assessment of Washington's real defects, see, for example, Bernhard Knollenberg, *Washington and the Revolution: A Reappraisal* (New York: Macmillan Co., 1940).

46. Gerry to Knox, February 7, 1778; Dyer to Williams, March 10, 1778; Laurens to Lafayette, January 12, 1778, *LDC*, 8:572; 9:45, 257.

47. *GW*, 4:606. The conspiracy itself has come to be associated with the name of Thomas Conway, an Irish-born French officer who was denied promotion in the American army by Washington, and who became Washington's loudest critic. Conway did not lead the conspiracy, but he was its most obnoxious member, and the man Washington most despised.

48. *VG*, October 17, 1777; October 24, 1777; January 17, 1777.

49. Rush (Notes), April 8, 1777, *LDC*, 6:558.

50. Buel, *Dear Liberty*, p. 38.

51. Royster, *A Revolutionary People at War*, p. 13.

52. Albanese, *Sons of the Fathers*, pp. 82–88.

53. Robert P. Hay, "Providence and the American Past," *Indiana Magazine of History* 65 (1969):79–101.

54. See, for example, three sermons—Nicholas Street, "The American States Acting over the Part of the Children of Israel in the Wilderness and Thereby Impeding Their Entrance Into Canaan's Rest" (1777); Ezra Stiles, "The United States Elevated to Glory and Honour" (1783); and Samuel Langdon, "The Republic of the Israelites An Example to the American States" (1788)—reprinted in Conrad Cherry, ed., *God's New Israel: Religious Interpretations of American Destiny* (Englewood Cliffs, N.J.: Prentice-Hall, 1971), pp. 67–105.

55. Gaillard Hunt, ed., *The History of the Seal of the United States* (Washington, D.C.: Department of State, 1909), p. 12.

56. *BG,* March 25, 1776.

57. For details, see Hay, "George Washington: American Moses"; Kerr, "Character of Political Sermons," pp. 59–89.

58. Albanese, *Sons of the Fathers,* pp. 86, 89.

59. "[T]hings are arbitrarily simplified," Emile Durkheim explains, "when religion is seen only on its idealistic side: in its way, it is realistic. There is no physical or moral ugliness, there are no vices or evils which do not have a special divinity. There are gods of theft and trickery, of lust and war, of sickness and death. Christianity itself, however so high the idea which it has made of the divinity may be, has been obliged to give the spirit of evil a place in its mythology. Satan is an essential piece of the Christian system; even if he is an impure being, he is not a profane one" *EF,* p. 468).

60. Davidson, *Propaganda and the American Revolution,* p. 373; Paul K. Longmore, "The Invention of George Washington" (Ph.D. diss., Claremont Graduate School, 1984), pp. 399–405.

61. Turner, *Dramas, Fields, and Metaphors,* pp. 64, 67–69.

62. Walter Bagehot believed that the Crown's ability to focus upon itself the sentiment and loyalty of the masses imparted to the institution of monarchy a decided psychological advantage over republics, which have no comparable way of simplifying, and objectifying, the otherwise incomprehensible authority of the state (*The English Constitution* [New York: Garland Publishing, 1978], p. 39).

63. Louise Burnham Dunbar, "A Study of 'Monarchical' Tendencies in the United States from 1776 to 1801," *University of Illinois Studies in the Social Sciences* 10 (1922):82.

64. *Ibid.,* 127.

65. *Ibid.,* 26, 56.

66. *HGW,* p. 12. See also *VG,* February 24, 1776.

67. George R. Stewart, *Names on the Land* (Boston: Houghton Mifflin

Company, 1967), pp. 164, 192; Walton C. John and Alma H. Preinkert, eds., "The Educational Views of George Washington," in *History of the George Washington Bicentennial Celebration,* 4 vols. (Washington, D.C.: George Washington Bicentennial Commission, 1932), 1:553.

68. Jane M. Hatch, ed., *The American Book of Days* (New York: Wilson, 1978), p. 129.

69. *VG,* March 30, 1776; Pattee, *Poems of Philip Freneau,* 2:98; Henry Hayden Clark, *Poems of Freneau* (New York: Harcourt Brace, 1929), p. 88.

70. Quoted in Moore, *Diary of the American Revolution,* 2:493.

71. Hetty J. Roozemond-Van Ginhoven, *Ikon: Inspired Art* (Echteld, Netherlands: The Wijenburgh Foundation, 1980), p. 13.

72. Roy C. Strong, *Portraits of Queen Elizabeth* (Oxford: Clarendon Press, 1963), p. 36.

73. Supreme Executive Council of the Commonwealth of Pennsylvania, *Minutes of the Supreme Executive Council* 2 (January 18, 1779), p. 671.

74. *Freeman's Journal,* September 12, 1781, reprinted in Moore, *Diary of the American Revolution,* 2:493. Indignation over the vandals' destruction of the Washington portrait was intensified by their simultaneous destruction of an image of General Richard Montgomery, killed in 1776 while leading an attack on Quebec under Washington's command. For a fuller discussion of the political significance of the Washington portraits, see Eugene F. Miller and Barry Schwartz, "The Icon of the American Republic," *Review of Politics* 47 (1985):516–43.

75. *EF,* pp. 134–40, 264; H. P. Gerhard, *The World of Icons* (New York: Harper and Row, 1971), pp. 11–41; Marianna Jenkins, *The State Portrait: Its Origin and Evolution,* College Art Institute of America, Study No. 3 (1947).

76. John Hill Morgan and Mantle Fielding, *The Life Portraits of Washington and Their Replicas* (Philadelphia: Printed for the Subscribers, 1931), p. 18.

77. However, the 1783 resolution eventually did lead to the erection of the Washington Monument. For details, see U.S., "Washington National Monument," *House of Representatives Report no. 485,* May 1, 1874.

78. Henry T. Tuckerman, *The Character and Portraits of Washington* (New York: G. P. Putnam, 1859), pp. 33–34.

79. Bagehot, *The English Constitution,* p. 39.

80. J. G. A. Pocock, "The Classical Theory of Deference," *American Historical Review* 81 (1976):516.

81. Daniel Shute, "An Election Sermon" (1768), reprinted in *American Political Writing during the Founding Era,* ed. Charles S. Hyneman and Donald S. Lutz, 2 vols. (Indianapolis: Liberty Press, 1983), 1:126; Phil-

lips Payson, *A Sermon Preached before the Honorable Council and Honorable House of Representatives of the State of Massachusetts-Bay* (Boston: John Gill, 1778), p. 32.

82. Rush, *Autobiography*, p. 139.

CHAPTER 2

1. Cherry, *God's New Israel*, pp. 88–89.
2. Washington to Francis Hopkinson, May 16, 1785, *WGW*, 28:140–41.
3. *New York Gazette*, February 11, 1784.
4. *Freeman's Journal*, December 5, 1781.
5. *Ibid.*, December 19, 1781.
6. William Tudor, *An Oration Delivered ... to Commemorate the Bloody Tragedy of the Fifth of March, 1770* (Boston: Edes and Gill, 1779), p. 11.
7. John Adams to Abigail Adams, October 26, 1777, *AFC*, 2:361.
8. Daniel, "Oration," p. 274.
9. Chinard, *George Washington as the French Knew Him*, p. 56.
10. Weber, *Economy and Society*, 1:246–54; 3:1121–23.
11. Seymour M. Lipset, *The First New Nation* (New York: W. W. Norton, 1979), p. 18.
12. *CIN*, pp. 151–72.
13. Monroe to Jefferson, July 27, 1787, *PTJ*, 11:631.
14. Hamilton, in recollection of the New York State (Ratification) Convention, March 7, 1789, *PAH*, 5:291.
15. Flexner, *George Washington*, 3:211; Monroe to Jefferson, July 12, 1788, *PTJ*, 13:351.
16. Clinton Rossiter, *The American Presidency* (New York: New American Library, 1960), p. 76. See also Jackson Turner Main, *The Anti-Federalists* (New York: W. W. Norton, 1974), p. 141.
17. Lewis to Thomas Shippen, October 11, 1787, *PTJ*, 12:230.
18. Monroe to Jefferson, July 12, 1788, *PTJ*, 13:352.
19. Dixon Wector, *The Hero in America: A Chronicle of Hero-Worship.* (Ann Arbor: The University of Michigan Press, 1972) p. 125.
20. Washington to Clinton, March 25, 1789, *WGW*, 30:252.
21. *GUS*, April 29, 1789. As he listened to these lyrics, Washington crossed over a laurel-decked bridge bearing a banner that read: "The Hero Who Defended the Mothers Will Protect the Daughters." The slogan reminded those present of the atrocities committed by British soldiers against American women, and of the Amer-

ican soldiers' determination to "free the land from rapine, devastation, and burnings, and female innocence from brutal lust and violence" *VG,* September 26, 1777).

22. *GUS,* April 29, 1789.

23. George Washington, *The Diaries of George Washington,* ed. Donald Jackson and Dorothy Twohig, 6 vols. (Charlottesville: University of Virginia Press, 1976–79), 5:447.

24. *GUS,* April 22, 1789.

25. Adams to Jefferson, October 9, 1787, *PTJ,* 12:220.

26. *New York Journal,* August 20, 1790.

27. *NG,* March 2, 1793.

28. Rush to Marshall, September 15, 1798, *LBR,* 2:807.

29. Dunbar, "A Study of 'Monarchical' Tendencies," pp. 57, 71, 58, 77, 107, 104, 108–11.

30. *NG,* September 12, 1792.

31. *CIN,* pp. 171–72.

32. Jenkins, *The State Portrait.*

33. (Charleston) *South Carolina State Gazette,* October 3, 1796.

34. Adams to Jebb, August 21, 1785, *Works of John Adams,* 9:532–36.

35. Adams to Jebb, September 10, 1785, *Ibid.,* 541.

36. *Ibid.,* 542.

37. *Ibid.*

38. *Annals of Congress,* 1st Congress, Vol. 2, Appendix, December 13, 1790, p. 2085.

39. *Ibid.,* 2nd Congress, March 24, 1792, p. 484.

40. *Ibid.,* March 26, 1792, pp. 488–89.

41. *Ibid.,* March 24, 1792, p. 484.

42. R. S. Yeoman, *A Guidebook of United States Coins,* 37th ed. (Racine, Wis.: Western Publishing Company, 1984), pp. 52–55.

43. Washington to David Stuart, June 15, 1790, *WGW,* 31:53–54.

44. See Washington to Jefferson, April 8, 1784; Jefferson to Washington, April 16, 1784, *PTJ,* 7:88–89; 105–10.

45. Edward A. Shils, *Center and Periphery* (Chicago: University of Chicago Press, 1975), p. 154.

46. Hamilton to Washington, May 5, 1789, *PAH,* 5:335–36.

47. (New York) *Daily Advertiser,* June 15, 1789.

48. *NG,* December 26, 1792.

49. *Ibid.,* January 30, 1793.

50. *Ibid.,* February 2, 1793.

51. *Ibid.*, March 2, 1793.
52. *Ibid.*, March 13, 1793.
53. Main, The Anti-Federalists, pp. 280–81.
54. Marshall Smelser, quoted in Lipset, *The First New Nation*, p. 38.
55. *ARA,* March 4, 1797.
56. Richard Hofstadter, *The American Political Tradition* (New York: Random House, 1973), p. 8.
57. The *National Gazette,* flagship of the anti-administration press, joined in this support (October 10, 1792).
58. Beckley to Madison, quoted in *GW,* 7:303.
59. *GW,* 7:303.
60. Charles Warren, *Jacobin and Junto; or, Early American Politics as Viewed in the Diary of Dr. Nathaniel Ames* (Cambridge: Harvard University Press, 1931), p. 63.
61. Jasper Dwight, *A Letter to George Washington ... Containing Strictures on His address of the 17th of September, 1796 Notifying his Relinquishment of the Presidential Office* (Philadelphia: Printed for the Author, 1796), p. 5. This loss, Dwight goes on to say, is to be lamented, since it may lead to the nation's fall. (Many Federalists attributed Jasper Dwight's letter to William Duane—an accusation that Duane himself denied. See Worthington Chauncey Ford, *The Spurious Letters Attributed to Washington* [Brooklyn, N.Y.: Privately printed, 1889], p. 158.)
62. Charles Adams to John Quincy Adams, December 30, 1793, quoted in *GW,* 7:143.
63. Adams to William Cunningham, October 15, 1808, *Correspondence Between the Honorable John Adams ... and William Cunningham, Esq.* (Boston: True and Greene, 1823), p. 34.
64. *NG,* June 1, 1793.
65. *ARA,* January 23, 1796.
66. Beckley to Madison, quoted in *GW,* 7:303.
67. (Boston) *Independent Chronicle,* September 7, 1795.
68. *ARA,* September 9, 25, 1795.
69. (Boston) *Independent Chronicle* September 27, 1795.
70. *GW,* 7:431.
71. *ARA,* August 22, 1795.
72. *BG,* September 26, 1796.
73. *GW,* 7:303.
74. *ARA,* September 21, 1795; February 20, 1796.
75. (New York) *Argus,* December 26, 1795, quoted in *GW,* 7:321.

76. *New York Journal,* December 7, 1793. Editor Thomas Greenleaf was forced to apologize publicly for publishing this statement.

77. *ARA,* January 23, 1797.

78. For details on the charges and defense, see Hamilton to Washington, October 26, 1795; Hamilton to Wolcott, October 26, 27, 28, 1795; Wolcott to Hamilton, October 29, 1795; Hamilton to (New York) *Daily Advertiser,* November 11, 1795, *PAH,* 19:350–54, 364, 400–404. The circle of charge and countercharge is widened in William Cobbett, *Porcupine's Works ... Exhibiting a Faithful Picture of the United States of America,* 12 vols. (London: Crown and Mitre, 1801), 403–42.

79. (Boston) *Independent Chronicle,* September 7, 1795.

80. *ARA,* October 21, 1795.

81. Included in *The Life and Works of Thomas Paine,* ed. William M. Van der Weyde (New Rochelle, N.Y.: Thomas Paine National Historic Association, 1925), pp. 139–201.

82. For details, see Ford, *The Spurious Letters.*

83. *ARA,* January 9, 1797.

84. *Ibid.,* March 6, 1797.

85. Richard Hofstadter, *The Paranoid Style in American Politics* (Chicago: University of Chicago Press, 1979), pp. 3–40.

86. It is almost as if "a set of people whether consciously, preconsciously, or unconsciously take on roles which carry with them, if not precisely recorded scripts, deeply engraved tendencies to act and speak in suprapersonal or 'representative' ways appropriate to the roles taken. . . . " (Turner, *Dramas, Fields, and Metaphors,* p. 123).

87. *IO,* p. 97.

88. *Ibid.,* pp. 119–21.

89. Lucas, *Portents of Rebellion,* pp. 112, 113.

90. *Ibid.,* pp. 113, 168, 176–77.

91. *IO,* p. 95.

92. Herbert Storing, *What the Anti-Federalists Were For* (Chicago: University of Chicago Press, 1981), p. 49.

93. James Flexner, *Washington: The Indispensable Man* (New York: New American Library, 1974), p. 287.

94. *NG,* June 1, 1793.

95. *Dictionary of American Biography,* ed. Allen Johnson and Dumas Malone, 21 vols. (New York: Charles Scribner's Sons, 1928–36), 7:584–85.

96. *Ibid.,* 4:248–49.

97. *Ibid.,* 3:425–26

98. *Ibid.,* 5:467–68.

99. *Ibid.,* 1:431–32.

100. *Ibid.,* 14:159–66.

101. *Ibid.,* 4:47.

102. *ARA,* January 24, 1797.

103. Chinard, *Washington as the French Knew Him,* p. xvi.

104. *GUS,* May 21, 1791.

105. *Ibid.,* May 25, 1791; June 1, 1791.

106. *Ibid.,* May 21, 1791.

107. *Ibid.,* May 21, 1791.

108. *Ibid.,* May 25, 1791; June 1, 1791.

109. Washington, *Diaries of George Washington,* 6:140.

110. Archibald Henderson, *Washington's Southern Tour* (Boston: Houghton Mifflin Co., 1923).

111. *GW,* 6:322.

112. Plumer to Jeremiah Smith, April 19, 1796, quoted in *GW,* 7;356.

113. Rush to Samuel Bayard, March 1, 1796; Rush to Adams, June 13, 1811, *LBR,* 2:768–69; 1084.

114. Jefferson to Monroe, June 12, 1796, *Writings of Thomas Jefferson,* 8:243.

115. Harper to Hamilton, November 4, 1796, *PAH,* 20:370–71.

116. *PG,* March 2, 1791.

117. *GW,* 7:343.

118. *EF,* p. 474–75.

119. (New York) *Argus,* March 6, 1776.

120. *PG,* March 9, 1796.

121. *Ibid.,* February 23, 1793; March 9, 1796.

122. *GUS,* July 9, 1796.

123. C. McCombs, *George Washington, 1732–1932: An Exhibition Held at the New York Public Library* (New York: New York Public Library, 1932), p. 1.

124. Jane Stuart, "The Stuart Portraits of Washington," *Scribner's Monthly* 21 (1876):367–74.

125. *PG,* January 8, 1800.

126. Sigmund Freud, *Group Psychology and the Analysis of the Ego* (New York: Bantam Books, 1960), p. 61.

127. Georg Simmel, *The Sociology of Georg Simmel,* ed. Kurt Wolff (New York: The Free Press, 1950), pp. 190, 192.

128. Ebanezer Davenport, *An Oration on the Death of General George Washington* (New York: John Furman, 1800), p. 12.

129. Osgood to Adams, January 14, 1784, *Letters of Members of the Continental Congress*, ed. Edmund C. Burnett, 8 vols. (Washington, D.C.: Carnegie Institute, 1921–36), 7:415.

130. Isaac Parker, *An Oration on the Sublime Virtues of General George Washington* (Portland, Me.: Elezer Jenks, 1800), p. 19.

131. *PG*, March 9, 1796.

132. Emile Durkheim, *The Division of Labor in Society* (New York: The Free Press, 1964).

133. Paul F. Boller, Jr., *George Washington and Religion* (Dallas: Southern Methodist University Press, 1963), pp. 116–62.

134. *ARA*, January 6, 1797.

135. Adams to Rush, April 4, 1790, *Old Family Letters* (see Introd., n. 15), 1:55.

136. Rush to Adams, February 24, 1790, *LBR*, 1:534.

137. John Adams, *Discourses on Davila: A Series of Papers on Political History* (Boston: Russell and Cutler, 1805), p. 59.

138. Jefferson to the President of the United States, May 23, 1792, *The Writings of Thomas Jefferson*, ed. Andrew A. Lipscomb, 20 vols. (Washington, D.C.: Thomas Jefferson Memorial Association, 1903–4), 8:347. (All previous and subsequent references to *The Writings of Thomas Jefferson* refer to the Worthington Ford edition.)

139. Charles, *Origins of the American Party System* (see Introd., n. 17), p. 52.

140. Hamilton eulogy on General Greene, July 4, 1789, *PAH*, 5:350.

141. Hamilton to Philip Schuyler, February 18, 1781, *ibid.*, 2:507.

142. Rush to Adams, February 12, 1812, *LBR*, 2:1123.

CHAPTER 3

1. (Charleston) *City Gazette of South Carolina*, January 8, 1800.

2. *Ibid.*

3. Adams to Jefferson, September 3, 1816, *The Adams-Jefferson Letters*, ed. Lester J. Cappon, 2 vols. (Chapel Hill: University of North Carolina Press, 1959), 2:488.

4. *EF*, p. 443.

5. *GW*, 7:649.

6. Morris was not only "pathetic and nervous" in the delivery of his address but also wanting in its conception. According to one observer, his oration was like a "cold, historical narrative, not that of a warm, impassioned address" (Howard Swiggart, *The Extraordinary Mr. Morris* [Garden City, N.Y.: Doubleday, 1952], p. 342). Evidently, the audience's emotional reaction to Morris's eulogy was not provoked by Morris's eulogical skill.

7. *GW,* 7:650–51.

8. *Russell's Gazette,* December 26, 1799.

9. *Ibid.*

10. *Ibid.,* December 30, 1799 to January 9, 1800. CF. William Lloyd Warner, *The Living and the Dead* (New Haven: Yale University Press, 1959), pp. 248–79.

11. *Russell's Gazette,* January 13, 1800.

12. *Ibid.*

13. Bostonian Society, *Funeral Processions in Boston from 1770 to 1800* (Boston: Bostonian Society Publications, 1907), 4:127–30. (See also 130–49.)

14. *Russell's Gazette,* January 13, 1800. See also George R. Minot, *An Eulogy on George Washington* (Boston: Manning and Loring, 1800).

15. William A. Bryan, *George Washington in American Literature* (New York: Columbia University Press, 1952). p. 55.

16. The eulogists cited in this book are part of a sample of fifty-five eulogists, whose orations were drawn from the *Early American Imprints.* Forty of these men were prominent enough to be listed in either the *Dictionary of American Biograpy* or *Appleton's Cyclopedia of American Biography.* About half of those listed (nineteen out of forty) pursued secular careers, mainly law and statecraft; the other half were clergymen. Among the six secular leaders whose religious preference is mentioned, there were two Quakers, a Presbyterian, a Unitarian, an Episcopalian, and a Deist; in this same group were found two Masonic grandmasters. Clergymen, on the other hand, tended to be drawn from the neo-Calvinist denominations (thirteen out of twenty-one were Presbyterians or Congregationalists). Whatever their denomination, only three of the twenty-one clergymen were personally acquainted with Washington, compared with nine of the nineteen secular leaders. As to regional background, twenty-two of the orators were born in New England, thirteen in the Middle states, and two in the South. Of the twenty men whose political preferences are reported, nineteen were Federalists. The lopsided regional and political representation reflects in part the distribution of printing presses, which in 1800 were concentrated in Federalist New England. (See Bernard Bailyn and John B. Hench, eds., *The Press and the American Revolution* (Worcester, Mass.: American Antinquarian Society, 1980.)

17. In the election year of 1800, the declining Federalist party certainly did itself no harm by playing a conspicuous role in the Washington funeral observances. Yet, most Republicans adored Washington as much as the Federalists did, and their eulogies, which were more likely to be delivered outside New England and therefore less likely

to be published (see note 16), probably gave the same account of his virtues. Even those who had opposed Washington at different points in his career, like Thomas Paine and Henry Lee, employed in their published eulogies terms of veneration that were similar to those used by steady supporters. Perhaps what is most important to stress, however, is that for half the eulogists no information can be found on their political preference. This lack of information may be due to the biographers' oversight, but it is also consistent with the fact that in 1800 about half the Congress, and probably far more than half the population, embraced no political faction.

18. Henry Holcombe, *A Sermon Occasioned by the Death of Lieutenant General George Washington* (Savannah: Seymour and Wollhopter, 1800), p. 4.

19. Mason, *A Funeral Oration* (see Introd., n. 19), p. 4.

20. Thomas Baldwin, *A Sermon Delivered to the Second Baptist Society . . . Occasioned by the Death of General George Washington* (Boston: Manning and Loring, 1800), p. 17.

21. *Ibid.,* p. 26.

22. Uzal Ogden, *Two Discourses Occasioned by the Death of General George Washington* (Newark, N.J.: Matthias Day, 1800), p. 42.

23. Baldwin, *A Sermon,* p. 27.

24. David Tappan, *A Discourse Delivered . . . in Solemn Commemoration of General George Washington* (Charlestown, Mass.: Samuel Etheridge, 1800), p. 5.

25. Samuel Tomb, *An Oration on the Auspicious Birth, Sublime Virtues, and Triumphant Death of General George Washington* (Newburyport, Conn.: Edmund M. Blunt, 1800), p. 13.

26. David McClure, *A Discourse, Commemorative of the Death of General George Washington* (East Windsor, Conn.: Luther Pratt, 1800), p. 15.

27. *PG,* December 24, 1799.

28. Jonathan M. Sewall, *An Eulogy on the Late General Washington at St. John's Church* (Portsmouth, N.H.: William Treadwell, 1799), p. 16.

29. Fisher Ames, *An Oration on the Sublime Virtues of General George Washington* (Boston: Young and Minns, 1800), p. 4.

30. *HGW,* p. 60.

31. (New York) *Daily Advertiser,* December 31, 1799.

CHAPTER 4

1. *EF,* p. 101. See also "Address to the Lycéens of Sens" (1883), in *Emile Durkheim on Morality and Society,* ed. Robert N. Bellah (Chicago: University of Chicago Press, 1973), p. 32.

2. A. Dulles, "Theology of Revelation," in *New Catholic Encyclopedia,* 12 vols. (New York: McGraw-Hill, 1967), 12:441.

3. Shute, "An Election Sermon" (1768), in Hyneman and Lutz, eds., *American Political Writing,* 1:122. See also Payson, *A Sermon,* p. 24. Specific references to Washington, in this regard, are found in Joseph McKeen, *Sermon Preached Before the Council, the Senate, and House of Representatives of the Commonwealth of Massachusetts* (Boston: Young and Minns, 1800), p. 9, and Zephaniah Swift Moore, "An Oration on the Anniversary of the Independence of the United States," in *American Political Writing,* ed. Hyneman and Lutz, p. 1217. (For Shute and Moore, see chap. 1, n. 81.)

4. *EF,* pp. 393–414.

5. United States, *History of the George Washington Bicentennial Celebration,* 4 vols. (Washington, D.C.: U.S. George Washington Bicentennial Commission, 1932), 4:9–14; 131, 139. (See also 24–32.)

6. "George Washington," in *The Great Soviet Encyclopedia,* 3rd edition, ed. A. M. Prokhorov, 31 vols. (New York; Macmillan, 1974), 4:672. "Leftist" leaders receive more positive coverage. Thomas Jefferson, for example, "was an outstanding representative of the left-wing of the eighteenth-century Enlightenment.... Progressive forces in the United States [now] draw on the best Jeffersonian traditions in the struggle for peace and democracy" (8:549). Likewise, Abraham Lincoln is "the bearer of the revolutionary traditions that are followed by all progressive people in the United States...." (4:505).

7. Quoted by Representative Roncalio in 94th Congress, 2nd Session, Vol. 122, Pt. 3, February 18, 1976, p. 3159.

8. Trevor H. Colbourn, *The Lamp of Experience* (Chapel Hill: University of North Carolina Press, 1965); *IO,* pp. 34–35. See also Caroline Robbins, *The Eighteenth-Century Commonwealthmen* (Cambridge: Harvard University Press, 1959).

9. On the role of the press, see Davidson, *Propaganda and the American Revolution* (see chap. 1, n. 7). On the role of the pulpit, see Harry Stout, "Religion, Communications, and the Ideological Origins of the American Revolution," *William and Mary Quarterly,* 3rd series, 34 (1977):519–41.

10. Clinton Rossiter, *Seedtime of the Republic* (New York: Harcourt, Brace & World, 1953), p. 143.

11. William A. Benton, *Whig-Loyalism* (Rutherford, N.J.: Fairleigh Dickinson University Press, 1969).

12. Rossiter, *Seedtime of the Republic,* p. 353.

13. *IO,* pp. 56–57.

14. Cecilia M. Kenyon, "Men of Little Faith: The Antifederalists on the

Nature of Representative Government," *William and Mary Quarterly*, 3rd series, 12 (1955):3–46; Main, The Anti-Federalists, p. 127.

15. *IO*, p. 60.

16. Jack P. Greene, *Landon Carter: An Inquiry into the Personal Values and Social Imperatives of the Eighteenth-Century Virginia Gentry* (Charlottesville: University Press of Virginia, 1965), p. 27.

17. Rossiter, *Seedtime of the Republic*, p. 372.

18. Samuel Adams, *The Writings of Samuel Adams*, ed. Harry A. Cushing, 4 vols. (New York: Octagon Books, 1968), 4:124–25.

19. (Boston) *Independent Advertiser*, May 29, 1749.

20. Meyer Rheinhold, "The Classics and the Quest for Virtue in Eighteenth-Century America," in *The Usefulness of Classical Learning in the Eighteenth Century* (University Park, Pa.: American Philosophical Association, 1977), p. 8.

21. *Ibid.*, p. 7.

22. According to Lawrence Friedman, the symbolic Washington pointed to deep-seated ideological and psychological problems stemming from the new republic's failure to live up to its own aspirations. The Americans, Friedman explains, tried hard to realize a perfect nation and to find a secure place within it, but then, how does one progress and remain in place at the same time? To soften, if not deny, this dilemma was the function of what Friedman calls "the mythical Washington." If Washington's countrymen found him to be the "perfect man," a man "inaccessible to human weakness," it was because a flawless hero was "helpful to patriots who fretted over the American experience in nation making. . . . A superior, united, independent New Nation followed from Washington's personal perfection." Correspondingly, if Americans attributed to Washington the virtues of steadiness, prudence, serenity, resoluteness, orderliness, and self-control, it was to create a man with the kind of secure, well-rooted existence they sought for themselves. In the revelation of Washington, Friedman concludes, the people found a model that reconciled their own aggressive striving toward infallibility with calm stability and a sense of place (*Inventors of the Promised Land*, pp. 44–78) [see Introd., n. 8].

23. Political and family life, in Jay Fliegelman's view, had always been as closely connected in the American colonies as they had been elsewhere. In the early colonial families, stern, authoritarian fathers had kept a distance between themselves and their children. By the mid–eighteenth century, however, the traditional patriarchal family had given way to an Enlightenment ideal characterized by affectionate and egalitarian relationships between parents and children. Since these relationships prepared children for independence and moral

self-sufficiency rather than emphasizing dependence and deference, their rationale "easily extended," in Fliegelman's opinion, "to an argument for colonial rights." Seeking a material sign, a monument, to this development, it was natural that Americans would turn to their "Father, Friend and Guardian," George Washington. He was "the embodiment of the new understanding of paternity." He was not a political hero pressed into the service of domestic needs, but rather a domestic hero pressed into the service of political needs. The replacement of enslaving fathers by liberating fathers "permitted Americans to transfer both their filial affection and the title of parent from King George to President Washington." Accordingly, Washington's "idealization as the nation's father served to complete the transformation of the antipatriarchal ideology into a national dogma" (*Prodigals and Pilgrims,* pp. 197–226) [see Introd., n. 8].

24. For Garry Wills, who regards George Washington as a symbol of the Enlightenment itself, political and family life exist in a relationship of tension, not collaboration. Washington's heroism entails the renunciation of the family in favor of the state. The heroic ideal itself, however, is subdued. "Unlike Carlyleans, who praise a happy thirst for power, men of the Enlightenment tried to instill a considered reluctance to exercise it," Wills argues. Washington's studied resistance to being drawn into positions of power and his timely resignations of power prove that he learned his lessons well. That Washington was not merely admired but venerated for such deeds affirms the Enlightenment's encouragement of "rational" hero worship, a disposition which, in Wills's view, reconciles the adoration of great men with libertarian ideals (*CIN,* p. 23. See also pp. 1–27; 173–194).

25. Since America's political culture had evolved before independence, when the needs of progress and stability became most salient, and since most Americans understood Washington as an exemplar of that culture, the dilemma that Lawrence Friedman describes—the inherent irreconcilability of progress and order (see note 22)—probably did not play a major role in the shaping of Washington's image. Jay Fliegelman's interpretation (see note 23) seems also to be pushed too far. To regard the virtues attributed to Washington as a reflection of the emerging antipatriarchal household is to trace the culture he represented to the makeup of the family, rather than vice versa—a procedure once favored by neo-Freudians, but long since discredited. Eighteenth-century Americans certainly did not understand their political heritage, or their Washington, in this way. However, Garry Wills's argument, that Washington incarnated Enlightenment ideals (see note 24), cannot be as quickly dismissed. We know that Washington was deeply admired in other countries (France and England especially) whose cultures were strongly influenced by the En-

lightenment. An entire volume by Gilbert Chinard, for example (*Washington as the French Knew Him*), documents the affection with which Washington was regarded in both imperial and republican France. As to England, the evidence is less voluminous but still compelling. In 1797, Rufus King reported: "The King is without doubt a very popular character among the People of this Nation; it would be saying very much, to affirm that next to him, General Washington is the most popular character among them, and yet I verily believe this to be the fact" (King to Hamilton, February 6, 1797, *PAH*, 20:505). In both countries, France and England, George Washington was a symbol of the struggle of free men against tyranny, and this fact is consistent with Wills's linkage of Washington with the aspirations of the Enlightenment. There is every reason to raise questions about the meaning of this linkage, however. The English people may have admired Washington, but they were prepared to endorse neither the republican values he symbolized nor the political system in which he participated. And although many of the French intellectuals cited by Chinard would have preferred a Washington to a Napoleon, the French people did not agree. Thus, the Americans' veneration of Washington was based on Enlightenment values that differed from those which prevailed elsewhere.

26. Howard Mumford Jones, *O Strange New World* (New York: The Viking Press, 1952), pp. 262–64; Cunliffe, *George Washington*, pp. 151–57; Smylie, "The President as Republican Prophet" (see Introd., n. 8); Albanese, *Sons of the Fathers*, pp. 143–81.

27. *IO*, pp. 23–34.

28. Thaddeus Fiske, *A Sermon ... Immediately Following the Melancholy Intelligence of the Death of General George Washington* (Boston: James Cutler, 1800), p. 11.

29. Joseph Blyth, *An Oration on the Death of General Washington* (Georgetown, S.C.: John Burd, 1800), p. 22; John T. Kirkland, *A Discourse Occasioned by the Death of General George Washington* (Boston: I. Thomas and E. T. Andrews, 1800), pp. 21–22; Timothy Bigelow, *An Eulogy on the Life, Character and Services of Brother George Washington* (Boston: Thomas and Andrews, 1800), pp. 16, 19.

30. Peter Karsten, *Patriot-Heroes in England and America* (Madison: University of Wisconsin Press, 1978), pp. 13–37; Ralph Ketcham, *Presidents above Party* (Chapel Hill: University of North Carolina Press, 1984), pp. 57–68; 89–93.

CHAPTER 5

1. Gordon S. Wood, *The Creation of the American Republic, 1776–1787* (Chapel Hill: University of North Carolina Press, 1969), p. 55.

2. *Ibid.*, p. 61.

3. *Ibid.*

4. *VG,* August 5, 1775.

5. John Fitch, *A Sermon Delivered . . . as a Tribute of Respect for the Memory of the Late General George Washington* (Peachah, Vt.: Farley and Goss, 1800).

6. Weber, *Economy and Society,* 3:1113.

7. Alexander MacWhorter, *A Funeral Sermon Preached for the Universally Lamented General Washington* (Newark, N.J.: Jacob Halsey, 1800), p. 15.

8. Elisha Dick, "Oration," in *The Washingtoniana* (Baltimore, Md.: Samuel Sawyer, 1800), pp. 198, 203.

9. Adams to Gerry, June 18, 1775, *LDC,* 1:504.

10. Silas Deane to Elizabeth Deane, June 16, 1775, *LDC,* 1:494.

11. *BG,* April 8, 1776.

12. *Ibid.*

13. *VG,* January 24, 1777.

14. *Ibid.*

15. Bryan, *George Washington in American Literature,* pp. 148, 128, 132, 156.

16. *Freeman's Journal,* April 22, 1789. See also *Freeman's Journal,* May 27 and September 23, 1789.

17. Washington to Gordon, January 23, 1778, *WGW,* 10:338.

18. Washington to Clinton, December 28, 1783, *ibid.,* 27:288.

19. Washington to Congress (First Inaugural Address), April 30, 1789, *ibid.,* 30:292.

20. Jefferson, Notes, August 2, 1793, *Writings of Thomas Jefferson,* 1:82.

21. Washington, "Farewell Address," September 19, 1796, *WGW,* 35:215–16.

22. Washington to the President of the United States, July 13, 1798, *ibid.,* 36:328–29.

23. Tomb, *An Oration,* p. 12.

24. *HGW,* pp. 30–31. See also Kirkland, *A Discourse,* p. 14.

25. *HGW,* p. 25.

26. John Adams, August 31, 1774, *Diary and Autobiography of John Adams,* ed. L. H. Butterfield, 4 vols. (Cambridge: Harvard University Press, 1961–62), 3:308.

27. *VG,* April 20, 1776.

28. Madison to Jefferson, January 22, 1786, *PTJ,* 9:196; Washington to Congress (First Inaugural Address), *WGW,* 30:295–96. The House

of Representatives' public reaction to the Inaugural Address is found in *Freeman's Journal,* May 20, 1789, and elsewhere.

29. Charles Atherton, *An Eulogy on General George Washington* (Amherst, N.H.: Samuel Preston, 1800), p. 21.

30. Mason, *A Funeral Oration,* pp. 6–7.

31. Samuel Macclintock, *An Oration Commemorative of the Late Illustrious General Washington* (Portsmouth, N.H.: Charles Pierce, 1800), p. 7.

32. *VG,* February 7, 1777.

33. John C. Dunn, ed., *The Revolution Remembered: Eyewitness Accounts of the War for Independence* (Chicago: University of Chicago Press, 1980), pp. 239–40.

34. Thomas Thacher, *An Eulogy on George Washington* (Dedham, Mass.: Mann, 1800), p. 10.

35. Henry Lee, *A Funeral Oration Prepared and Delivered at the Request of Congress* (Brooklyn: Thomas Kirk, 1800), p. 4.

36. Baldwin, *A Sermon,* p. 20. See also Thacher, *Eulogy,* p. 14.

37. Edward Carrington to Jefferson, June 9, 1787, *PTJ,* 11:407–8.

38. Hamilton to New York State (Ratification) Convention, July 17, 1788, *PAH,* 5:176–77.

39. Monroe to Jefferson, July 12, 1788, *PTJ,* 13:352.

40. Jefferson to Washington, May 10, 1789, *ibid.,* 15:118.

41. MacWhorter, *A Funeral Sermon,* p. 11.

42. Washington to Lee, September 22, 1788, *WGW,* 30:98.

43. Lee, *A Funeral Oration,* p. 7.

44. Fredric M. Litto, "Addison's *Cato* in the Colonies" *William and Mary Quarterly,* 3rd series, 23 (1966):431–49; Henry C. Montgomery, "Addison's Cato and George Washington," *Classical Journal* 55 (1960):210–12; Henry C. Montgomery, "Washington the Stoic," *Classical Journal* 31 (1936):371–73; Albert Furtwangler, "Cato at Valley Forge," *Modern Language Quarterly* 41 (1980):38–53.

45. Joseph Addison, "Cato," in *The Works of Joseph Addison,* ed. Henry G. Bohn, 6 vols. (London: George Bell and Sons, 1893), 1:180–81.

46. Richard Buel, "Political Thought Before the Revolution," in *Politics and Society in Colonial America,* ed. Michael Kammen (Hinsdale, Ill.: Dryden Press, 1973), p. 105.

47. *VG,* July 14, 1775.

48. *Ibid.*

49. John Page to Jefferson, July 6, 1776, *PTJ,* 1:455.

50. *Pennsylvania Journal,* February 19, 1777, reprinted in Moore, *Diary of The American Revolution,* I:397.

51. Joseph Campbell, *The Hero with a Thousand Faces* (Princeton: Princeton University Press, 1973), pp. 97–109.

52. Duché to Washington, October 16, 1777, *WGW*, 9:382–83.

53. Nathaniel Folsom to Josiah Bartlett, October 30, 1777, *LDC*, 8:213.

54. Paul F. Boller, Jr., "Washington and Civilian Supremacy," *Southwest Review* 39 (1954):13.

55. (New Haven) *Connecticut Journal*, December 6, 1781.

56. Washington to Lee, February 13, 1789, *WGW*, 30:202–3.

57. Gouverneur Morris, *An Oration on the Death of General Washington* (New York: John Furman, 1800), p. 9.

58. Washington to Nicola, May 22, 1782, *WGW*, 24:272.

59. See, for example, Orrin E. Klapp, *Heroes, Villains, and Fools* (Englewood Cliffs, N.J.: Prentice-Hall, 1962), and *Symbolic Leaders* (Chicago: Aldine, 1964).

60. Dunbar, "A Study of 'Monarchical' Tendencies," p. 40.

61. *Ibid.*, p. 51.

62. Madison to Randolph, March 17, 1783, *The Writings of James Madison*, ed. Gaillard Hunt, 9 vols. (New York: G. P. Putnam's Sons, 1900–1910), 1:407.

63. Flexner, *Washington: The Indispensable Man*, p. 178.

64. Adams to Livingston, June 16, 1783, *Works of John Adams*, 8:73.

65. Clark, *Poems of Freneau*, p. 89.

66. *HGW*, p. 11.

67. Sewall, *Eulogy*, p. 12.

68. Josiah Dunham, *A Funeral Oration on George Washington* (Boston: Manning and Loring, 1800), p. 6.

69. George Blake, *A Masonic Eulogy on the Life of the Illustrious Brother George Washington* (Boston: John Russell, 1800), p. 17.

70. Wood, *Creation of the American Republic*, p. 21.

71. Thacher, *Eulogy*, p. 14.

72. "Explanation of the Frontispiece" in *Philadelphia Magazine and Review*, January, 1799, quoted by Wendy C. Wick, *George Washington: An American Icon* (Charlottesville: University of Virginia Press, 1982), p. 133.

73. Raymond Firth, *Symbols: Public and Private* (Ithaca, N.Y.: Cornell University Press, 1973), p. 311. See also Barry Schwartz, *Vertical Classification* (Chicago: University of Chicago Press, 1981).

74. Washington to president of Congress, December 20, 1783, *WGW*, 27:277–78.

75. These symbolic devices were exploited in the protocol used by Con-

gress to receive Washington's resignation speech and commission. The details, drawn up by Thomas Jefferson, Elbridge Gerry, and James McHenry (Editor's note, *PTJ*, 6:409–10), are presented below:

[22 DECEMBER 1783]

Order for a publick Audience of General Washington.

1st. The president and Members are to be seated and covered, and the Secretary to be standing by the Side of the president.

2ndly. The Arrival of the General is to be announced by the Messenger to the Secretary, who is thereupon to introduce the General attended by his Aids to the Hall of Congress.

3dly. The General being conducted to the Chair by the Secretary, is to be seated with an Aid on each side, standing, and the Secretary is to resume his place.

4thly. After a proper Time for the Arrangement of Spectators Silence is to be ordered by the Secretary if necessary, and the president is to address the General in the following Words "*Congress sir are prepared to receive your Communications.*" Whereupon the General is to rise and address Congress, after which he is to deliver his commission and a Copy of his Address to the president.

5thly. The General having resumed his place, the president is to deliver the Answer to Congress, which the General is to receive standing.

6thly. The president having finished, the secretary is to deliver the General a Copy of the Answer from the president, and the General is then to take his leave.

N.B. When the General rises to make his Address, and also when he retires, he is to bow to Congress, which they are to return by uncovering without bowing.

76. The elevation of the President's chair is evident in John Trumbull's portrait, *The Resignation of General Washington.*

77. *PTJ*, 6:410.

78. *Ibid.*

79. See Barry Schwartz, *Queuing and Waiting: Studies in the Social Organization of Access and Delay* (Chicago: University of Chicago Press, 1975).

80. McHenry to Caldwell, December 23, 1783, *Letters of Members of the Continental Congress,* 7:394–95.

81. *Ibid.*

82. Pattee, *Poems of Philip Freneau,* 2:228. On the press coverage, see, for example, Jefferson to Benjamin Harrison, December 24, 1783, *PTJ*, 6:419.

83. Washington to the States (Circular Letter), June 8, 1783, *WGW*, 26:486–87; 495.

84. Washington to Hamilton, August 28, 1788, *ibid.*, 30:67.

85. Washington to Knox, March 8, 1787, *ibid.*, 29:171.

86. Washington to Randolph, April 9, 1787, *ibid.*, 198.

87. Washington to Benjamin Lincoln, October 26, 1788, *ibid.*, 30:119.

88. See, for example, *CIN*, pp. 151–54.

89. See Washington's letters to Madison, November 18, 1786; David Stuart, November 19, 1786; Madison, December 16, 1786; Randolph, December 21, 1786; David Humphreys, December 26, 1786; Knox, February 3, 1787; Knox, March 8, 1787; Secretary for Foreign Affairs, March 10, 1787; James Mercer, March 15, 1787; Randolph, March 28, 1787; Knox, April 2, 1787; Randolph, April 9, 1787, *WGW*, 29:70–72, 75–77, 113–15, 119–20, 125–29, 151–53, 170–73, 177, 179–81, 186–88, 193–95, 197–98.

90. See Washington's letters to Lee, September 22, 1788; Hamilton, October 3, 1788; Benjamin Lincoln, October 26, 1788; Gouverneur Morris, November 28, 1788; Jonathan Trumbull, December 4, 1788; Lewis Morris, December 13, 1788; William Gordon, December 23, 1788; William Pierce, January 1, 1789; Samuel Hanson, January 10, 1789; Lafayette, January 29, 1789, *ibid.*, 30:97–98, 109–12, 118–21, 143, 149–50, 157, 168–69, 175, 177–78, 185–86.

91. Madison to Jefferson, May 15, 1787, *PTJ*, 11:363.

92. Humphreys to Jefferson, November 29, 1788, *ibid.*, 14:302.

93. Jefferson to William Carmichael, March 4, 1789, *ibid.*, 14:615.

94. Benjamin Orr, *An Oration in Commemoration of the Life of General George Washington* (Amherst, N.H.: Samuel Preston, 1800), p. 137.

95. Bigelow, *Eulogy*, pp. 15–16.

96. Lee, *A Funeral Oration*, p. 13.

97. Aaron Bancroft, *An Eulogy on the Character of the Late General George Washington* (Worcester, Mass.: Isaiah Thomas, 1800), p. 12.

98. *Russell's Gazette*, January 2, 1800.

99. Mason, *A Funeral Oration*, p. 17.

100. Holcombe, *A Sermon*, p. 11.

101. Ames, *An Oration*, pp. 20, 26–27.

102. Samuel West, *Greatness the Result of Goodness: A Sermon Occasioned by the Death of George Washington* (Boston: Manning & Loring, 1800), p. 12. See also Talleyrand's comment on "the new type of heroism of which Washington and America were models for the world at large" (Chinard, *Washington as the French Knew Him*, p. 128).

103. Tappan, *A Discourse*, p. 25.

104. West, *Greatness the Result of Goodness,* pp. 12–13.

105. Baldwin, *A Sermon,* p. 23.

106. Bancroft, *Eulogy,* p. 16.

CHAPTER 6

1. Aristotle, "Nichomachean Ethics," in Richard McKeon, ed., *Introduction to Aristotle* (New York: Modern Library, 1947), p. 34.

2. *GW,* 3:7.

3. *BG,* August 14, 1775; Abigail Adams to John Adams, July 16, 1775, *AFC,* 1:246.

4. *Georgia Gazette,* August 23, 1775.

5. Washington to Congress, December 23, 1783, *WGW,* 27:284.

6. *Freeman's Journal,* April 29, 1789.

7. Ames to Minot, May 3, 1789, quoted in *GW,* 6:195.

8. ' LaRochefoucauld, quoted in Peter Blau, *Exchange and Power in Social Life* (New York, John Wiley and Sons, 1967), p. 33. See also pp. 49, 57.

9. Payson, *A Sermon,* p. 24.

10. Adams to Rush, June 21, 1811, in Schutz and Adair, eds., *The Spur of Fame,* p. 181.

11. Flexner, *George Washington,* 2:507.

12. Benjamin Tallmadge, *Memoir of Benjamin Tallmadge* (New York: New York Times and Arno Press, 1968), pp. 63–69.

13. Washington, "Farewell Address," September 19, 1796, *WGW,* 35:216–17.

14. Abiel Holmes, *A Sermon ... Occasioned by the Death of General George Washington* (Boston: Samuel Hall, 1800), p. 16; MacWhorter, *A Funeral Sermon,* p. 2; Lee, *A Funeral Oration,* p. 10.

15. (Boston) *Independent Chronicle,* June 21, 1787. Moreover, Americans cannot prevent money from leaving the country when "there is an inordinate consumption of foreign geegaws" (*Freeman's Journal,* January 5, 1785). For more on the ascetic tradition in American culture, see Edmund S. Morgan, "The Puritan Ethic and the American Revolution," in *The Challenge of the American Revolution* (New York: W. W. Norton, 1978), pp. 88–138.

16. (Charleston) *South Carolina Gazette,* October 6, 1766, quoted in Hyneman and Lutz, *American Political Writings,* 1:93, 95.

17. Payson, *A Sermon,* p. 17. For a detailed discussion of the relationship between luxury and public virtue, see *VG,* June 8, 1776.

18. *HGW,* p. 28.

19. Joseph Lathrop, "Frugality," in Hyneman and Lutz, *American Political Writings*, 1:663.

20. *VG*, January 24, 1777.

21. John Adams to Abigail Adams, September 1, 1777, *LDC*, 7:580.

22. Greene to Rainald McDougall, April 11, 1779, quoted in *GW*, 5:91.

23. *HGW*, pp. 30, 32–33.

24. *Ibid.*, p. 33.

25. Quoted in Bryan, *George Washington in American Literature*, p. 138. The passage is from Timothy Dwight's "The Conquest of Canaan," a poem that many have regarded, and still regard, as an allegory of the American Revolution. The object of this passage, Joshua, is supposedly Washington's stand-in. Dwight denied that he ever intended to make such a parallel, but many doubt his word.

26. Thacher, *An Eulogy on George Washington*, p. 19.

27. Tuckerman, *The Character and Portraits of Washington*, pp. 91–92. For futher analysis of the visual depiction of Washington's moral character, see Barry Schwartz and Eugene F. Miller, "The Icon and the Word," *Semiotica*, 61½ (1986):69–99.

28. Wick, *George Washington: An American Icon*, p. 62.

29. *Ibid.*, p. 58; *CIN*, p. 79.

30. *GUS*, May 2, 1789.

31. Samuel Mead, *A Sermon Occasioned by the Death of General George Washington* (Salem, Mass.: Joshua Cushing, 1800), p. 8.

32. Timothy Dwight, *A Discourse, Delivered at New Haven, on the Character of George Washington, Esq. at the Request of the Citizens* (Thomas Green and Son, 1800) p. 23.

33. Morris, *An Oration on the Death of General Washington*, p. 5.

34. Using the term "genius" in the sense of a strongly marked aptitude rather than a transcendent mental supriority, Edmund Morgan's essay, *The Genius of George Washington* (New York: W. W. Norton, 1980), provides a twentieth-century assessment of Washington's intellect. It was especially Washington's ability to preserve both order and liberty, Morgan suggests, that set him apart from others. He knew when and how to concentrate power for military and national purposes, and he was acutely sensitive to the dangers of political decentralization. Washington's contemporaries would have interpreted his balancing act a little differently. The effective exercise of power, in their view, did require a "marked aptitude"; however, sensitivity to the proper distribution of power stemmed from *moral* preference. Not in aptitude or morality alone, moreover, but in their reconciliation in decision and conduct was where Washington's wisdom was seen to be best demonstrated.

35. *CIN,* p. 162.

36. Pattee, ed., *Poems of Philip Freneau,* 1:149.

37. *VG,* January 17, 1777.

38. See, for example, *PG,* March 18, 1789.

39. Sewall, *Eulogy,* pp. 24, 27.

40. Macclintock, *An Oration,* p. 10.

41. MacWhorter, *A Funeral Sermon,* pp. 5, 10.

42. John Brooks, *An Eulogy on General Washington* (Boston: Samuel Hall, 1800), p. 11.

43. *BG,* January 22, 1776.

44. John Trumbull, *The Poetical Works,* 2 vols. (Hartford, Conn.: Samuel G. Goodrich, 1820), 2:99.

45. Tappan, *A Discourse,* p. 28.

46. Tomb, *An Oration,* p. 11.

47. Mason, *A Funeral Oration,* pp. 8–9.

48. Joseph Addison, "Cato," in *The Works of Joseph Addison,* 1:181.

49. Shute, "An Election Sermon" (1768), in Hyneman and Lutz, eds., *American Political Writing,* 1:124. See also John Tucker, "An Election Sermon" (1771), in *American Political Writing,* 1:167; T. H. Breen, *The Character of the Good Ruler, 1630–1730* (New Haven: Yale University Press, 1970).

50. Shute, *ibid.*

51. Kirkland, *A Discourse,* p. 14.

52. Quoted in Tuckerman, *The Character and Portraits of Washington,* p. 104.

53. *Ibid.,* p. 54.

54. *PG,* August 8, 1787.

55. Lee, *A Funeral Oration,* p. 7.

56. Caleb Alexander, *A Sermon Occasioned by the Death of His Excellency George Washington* (Boston: Samuel Hill, 1800), p. 22.

57. Jeremiah Smith, *An Oration on the Death of George Washington* (Exeter: Henry Raulet, 1800), p. 70.

58. Shute, "An Election Sermon" (1768), in Hyneman and Lutz, eds., *American Political Writing,* 1:124.

59. Smith, *An Oration,* p. 64.

60. Parker, *An Oration,* p. 21; see also Nathan O. Hatch, *The Sacred Cause of Liberty* (New Haven: Yale University Press, 1977).

61. Barry Schwartz, "Vengeance and Forgiveness," *School Review* 86 (1978):655–68.

62. This early nineteenth-century poem is quoted in Bryan, *George Washington in American Literature,* p. 141.

63. *HGW,* p. 41.

64. Thacher, *Eulogy,* p. 11.

65. Boller, *George Washington and Religion,* pp. 86, 89.

66. Payson, *A Sermon,* p. 26.

67. Donald S. Lutz, "The Relative Influence of European Writers on Late Eighteenth Century American Political Thought," *American Political Science Review* 78 (1984):189–97.

68. Quoted in Hatch, *The Sacred Cause of Liberty,* p. 97.

69. Fiske, *A Sermon,* p. 11.

70. McClure, *A Discourse,* p. 20.

71. Abraham Clarke, *A Discourse Occasioned by the Death of General Washington* (Providence, R.I.: 1800), p. 8.

72. Smith, *An Oration,* p. 76.

73. Moses Cleaveland, *An Oration, Commemorative of the Life and Death of General George Washington* (Windham, Conn.: John Byrne, 1800), p. 14.

74. Fitch, *A Sermon,* p. 7; Blyth, *An Oration,* p. 7; Abraham Wood, *A Funeral Elegy on the Death of General George Washington* (Boston: I. Thomas and E. T. Andrews, 1800), p. 9.

75. Ralph Waldo Emerson, "Lines on Washington Written at Concord Dec. 24th, 1814," in Ralph Waldo Emerson, *The Letters,* ed. Ralph L. Rusk, 6 vols. (New York: Columbia University Press, 1939), 6:329.

76. Lee, *A Funeral Oration,* p. 9.

77. Quoted in *HGW,* p. 9

78. See, for example, Fiske, *A Sermon,* p. 20.

79. Sewall, *Eulogy,* pp. 17–18.

80. (Charleston, S.C.) *City Gazette and Daily Advertiser,* December 3, 1800.

81. Boller, *George Washington and Religion,* pp. 33–34.

82. *Ibid.,* pp. 92–115.

83. *HGW,* pp. 14, 15, 60, 61, 66.

84. *Ibid.,* p. 70.

85. The ratio of classical allusions to biblical allusions in the portrayal of Washington is for Garry Wills an index of America's secularism. Mason Weems's reliance on classical allusions, according to Wills, made his portrayal secular; the eulogists' reliance on Mosaic allusions made their portrayals religious. Correspondingly, the disappearance of Mosaic images in the early nineteenth century could only mean that the tension between America's secular and religious

trends had been resolved in favor of the former; thus, Weems's life of Washington can be read as a sign of the emerging dominance of the Enlightenment. Wills' theory is imaginative, but falls short on two counts. Mosaic allusions faded not during an age of reason but during a thirty-year wave (1800–1830) of anti-secular religious feeling that culminated in America's "Second Great Awakening." The florid reappearance of these allusions in eulogies in 1865, as part of the nation's efforts to understand the significance of Abraham Lincoln's life and death (a development that Wills overlooks), attests to their enduring relevance. On Wills's related point, the lack of iconic portrayals of Washington as an American Moses, one can only observe that biblical devices were rarely used in America—or, for that matter, in Europe—to portray any political leader. From its sixteenth-century inception, state portraiture drew on classical symbols, whose uses were never deemed incompatible with religion, and never undermined the religious legitimation of political authority. (See *CIN*, 27–53; William McLoughlin, *Revivals, Awakenings, and Reform* [Chicago: Univeristy of Chicago Press, 1978], pp. 98–140; Jenkins, *The State Portrait*.)

86. Isaac Braman, *An Eulogy on the Late General George Washington,* quoted in Robert P. Hay, "George Washington: American Moses," p. 783.

87. Most of the eulogies touch on one or more aspects of this analogy. For the best example, see Jedidiah Morse, *A Prayer and Sermon . . . on the Death of General Washington* (Charlestown, Mass.: Samuel Etheridge, 1800). For a discussion of the analogy itself, see Robert P. Hay, "George Washington: American Moses."

88. Morse, *A Prayer and Sermon,* pp. 22–29.

CHAPTER 7

1. Adams to Jebb, September 10, 1785, *Works of John Adams,* 9:541.

2. Mason L. Weems, *The Life of George Washington,* 6th ed. (Philadelphia: Mathew Cary, 1808), p. 4.

3. Hatch, *The Sacred Cause of Liberty,* p. 113.

4. Tomb, *An Oration,* p. 7.

5. Thacher, *Eulogy,* p. 8.

6. Dick, "Oration," p. 199.

7. *HGW,* p. 61.

8. Lee, *A Funeral Oration,* pp. 14–15.

9. See, for example, Davenport, *An Oration,* p. 7; Bigelow, *Eulogy,* pp. 15–16; Kirkland, *A Discourse,* pp. 7–8; Blyth, *An Oration,* p. 13; Alexander, *A Sermon,* p. 13.

10. *HGW,* pp. 42–43. For one eyewitness account, see James Butler (Wash-

ington's former overseer) to Hamilton, December 1, 1795, *PAH,* 19:467–68.

11. Figure 46 depicts an imaginary scene first described in the sixth (1805) edition of Mason Weems's biography.

12. Thacher, *Eulogy,* p. 17.

13. David Ramsay, *An Oration on the Death of Lieutenant-General George Washington* (Charleston, S.C.: W. P. Young, 1800), p. 22.

14. (Charleston, S.C.) *City Gazette and Advertiser,* January 9, 1800.

15. *Ibid.,* February 26, 1800.

16. Washington to William Pearce, February 15, 1795; March 8, 1795; July 5, 1795; March 20, 1796, *WGW,* 34:118, 135, 231, 502–503.

17. Washington to William Pearce, March 22, 1795, *WGW,* 34:154.

18. Washington to the President of Congress, September 24, 1776, *WGW,* 6:114.

19. *GW,* 5:245.

20. Flexner, *Washington: The Indispensable Man,* p. 150.

21. Knollenberg, *Washington and the Revolution.*

22. There is one exeption: William E. Woodward. He found Washington to be totally devoid of idealism, and compared his character to that of a petty banker (*George Washington*).

23. Douglass Adair, "Fame and the Founding Fathers," in Trevor Colbourn, ed., *Fame and the Founding Fathers: Essays by Douglass Adair* (New York; W. W. Norton, 1974), pp. 3–26; *CIN,* pp. 109–22.

24. Washington to John Augustine Washington, March 31, 1776, *WGW,* 4:450.

25. Washington to the South Carolina Senate and House of Representatives, May 28, 1784, *WGW,* 27:407–8.

CODA

1. Wayne Whipple, *The Story Life of Washington,* 2 vols. (Philadelphia: John C. Winston Co., 1911), 1:xvi.

2. Johannes Kuhn, "Address to George Washington Bicentennial Banquet: Dresden" in *History of the George Washington Bicentennial Celebration,* 4:142.

3. The American counterpart of Weber's sociological conception (*Economy and Society,* 3:1112–13) is also rooted in this republican ideal. See Barry Schwartz, "Emerson, Cooley, and the American Heroic Vision," *Symbolic Interaction* 8 (1985):103–20.

4. *EF,* p. 420. See also Barry Schwartz, "The Social Context of Commemoration," *Social Forces* 61 (1982):374–402.

5. William S. Baker, *Bibliotheca Washingtoniana.*

6. Schutz and Adair, *The Spur of Fame* (see Introd., n. 25), p. 229.

7. Abraham Yarmolinsky, *Picturesque United States of America . . . A Memoir on Paul Svinin* (New York: William E. Rudge, 1930) p. 34.

8. Quoted in Lipset, *First New Nation*, p. 19.

9. Carl Bode, *The Anatomy of American Popular Culture, 1840–1861* (Berkeley: University of California Press, 1959), p. xii.

10. Walt Whitman, *I Sit and Look Out,* ed. Emory Holloway and Vernolian Schwarz (New York: Columbia University Press, 1932), p. 59. For more details on the antebellum deification of Washington, see Frank Craven, *The Legend of the Founding Fathers* (New York: New York University Press, 1956); Richard W. Van Alstyne, *Genesis of American Nationalism* (Waltham, Mass.: Blaisdell, 1970); Kammen, *A Season of Youth* (see Introd., n. 8); Forgie, *Patricide in the House Divided* (see Introd., n. 8.).

11. For details, see William A. Bryan, "George Washington: Symbolic Guardian of the Republic, 1850–1861," *William and Mary Quarterly* 7 (1950):53–63.

12. *New York Times,* February 23, 1865, p. 8.

13. Quoted in Wector, *The Hero in America,* p. 262.

14. E. S. Atwood, *A Discourse Delivered on . . . the Assassination of President Lincoln* (Salem, Mass.: Salem Gazette, 1865), p. 6; George Bancroft, *Memorial Address on the Life and Character of Abraham Lincoln . . . at the Request of Both Houses of the Congress* (Washington, D.C.: Government Printing Office, 1865), p. 43; George W. Briggs, *Eulogy on Abraham Lincoln* (Salem, Mass.: City Council, 1865), pp. 4–5, 18–19, 24; Edward F. Cutter, *Eulogy on Abraham Lincoln* (Boston: D.C. Colesworthy, 1865), p. 10; J. G. Holland, *Eulogy on Abraham Lincoln* (Springfield, Mass.: Samuel Bowles & Co., 1865), pp. 5, 8, 10–11; Charles P. Krauth, *A Discourse* (Pittsburgh: W. S. Haven, 1865), pp. 12, 16, 19; John Mc-Clintock, *Discourse Delivered on the Day of the Funeral of President Lincoln* (New York: J. M. Bradstreet and Son, 1865), pp. 8, 13, 16, 18, 22. See also David S. Coddington, *Eulogy on President Lincoln* (New York: Baker and Godwin, 1865).

15. Cutter, *Eulogy,* p. 13; Briggs, *Eulogy,* p. 40.

16. Fred Greenstein, *Children and Politics* (New Haven, 1965), p. 138.

17. For details, see "Hall of Fame," *Encyclopedia Americana,* 30 vols. (Danbury, Conn.: Grolier, Inc., 1985), 13:720–21.

18. George Gallup, *The Gallup Poll: Public Opinion, 1935–1971,* 3 vols. (New York: Random House, 1972), 1:489.

19. Gallup, *ibid.,* 2:1560.

20. *Chicago Tribune,* January 10, 1982.

21. Criticism of the "Monday Holiday" law, enacted in 1968, resurfaced during the 1976 Bicentennial. See, for example, Representative Wil-

liam M. Ketchum, "Monday Holiday Act," in *Congressional Record,* 94th Congress, 2nd Session, Vol. 122, Pt. 4, February 24, 1976, pp. 4244–45; Representative Henry J. Hyde, "When Should Americans Celebrate George Washington's Birthday?" in *Congressional Record,* 94th Congress, 2nd Session, Vol. 122, Pt. 7, March 30, 1976, pp. 8715–16.

22. Whitman, *I Sit and Look Out,* p. 59.

23. Frances D. Whittemore, *George Washington in Sculpture* (Boston: Marshall Jones Company, 1933); United States, *United States Postage Stamps: An Illustrated Description of all United States Postage and Special Service Stamps* (Washington, D.C.: U.S. Government Printing Office [updated periodically]); James M. Goode, *The Outdoor Sculpture of Washington, D.C.* (Washington, D.C.: Smithsonian Institution Press, 1974); United States Congress, *Arts in the United States Capitol* (Washington, D.C.: U.S. Government Printing Office, 1978).

24. Stewart, *Names on the Land,* p. 164.

25. *Roanoke Times,* August 31, 1980, pp. 3–5; *Public Law* 94–512 [H.R. 2749], October 15, 1976; *Congressional Record,* 94th Congress, 1st Session, Vol. 121, Pt. 14, June 11, 1975, p. 18522; 94th Congress, 2nd Session, Vol. 122, Pt. 21, August 24, 1976, pp. 27495–502; Pt. 22, August 25, 1976, p. 27805; Pt. 25, September 28, 1976, pp. 32931–32; *New York Times,* February 17, 1980, p. 18.

26. Augusta Stevenson, *George Washington: Boy Leader* (New York: Bobbs-Merrill, n.d.), pp. 180–81.

27. Stewart Graff, *George Washington: Father of Freedom* (Champaign, Ill.: Garrard, 1964), pp. 68–69.

28. James T. Flexner, "George Washington is Alive," *Reader's Digest,* February 1982, p. 160.

29. *New York Times,* February 22, 1973, p. 38.

30. *New York Times,* February 18, 1975, p. 29.

31. See also David F. Musto, *George Washington and the Temptations of Political Life: An Address delivered on the 250th Anniversary of the Birth of George Washington at the Smithsonian Institution, Washington, D.C.* (Connecticut: Society of the Cincinnati, 1982).

32. Butler B. Hare, "George Washington, the Citizen–Soldier–Statesman," in *Congressional Record,* 78th Congress, 1st Session, Vol. 89, Pt. 9, February 22, 1943, p. A723.

33. Wilma Pitchford Hay, *George Washington's Birthdays* (New York: Coward-McCann, 1963), pp. 20–21.

34. *New York Times,* February 22, 1965, p. 20.

35. *New York Times,* February 22, 1976, sec. 4, p. 13.

36. Flexner, *George Washington,* 1:5.

37. H. L. Rogers quoted by Barry Goldwater, "Selected Favorable and

Unfavorable Criticism," in *Congressional Record,* 84th Congress, 1st Session, Vol. 101, Pt. 1, January 21, 1955, p. 585. (The unfavorable criticisms of Washington and two other American Presidents are presented as examples of character assassination. Goldwater assembled these materials in response to widespread criticism of Vice-President Richard Nixon.

38. Senator A. Willis Robertson, "The Spirit of George Washington," in *Congressional Record,* 84th Congress, 1st Session, Vol. 101, Pt. 2, February 22, 1955, p. 1894.

39. Norma C. Camp, *George Washington: Man of Courage and Prayer* (Melford, Mich.: Mott Media, 1977).

Index